JUST WAR

RICHARD J. REGAN

JUST WAR

PRINCIPLES AND CASES

THE CATHOLIC UNIVERSITY OF AMERICA PRESS

WASHINGTON, D.C.

The paper used in this paper meets the minimum requirements of American
National Standards for Information Science—Permanence of Paper for Printed
Library materials, ANSI Z39.48-1984.

Library of Congress Cataloging-in-Publication Data
Regan Richard J.
    Just war : principles and cases / by Richard J. Regan.
      p.   cm.
    Includes bibliographical references and index.
    1. Just war doctrine.   I. Title.
B105.W3R44   1996
172'.42—dc20
95-46533
      ISBN 0-8132-0855-6 (cl : alk. paper)
      ISBN 0-8132-0856-4 (pbk. : alk. paper)

CONTENTS

Preface   vii

PART 1. PRINCIPLES

1. **Justifying War**   3

   Why War Needs to Be Morally Justified 3 / The Pacifist
   Position 4 / The Marxist Critique of War 7 / God's Will as
   the Moral Norm of Just War 8 / Right Reason as the Moral
   Norm of Just War 10 / Just-War Theory 14

2. **The Just War Decision: Legitimate Authority**   20

   The U.S. Constitution 23 / The U.N. Charter 24 / Article 42
   and U.S. Constitutional Processes 28 / The United Nations,
   Human Rights, and Military Action 34 / The War Powers
   Resolution 39 / Conclusion 41

3. **The Just War Decision:**
   Traditional Just-Cause Considerations   48

   Defense of National Territory and International Space 48 /
   Preventive Attack 51 / Rescue of Nationals 52 / Terrorism 53 /
   Rectifying Economic Injury 56 / Vindicating Territorial
   Claims 59 / Proportionality 63 / Last Resort 64 / Cessation of
   Just Cause 66

4. **The Just War Decision: Just Cause and**
   Interventionist Wars   68

   Intervention in Other Nations' Internal Affairs and Civil
   Wars 68 / Secession and Intervention in Secessionist Wars 73

v

5. The Just War Decision: Right Intention 84

6. Just War Conduct 87

The Principle of Discrimination 87 / The Principle of
Proportionality 95 / Effect of Unjust War Conduct on Just
Cause 98 / Observance of International Conventions 98

7. Nuclear Weapons and Just War Conduct 100

The Bipolar Cold War Context 101 / The New Nuclear
Superpower Context 106 / The China Context 108 / The
Context of Other Nations' Nuclear Capability and the Problem
of Proliferation 111 / Nuclear Proliferation and Terrorism 117

PART 2. CASES — AND QUESTIONS

World War I (1914–18) 123

The Vietnam Wars (1946–75) 136

The Falklands War (1982) 151

Revolution and Civil War in Nicaragua (1978–90) 159

The Civil War in El Salvador (1979–92) 165

The Gulf War (1991) 172

The Intervention in Somalia (1992–94) 179

The Bosnian War (1992–95) 192

Appendix 1. The United Nations Charter 213
Appendix 2. The War Powers Resolution 232
Selected Bibliography 238
Index 243

PREFACE

No one who has experienced combat or read history is likely to doubt that war is hell. Nor does it require much reflection to realize that human beings have a moral obligation to avoid the evil of war. This realization raises a host of questions: Is war ever justified? If so, for what purposes? Who has the authority to decide to wage war? What is acceptable war conduct? Just-war theorists have considered such questions, and reflective citizens should do likewise.

The first part of this book summarily explains the basic principles of just-war theory in a modern context. I particularly emphasize the importance of the United Nations' role in contemporary just-war theory. The second part of the book consists of eight case studies and sets of questions about the cases. The cases invite students and readers to apply just-war principles to often complex war-related situations, and the questions after the cases invite students and readers to consider hypothetical factual variations—and to appreciate the need for more facts. The case studies are brief, but I hope adequate for their purpose. The Suggested Readings after the text of the cases, and the Selected Bibliography, should both provide material and open avenues for further investigation. For the convenience of the student and reader, I have appended the most relevant provisions of the U.N. Charter and the entire War Powers Resolution.

The book is most suitable for undergraduate and graduate courses on the morality of war, but the material, especially the cases, is suitable for discussion groups. I have selected some cases of a traditional character (e.g., World War I) and others of an untraditional character (e.g., the revolutionary wars in Nicaragua and El Salvador). The emphasis is on contemporary relevance, and the cases include the most recent war situations in Somalia and Bosnia. The latter war situation is still evolving, and so no complete analysis of it is possible. Its inclusion in this book, however, may help to illustrate the elements of uncertainty and limited knowledge under which statesmen are called upon to make war decisions.

I wish to thank Dr. Mary G. Powers, the former dean of the Graduate School of Arts and Sciences of Fordham University, for her grant of a course reduction that facilitated the preparation of this book, and Joseph Vetter, my graduate assistant for several semesters, for his help in preparing the case studies.

Richard J. Regan
Bronx, New York

PART 1

PRINCIPLES

1

JUSTIFYING WAR

Why War Needs to Be Morally Justified

Ancient Greece and Rome regarded war as simply a fact of life, a regrettable but inevitable fact of life. In early modern times, Thomas Hobbes, a keen seventeenth-century student of the classics, imbued that stance with a basically amoral philosophical theory.[1] Individuals and societies seek to aggrandize their self-interests, and wars are the "natural" consequence of individual and societal acquisitive appetites. The resulting state of war and potential war is "natural" to individuals and societies unless there is a sovereign power to restrain those conflicting appetites. There is no norm of morality superior to self-interest, although the fundamental "law of nature" (self-preservation) morally obliges individuals and societies to desire peace, and reason dictates the only means to escape war: individuals need to surrender their freedom to a sovereign power in organized society that will guarantee their survival, and regionally organized societies likewise need to surrender their freedom to a sovereign international power that will guarantee their survival. In the absence of sovereign power, there is only a moral duty to desire peace, and wars can only be called "good" or "bad" insofar as they are successful or unsuccessful in furthering societal interests.

Only hardly needs to do more than glance at a daily newspaper

1. Cf. *Leviathan*, chap. 13.

in order to be aware of the human potential for conflict and violence. But human beings also have the potential to live in peace and to cooperate with one another for their common material and spiritual development. Moreover, human beings are endowed with the power of reason, and their reason can recognize that living in peace and working cooperatively with other human beings are specifically human goals. In other words, human beings through their power of reason to evaluate can recognize that they *should* live in peace and work together cooperatively.

Human beings engage in many activities that can and do result in the death of other human beings. Vehicular accidents, for example, result in many deaths. Although the negligence or recklessness of drivers may cause accidents that result in death, drivers of automobiles do not typically intend to kill anyone. In the case of war, however, combatants directly intend the death of enemy combatants unless the latter capitulate or agree to an armistice. Human beings are endowed with reason, and reason recognizes a prima facie moral obligation not to kill other human beings. Therefore, reason needs to determine whether the deliberately intended killing of human beings involved in war can ever be justified. Moreover, if such killing can be justified, reason needs to determine when it can, and when it cannot.

The Pacifist Position

The pacifist moral position on war is categorically negative: human beings, whether as private individuals or as agents of the public, are never justified in the use of killing force against other human beings. The historical origins of pacifism in the West can be traced to Christianity, and the pacifist movement continues to be largely rooted in that source. This is not surprising, since the Gospels clearly indicate the nonviolent thrust of Jesus' ethical teaching. His followers are commanded not only to love God but also to love their neighbor (Mt. 22:39; Lk. 10:27). In the Sermon on the Mount, Jesus admonished his followers: "You have heard that it was said, 'An eye for an eye, and a tooth for a tooth.' But I say to you, Do not resist one who is evil. But if anyone strikes you on the right cheek, turn to him the other also" (Mt. 5:38–39). And when Jesus was arrested in the Garden of Gethsemane, he rebuked Peter for striking the servant of the high priest and cutting off the servant's ear: "Put your sword back into its place, for all who take the sword will perish by the sword" (Mt. 26:52).

Fragmentary literary evidence from the second and third centuries of the Christian era indicates that Church leaders either disapproved or looked down on Christians' serving in the imperial Roman army[2]; one can cite Origen, Justin Martyr, and Clement of Alexandria for that view.[3] The attitude of Christians seems to have changed with the Edict of Milan (313 A.D.) and the conversion of Constantine, and the practice of pacifism by Christians to have waned. At the time of the Reformation, however, a number of Protestant sects revived the practice: the Anabaptists, the Quakers, the Mennonites, the Brethren, the Shakers. Indeed, it was in Pennsylvania in the late seventeenth century that the Quaker William Penn instituted his pacifist "holy experiment."

Although many contemporary pacifists are pacifist for religious reasons, many others are such for philosophical reasons. For the latter, human life is an absolute value, and so human beings should not resort to killing or maiming force even when wrongdoers do violence to them or threaten to do so. In the short run, of course, pacifist practitioners will suffer injustice and prefer to suffer injustice than to commit it. But in the long run, many pacifists claim, nonviolence and nonresistance will convert unjust aggressors and oppressors, and peace and justice will ultimately prevail. This was the vision of Mahatma Gandhi and Dr. Martin Luther King.

---

2. The pagan rites associated with Roman military service were an additional and perhaps decisive reason why early Christians shunned such service. See Edward A. Ryan, S.J., "The Rejection of Military Service by the Early Christians," *Theological Studies* 13 (March 1952): 1–32; G.E.M. Anscombe, "War and Murder," in *War and Morality,* ed. Richard A. Wasserstrom (Belmont, Calif.: Wadsworth, 1970), p. 48.

3. Origen, *Contra Celsum* III, 8; Justin, *Trypho* 110; Clement of Alexander, *Protrepticus* XI, 116; *Paedagogus* I, 12. For a brief survey of patristic comments on war, see Alfred Vanderpol, *La doctrine scholastique du droit de guerre* (Paris: Pedone, 1919), pp. 171–95; Yves de la Brière, *Le droit de juste guerre* (Paris: Pedone, 1938), pp. 15–17.

Just-war theorists reject the pacifist principle. In their view, it is the value of a victim's human life that justifies the use of killing force against a wrongdoer. The wrongdoer's right to life is contingent on his not threatening the victim's life, and when the wrongdoer does so, it is a question of which life is to be preferred. Why should the life of the aggressor be preferred to the life of the victim? Moreover, community leaders resort to killing action against wrongdoers in order to defend the community and all of its members, not to defend themselves as individuals. As noted later in this chapter, Saint Augustine, the most influential Western theologian of the early Middle Ages, thought that it was precisely this aspect of aid to one's neighbor that justified Christian statesmen's resorting to war to resist foreign aggressors. In other words, love of one's neighbor may justify or even require the use of killing force against wrongdoers.

Pacifists generally argue that nonviolence and nonresistance will ultimately win the minds and hearts of aggressors and oppressors, but that argument is neither convincing nor dispositive. The success of Gandhi or King may have been due (at least in part) to the appeal of their nonviolent campaigns to the conscience of their oppressors. But if that is true, it is because Gandhi could appeal to the moral conscience of a free British electorate over the heads of colonial administrators, and King could appeal to the moral conscience of the national American electorate over the heads of regional southern officials. There is no reason to believe that such campaigns would have been successful against the rulers of Nazi Germany. Second, the argument rests on an extremely optimistic view about the reformability of human behavior. Hobbes was surely correct in describing a persistent conflictual pattern of human behavior. To imagine that every or even most human beings will behave like saints seems to be wishful thinking. And even were human beings to be so transformed at some indefinite future point of time, why should innocent human beings suffer oppression in the intervening short run?

Christian pacifists may also interpret Jesus' teaching on resistance and the use of force too broadly.[4] Jesus evidently urged his

---

4. Cf. Joseph C. McKenna, "Ethics and War: A Catholic View," *American Political*

followers to practice nonresistance and nonviolence. But it is far from clear that Jesus urged the practice of nonviolence as a strict moral obligation rather than as a moral ideal. Second, there is nothing in the context to indicate that Jesus advised public authorities to forgo the use of killing force against wrongdoers. Indeed, St. Paul says that rulers are servants of God when they execute God's wrath on domestic wrongdoers (Rom. 13:4). Third, one needs to understand many of Jesus' statements as exaggerated expressions that emphasize the main point of his teaching. For example, Jesus advises his followers not to call any man their father (Mt. 23:9). Interpreting the Gospels, however, is a complex matter, and none of the preceding observations is intended to gainsay the need for scholarly exegesis of, and theological reflection on, the Gospel texts in order to assess their import on the legitimacy of war.

Individual pacifists are often called upon to give heroic witness to the value of human life. Nonpacifists should not only admire such witness but also be drawn by it to assess critically the putative justice of particular wars. But what is admirable and virtuous on the part of individuals may not be admirable or virtuous on the part of statesmen. Supposing that human beings may justly resort to force, including killing force, to resist wrongdoers, then those in charge of a community may have a duty to do so. The practice of pacifism by individuals directly affects only those individuals; the practice of pacifism by statesmen, on the other hand, would directly affect the entire community.

The Marxist Critique of War

Marxists trace war to the privatization of property and the dominant modes of production at a given stage of history (slavery, feudalism, capitalism). In the capitalist mode of production, entrepreneurs seek to maximize profits by acquiring foreign resources and markets, and capitalist regimes serve their capitalist masters by pursuing imperialist policies. Economic imperialism inevitably leads

---

Science Review 54 (September 1960): 648–49; Vanderpol, *Doctrine scholastique*, pp. 16–33.

capitalist regimes to wage wars both to acquire undeveloped resources and markets and to prevent competing capitalist regimes from doing the same. Moreover, capitalist regimes will forcibly repress Communist movements. When the Communist revolution succeeds, and private property is abolished, the cause of war will be eliminated, and perpetual peace will reign. In short, the only just causes of war are to defend Communist regimes and to overturn capitalist ones.

The Marxist causal explanation of war is simplistic. Although many wars may have economic causes, many others do not, at least not only economic causes. Wars are often fought for reasons of religion, ethnicity, political power, and personal glory, and Marxist attempts to reduce such causes to economic structures seem tortured.

Even if Marxists are correct about the injustices of capitalism and the inclination of capitalist nations to wage imperialist wars, there remain the injustices of communism and its own tendency to wage unjust wars. Communist regimes themselves are fundamentally unjust toward their peoples—and fundamentally more unjust than democratic capitalist regimes—insofar as they suppress freedoms of the human spirit (speech, press, religion, the arts), and Communist revolutionaries wage war to establish such unjust regimes. Moreover, Communist regimes have waged wars of aggression against other nations, including other Communist nations. We need, therefore, to look elsewhere for a more adequate just-war theory, one that fully reflects the nature of the human person and the human community.

God's Will as the Moral Norm of Just War

If the existence of the universe at all times depends on God's causal action, then every historical event is in some way the result of his will. And if human beings are free, then God wills some events to come about through human causality. We are not presently concerned with how human causality is compatible with God's, or how human freedom is compatible with God's omnipotence, but with God's will as the moral norm of human action. Moreover, we are here not concerned with God's will as the moral norm that human beings discover by exercising their reason, but with his will as a moral norm that God communicates about a particular war by special revelation. In short, we are here concerned with God's justifying war by specifically sanctioning it, and with his will's constituting the moral norm of just war in this way.

For ancient Israel, the will of God seems to have been deemed to determine the justice of war: Yahweh willed specific wars for the sake of his Covenant with Israel. Yahweh could sanction wars against the enemies of Israel in order to achieve and preserve the promises of the Covenant (Ex. 15:1–18), or Yahweh could sanction wars against Israel in order to punish its people for infidelity to the Covenant (Jer. 21:4–5; Is. 10:5–11; Is. 63:10). Moreover, God's will was deemed to require the destruction of every living creature associated with enemies residing within the confines of the Promised Land (Dt. 20:17; Jos. 6:17, 21), and the destruction of all male inhabitants, the slavery of all women and children, and the expropriation of all property in the case of enemies residing outside Israel's borders who refused to capitulate (Dt. 20:14–15).

"Holy wars" were not restricted to ancient times, and many religions have at one time or another appealed to God's will as the justification of war. In the Middle Ages, for example, Christians waged Crusades to wrest the "Holy Land" from Moslem control.[5] After the Reformation, German Protestants and Catholics waged the Thirty Years War in part for religious reasons. Moslems waged holy wars to bring their religion to the infidel by force of arms. Indeed, many fundamentalist Moslems continue to accept the concept of holy war, albeit only to maintain or gain control of regions of historical Moslem dominance (e.g., Lebanon, Palestine).

If God does indeed specifically sanction a war, then that war will of course be just. But does he? Since it is at least prima facie morally wrong for human beings to kill other human beings deliberately, it is also prima facie contrary to God's will to do so. The burden of proof is on those who assert that God wills a particular war. Second,

---

5. For a comprehensive history of the Crusades, see Steven Runciman, *A History of the Crusades*, 3 vols. (Cambridge: Cambridge University Press, 1951–54). For a shorter, more recent history, see Jonathan Riley-Smith, *The Crusades: A Short History* (New Haven, Conn.: Yale University Press, 1990).

rulers have no direct knowledge about the will of God that priests or prophets profess to communicate, and priests or prophets themselves may be communicating their own interpretation of God's will rather than any special revelation from him. Third, human agents are adept at appropriating God's will to their own. Fourth, human beings will in any case need to rely on their own natural power of reason to determine the morality of war when, as seems typically the case, God gives no special indication of his will. Moreover, biblical writers seem to have determined the justice of Israel's wars retroactively, that is, by their outcomes: if Israel won, then God willed the war to fulfill his Covenant promises, but if Israel lost, then God willed the war to punish Israel for the people's infidelity.

Right Reason as the Moral Norm of Just War

We have thus far argued (1) that war needs to be morally justified; (2) that war can be morally justified; (3) that God does not, at least in the ordinary course of events, give statesmen a special indication of his will. In the absence of such an indication, therefore, statesmen need to rely on their own faculty of reason to decide the justice of waging war.

Moral reasoning is an exercise of practical reason, that is, reason in relation to human action. This involves not only reasoning about appropriate means to ends but also understanding the appropriateness of ends themselves. Practical reason understands the proper goals of human activity, that activities of reason itself (the search for truth, the development of friendships, and the appreciation of beauty) and external activities in accord with right reason (morally virtuous activity) are properly human goods. Right reason in external activities determines the mean between too much and too little activity (e.g., the mean between eating too much or too little, the mean between taking too much or too little risk in the face of danger). In justice, right reason determines exactly (not too much, not too little) what one owes to another. In the light of these appropriate ends, practical reason determines the appropriateness of particular actions (e.g., when to study, what to eat or drink). Human beings cannot develop themselves in properly human ways other than in association with other human beings. A prime purpose of an organized community is to establish and defend the order of justice between members of the community, and between the community and other communities. And so rulers (who include citizens in democratic polities) need to weigh the justice of waging war. Justice will be wanting not only if rulers resort to war when right reason indicates that they should not, but also if they do not wage war when right reason indicates that they should. As in the case of all moral virtue, the justice of waging war consists in the mean between too much and too little.

Statesmanship in managing foreign affairs and in waging war involves practical skills. Statesmen need to have diplomatic skills to avert or end war, political skills to mobilize public support, and military skills to wage successful war. But practical reason primarily concerns the suitability of shrewdness to human ends, and skills need to be subordinated to human ends. The Nazi war machine, for example, demonstrated remarkable skills, but it was used for inhuman ends. In short, statesmen need practical reason to give direction to their use of skills.

In all polities, statesmen decide when and how to wage war. In democratic polities, citizens are also involved in the decisions, at least insofar as they elect their leaders. On the one hand, citizens need to recognize that their elected representatives are presumptively more expert than they and certainly have access to more information. On the other hand, citizens should not shirk their own responsibility to reach informed practical judgments about war decisions and to exercise their franchise accordingly.

The object of practical (moral) reason is to know how to act, whereas the object of theoretical reason is to understand things and actions in terms of their causes. These different kinds of reason result in different kinds of certitude. Theoretical reason achieves knowledge about necessary causal relations; practical reason achieves knowledge about appropriate human action. As a baseball umpire is called on to make close calls about whether or not pitches fall within the batter's strike zone, so practical reason needs to make close calls about whether or not human actions are appropriate. And as a baseball umpire's call, despite its closeness, may nonetheless be certain, so practical reason's judgment about the appropriateness of human action, despite the closeness of the judgment, may nonetheless be certain. But the certainty of practical reason about the appropriateness of human actions differs in kind from the certitude about necessary causal relations, and we call the former certitude moral or practical, and the latter certitude physical or metaphysical. Indeed, because of the manifold contingencies involved in human actions, the certitude of practical reason itself admits of degrees.

Most recognize the fact that moral judgments can be neither empirically verified nor philosophically demonstrated. Some erroneously conclude from this fact that moral judgments are purely subjective. Such a conclusion is untenable. Moral judgments are indeed subjective insofar as they are the judgments of individual human subjects, and individual human beings do disagree about many moral matters. But moral judgments are also objective insofar as they focus on a real object, namely, the human constitution and the relation of human actions to that constitution. And human beings use argument and evidence to evaluate moral judgments. Thus, although moral judgments about war do not enjoy the certitude of theoretical reason and rest on imperfect knowledge of contingent events, the judgments may be certain as to human action and objectively true in that respect.

Those who recognize a prima facie moral obligation not to wage war but demand the certitude of theoretical reason to justify it likewise misconceive the nature and function of practical reason. Practical reason concerns the suitability of human action, and this involves not only the human suitability of particular actions but also the human suitability of failure to act. In many circumstances, it will be more unsuitable for human beings not to act than to act in a particular way. If statesmen need the absolute certainty of theoretical reason to justify war, they will never be able to do so. Practically speaking, therefore, such a position is pacifism under a different name. But if statesmen need only the certitude of practical reason to justify war, they will need to judge the proportionality of waging a particular war by comparing the consequences of waging war with the consequences of not waging war. Statesmen thus may fail to act rightly just as much if they fail to resort to war when practical reason determines that they should, as they would act wrongly if they resort to war when they should not.

None of the foregoing discussion about practical reason is meant to imply that the concrete exercise of practical reason is a simple matter. Practical reason involves knowledge not only of principles but also of contingent facts. Because the subject matter of practical reason is contingent, application of principles in statecraft will often, perhaps typically, be difficult. Situations are fluid, and present actualities may not perdure. Moreover, political decision makers often have limited or uncertain information about past or present actualities. Many of the cases presented in the second part of this book illustrate these problems.

Although statesmen may be able to reach morally certain conclusions that some action should be taken, they will often, again perhaps typically, need to examine and debate collectively about alternate courses of action in the light of acceptable principles, available information, and likely future events before they can reach conclusions about what is to be done. For example, U.S. statesmen and those of other nations can have little doubt that the North Korean regime has attempted to develop nuclear-weapons materials, and that the possession of such weapons would pose a real threat to regional peace, but statesmen can differ about what should be done about the problem. Although every human being is radically capable of ordinary prudence, statecraft requires a specialized kind of prudence with respect to understanding both the appropriateness of ends and the appropriate means to proper ends.

Prudence is doubly related to the moral virtues. On the one hand, prudence, that is, right practical reason, plays a central role in the development and exercise of moral virtues. For example, human beings can only exercise the virtues of courage, moderation, and justice if they exercise their reason to determine the mean between excess and defect. On the other hand—and this is the relationship that has import for decisions to wage war and decisions about war conduct—human beings can make practical judgments according to right reason only if they have the requisite moral virtue to prevent passions from overwhelming reason. Moreover, the force of dominant customs may hinder human beings from exercising reason to assess the moral legitimacy of conventional wisdom about war decisions and war conduct.

Just-War Theory

Although Augustine is normally considered the originator of the just-war theory, a few pre-Christian thinkers contributed to the development of the theory. Chief among these contributors were Aristotle and Cicero.

Aristotle's main contribution was in the study of ethics as a rational discipline. Aristotle distinguished ethics as practical science from theoretical sciences and philosophy, and he related the rightness of human action to the proper development of human personality. Moreover, Aristotle considered the justice of human relations.

In the *Politics*, Aristotle deals with the internal right ordering of the polis, the Greek city-state. Although Aristotle was not primarily concerned about the relations of the Greek city-states to one another and to non-Greek polities, he did make some specific comments on war in connection with the role of education in a rightly ordered polis. He criticizes the Spartan constitution for training its citizens primarily or exclusively for war.[6] As a practical matter, such a polity will lose its raison d'être and peculiar way of life when it achieves or loses dominion over its neighbors. As a theoretical matter, a lawgiver ought not openly to approve the acquisition of mastery (dominion), for it is nobler and more in keeping with virtue to rule over free men than to have mastery over them. A city-state that trains its citizens to rule its neighbors provides no basis for calling itself happy. The principles that are good for nations are the same as those that are good for individuals. The lawgiver should aim generally to establish peace and a cultured life.

Military training itself has three purposes: (1) to preserve one's own city-state from subjection to others; (2) to obtain or maintain

6. *Politics* VII, 13. 1333b11–38.

leadership of one's own city-state over other city-states for their own benefit but not to exercise dominion over them; (3) to exercise dominion over those who are not fit to rule over themselves.[7]

The first objective (self-defense) is, as we shall see, a generally accepted justification of war. (By extension, although Aristotle does not mention it, city-states would seem to be as justified in waging war to defend other city-states as in waging war to defend themselves.)

The second objective (leadership over other Greek city-states) presupposes that the city-state resorting to military force is culturally and morally superior to other city-states and aims only at nondespotic rule over other Greeks for their own benefit. That goal in itself, however, hardly seems to justify the killing involved in war.[8]

The third objective (dominion over non-Greeks) was based on the common Greek assumption that non-Greeks were by nature, that is, genetically, inferior and unfit to rule. In discussing the acquisition of property and slaves, Aristotle is explicit: "It is part of nature's plan that the art of war, of which hunting is a part, should be a way of acquiring property, and that it must be used both against wild beasts and against such men as are by nature intended to be ruled over but refuse."[9] Individuals should acquire only a moderate amount of property (including slaves), that is, an amount sufficient for the proper human life of reason and activity in accord with reason, and a polis should not acquire too much wealth, which would incite attacks by envious neighbors.[10] Aristotle's justification of imperialism, however limited, and its underlying premise about the incapacity of

7. Ibid. 1333b38–1334a10.

8. Military action by one city-state against another, however, might arguably be necessary for self-defense in some circumstances. The other city-state, for example, might be giving sanctuary or right of passage to enemy forces.

9. *Politics* I, 3. 1256b23–27. The translation is by A. E. Sinclair, *The Politics* (Baltimore: Penguin, 1962), p. 40. Aristotle there calls such war "just by nature" (*"physei dikaion"*). In the *Rhetorica ad Alexandrum* 2 (1425a10–16, b11–16), Aristotle presents arguments for justifying war. Cf. Plato, *Republic* V (471a5–b5) and *Laws* XII (955b9–c6).

10. *Politics* II, 4. 1267a24–28.

non-Greeks for self-rule seem radically inconsistent with the rationality that he himself attributes to every human being. And if non-Greeks as human beings are capable of self-rule, then Greeks will not be justified in waging war to conquer and enslave them. But particulars of Aristotle's explanation of legitimate war are less important than the fact that he, untypical of ancient thinkers, limited the legitimate aims of war at all.

The other chief pre-Christian contributor to just-war theory (and also untypical of ancient thinkers) was Cicero, to whom Augustine attributed his pursuit of philosophy.[11] According to Cicero, who reflected the Stoic universal brotherhood of humankind, "no just war can be waged except for the purpose of punishment or repelling enemies,"[12] and "the only excuse . . . for going to war is that we may live in peace unharmed."[13] But Cicero nevertheless celebrated the benefits that Roman rule brought to subject peoples. A superior people (such as the Romans) justly rule inferior peoples, because thereby "the license to do wrong is taken away from wicked men," and "those subdued will be better off, because, when not subdued, they were worse off."[14] As Aristotle thought Greeks, so Cicero thought Romans superior to other peoples, but unlike Aristotle with respect to Greek rule over inferior peoples, Cicero seemed to hold that Roman rule was justified by the benefits it brought to inferior peoples. As in the case of Aristotle, particulars of Cicero's explanation of just war are less important than the fact that he required war to be somehow justified.

The triumph of Christianity in the Roman Empire posed a dilemma for Christian rulers. On the one hand, their religion was antithetical to the use of killing force; on the other, their failure to use

11. *Confessions* III, 4.

12. *De re publica* III, 23. The translation is mine.

13. *De officiis* I, 11. The translation is by Walter Miller, *De officiis* (Cambridge, Mass.: Harvard University Press, 1913), p. 37. Cicero there also comments on duties in war conduct and the legal authority to wage war.

14. Augustine, *De civitate Dei* XIX, 21. The translation is by William C. Greene, *The City of God* (Cambridge, Mass.: Harvard University Press, 1960), pp. 209–10. Augustine there claims to paraphrase what Cicero says in the *De re publica*, but the actual text has not survived.

killing force would entail dire consequences for the community. In short, Christian rulers lacked a moral theory on war that would reconcile their beliefs as Christians with their responsibilities as statesmen. Augustine provided the embryo of such a theory.

Augustine admits that the law of love prohibits Christians from killing or wounding others in their own defense, but the law of love itself obliges Christians to come to the aid of others and so justifies the use of force that inflicts harm on malefactors.[15] This duty to use force to aid others is incumbent on authorities as well as private persons, since "the injustice of the opposing side . . . lays on the wise man the duty of waging wars."[16] In carrying out such a duty, however, Christian statesmen and warriors should love the enemy they forcibly oppose. The necessity of war was the lamentable consequence of sin, and human beings, with the grace of God, were capable of avoiding war.

Thomas Aquinas, writing in the thirteenth century, went further: he held that individuals may use proportionate force, even killing force, not only to defend others from harm but also to defend themselves.[17] Even so, Aquinas held that private persons may not directly intend the death of life-threatening aggressors, and he interpreted Augustine to mean only this when the latter disapproved of Christians' killing others in self-defense.[18] Aquinas endorsed the position of Augustine on war and laid down three conditions: (1) legitimate, that is, constitutional, authority should make the war decision; (2) war should be waged for a just cause; (3) statesmen should resort to war with right intention.[19] The sixteenth- and seventeenth-century theologian-philosophers Francisco de Vitoria[20] and Francisco Suárez[21] added three further conditions: (4) the evils of war,

15. *Epistola* 47 (*ad Publicolam*). Cf. *De libero arbitrio* I, 5.

16. *De civitate Dei* XIX, 7. The translation is by David Knowles, *The City of God* (Harmondsworth, England: Penguin, 1972), p. 862.

17. *Summa theologiae* II–II, Q. 64, A. 7.

18. Ibid., reply to obj. 1.

19. *Summa theologiae* II–II, Q. 40, A. 1.

20. Francisco de Vitoria, *Reflectiones: De Indis et de jure belli*, ed. Ernest Nys (Washington, D.C.: Carnegie Endowment for International Peace, 1917).

21. Francisco Suárez, *De triplici virtute theologica: De caritate, disputatio* 13 [*de bello*]

especially the loss of human life, should be proportionate to the injustice to be prevented or remedied by war; (5) peaceful means to prevent or remedy injustice should be exhausted; (6) an otherwise just war should have a reasonable hope of success. (As we shall explain, the latter conditions are explications of the proportion implicit in the justness of the cause of war.)

Aquinas dealt with the morality of war conduct only implicitly. For example, he condemned any direct killing of innocent human beings,[22] and he permitted private individuals to use killing force against aggressors only if proportionate to the end of self-defense.[23] Vitoria and Suárez, however, explicitly considered the morality of war conduct, and so just-war theory developed to include both the decision to wage war (*jus ad bellum*) and the justice of conduct in war (*jus in bello*).

The Protestant tradition might seem to imply the impossibility of any war's being just. It is a central principle of traditional Protestantism that original sin tainted the whole human enterprise; human beings are intrinsically sinners, and their every action sinful. Every political act is consequently immersed in sin and contaminated with injustice. The decision to wage war, in common with every human decision, is fundamentally incapable of moral legitimation. In modern times, Reinhold Niebuhr forcefully articulated this view of national and international politics.[24]

But Niebuhr also recognized that war might be the lesser of two evils, and he can be said in that sense to have "justified" such wars even if he did not fully legitimate them morally. Niebuhr thus reached conclusions about the propriety of war not substantially different in most particulars from those of traditional just-war theorists. His position is clearly distinguishable from that of pacifists; although he and pacifists are one in condemning all war as immoral, he, unlike pacifists, would in a limited sense justify some wars as the lesser

---

in *Selections from Three Works*, ed. James Brown Scott, 2 vols. [Latin text and English translation] (Oxford: Clarendon Press, 1944).

22. *Summa theologiae* II–II, Q. 64, A. 6.
23. *Summa theologiae* II–II, Q. 64, A. 7.
24. *Christianity and Power Politics* (New York: Scribner's, 1940).

of two evils. Protestant tradition so interpreted, although it can never fully legitimate war, need not exclude just-war analysis. Indeed, the pronouncements of the National Council of Churches on war in recent years have used just-war analysis.

The principles of just war need to be explained and applied. This we shall do in the next four chapters.

2

THE JUST WAR DECISION

Legitimate Authority

Just-war theory requires that decisions to wage war be made by those who are legally authorized to do so.[1] One of the primary purposes of organized society is to protect its members from domestic and foreign violence, and to do so, organized society needs to regulate, that is, legitimate, any use of force. Therefore, since war involves killing force, organized society needs to rest the authority to wage war in certain institutions and personnel. The constitution and laws of nation-states specify the institutions and personnel authorized to make their war decisions, and the U.N. Charter authorizes the Security Council to make the international community's war decisions.

At the outset, it is appropriate to note that the war-related constitutional and legal questions that statesmen confront are concrete, practical questions, not abstract, theoretical questions. Statesmen are concerned about action, and action involves practical, not theoretical, reasoning. Statesmen act prudently, that is, with practical wisdom, when their reason determines the locus and limits of constitutional and legal authority in the context of prospective action. Moreover, they often must decide these war-related constitutional

1. Cf. Thomas Aquinas, *Summa theologiae*, I–II, Q. 40, A. 1.

and legal questions under severe time constraints. Constitutional and legal questions will often have no commonly accepted answers. Although statesmen should consult experts, they themselves must ultimately decide such war-related questions, and the community ultimately decides whether or not to accept the statesmen's judgments.

Second, we should recall what the prudence or practical wisdom of statesmen involves. We are accustomed to identify prudence with refraining from acting foolishly. This is indeed one aspect of prudent behavior; one should not act, or not act in a particular way, when practical reason determines that it would be unwise to do so. But there is another, complementary aspect of prudence: one should act, or act in a particular way, when practical reason so dictates. The more important the cause justifying military action, the more prudent prospective military action may be, and the more prudent the military action, the more constitutional leeway the statesman may enjoy.

In this connection, we should also note that few moral philosophers deem legitimate authority an absolutely indispensable condition of private or public morality. Given an extreme necessity—but only in such a case—statesmen may be justified in acting outside and even contrary to the letter of the law. President Abraham Lincoln, for example, claimed that it was justifiable for him to violate the U.S. Constitution in certain particulars in order to save the Constitution itself. In other words, extreme necessity may create legal authority. Although most would agree in principle that extreme necessity may justify resort to prima facie unconstitutional means, however, legal systems typically are flexible enough to accommodate situations of extreme necessity.

Third, fundamental law will change over time. This is evidently the case with respect to unwritten constitutions like that of the British, but it is also the case with respect to written constitutions like that of the United States. The Fourteenth Amendment, for example, is today understood to apply to matters that its framers never dreamed would fall within its compass. How fundamental law, especially written fundamental law, evolves, and what norms should govern its development are hotly disputed. Moreover, the present legal status of fundamental law on particular points may not yet be settled, that is, legitimated. This is particularly so with the presently evolving role of the United Nations in legitimating the use of outside military force to achieve intranational peace or end secessionist wars. A "new world order" is emerging since the collapse of the Soviet Union, and the United Nations seems destined to play a much larger role in that order than it played in the old order. But the dimensions of the new order are still undefined. Because peace is a universal human good, and because an international rule of law is the best, indeed the only, way to eliminate or reduce radically the scourge of war, morally responsible statesmen and citizens should welcome this expansion of the role of the United Nations in maintaining peace and security and respond positively. This is not to say, of course, that such developments are to be embraced without regard to the text of the charter or without regard to the practical consequences of doing so.

Fourth, as in the matter of just cause, so in the matter of constitutional authority, statesmen—and ultimately citizens in democratic polities—need to approach the question with a right intention. They should approach the question of constitutional authority as judges would rather than ex parte, as lawyers do. Statesmen's wishes should not dictate their judgments about their constitutional authority to wage war, although the objective weight of a just cause may properly influence them to interpret the constitution in a light favorable to military action (or vice versa). After democratic statesmen have prudently determined that they have constitutional authority to undertake military action (and just cause to do so), they will need to convince citizens that this course of action is legal and proper, and right intention requires democratic statesmen to accept the decision of their nations' courts and electorates on the legitimacy and justice of their action.

Lastly, we should especially note that citizens are the ultimate interpreters of a democratic constitution, at least in particular matters not expressly defined therein, and they may also amend their constitution. This means that legal authority in a constitutional democracy will ultimately reflect the will of the people. Democratic leaders who claim to have the constitutional authority to act in a particular way will consequently have to convince the electorate that their position is correct. Conversely, democratic leaders who fail to convince the electorate that they have the constitutional authority so to act will ultimately lack that authority. The practical conclusion is that democratic decision makers need to strive for a political consensus on the locus of constitutional authority, and prudence dictates that U.S. presidents, even if they reasonably judge that they have solid constitutional grounds for undertaking military action on their own authority, should seek congressional endorsement of longer-term military action.

The U.S. Constitution

In most parliamentary systems, executive officials are members of the legislature, and the executive power (the government) is directly responsible to the legislative power (the parliament). The government, as long as it enjoys the confidence of parliament, has a broad mandate to conduct foreign affairs. The government also has a broad mandate to undertake military action short of a declared war—unless, as in the case of Germany, the constitution forbids it to do so.

In a presidential-congressional system, on the other hand, there are separate executive and legislative personnel, and the executive power (the president and cabinet officers) is not directly responsible to the legislative power (the Congress). The president is popularly elected, although technically by Electors (Art. II, sec. 1, cls. 2 and 3). The president is subject to impeachment by Congress for failure to obey the Constitution and the laws made thereunder but is otherwise solely responsible to the electorate. The president has charge of foreign affairs (Art. II, sec. 2, cl. 2) and is commander in chief of the armed forces (Art. II, sec. 2, cl. 1). The Congress is elected independently of the president, and its members are responsible to the electorates of individual districts and states (Art. I, sec. 2, cl. 1, and Amendment XVII). The Congress has the power to raise armies (Art. I, sec. 8, cl. 12), to provide for the military (Art. I, sec. 8, cl. 1), and to declare war (Art. I, sec. 8, cl. 11).

The American division of power between that of the president to command the armed forces and that of Congress to declare war was well suited to the political, legal, and strategic environment of the United States from 1789 until the end of World War II. The domestic Indian wars and the Civil War were not deemed wars between sovereign states requiring a congressional declaration of war. Accordingly, Congress mounted no challenge to the president's decision to engage U.S. forces in those conflicts, although many northerners, including former president James Buchanan, thought that the president had no constitutional authority to use military force against the secessionist states. With respect to foreign nations, Congress did declare full-scale wars against Great Britain (1812), Mexico (1847), Spain (1898), the Central Powers (1917), and the Axis Powers (1941), but the president on his own authority ordered relatively minor military actions, such as the naval attacks against the Barbary Coast pirates (1801–5). A commonsense distinction between "war" and "police action" came to differentiate the respective powers of Congress to declare war and the president to order the armed forces into small-scale, short-term conflicts.

The U.N. Charter

In 1945, the U.S. government signed, and the Senate ratified, the United Nations Charter. Article VI of the U.S. Constitution recognizes valid treaties to be the "supreme law of the land," and the Supreme Court has held that valid treaties may grant power to the federal government not otherwise conferred by the Constitution, at least as long as the treaty's provisions are "not contravened by any prohibitory words" in the Constitution.[2] Thus the question arises, How, if at all, does the U.N. Charter affect the respective war-related powers of the president and Congress?

The first declared purpose of the United Nations according to Article 1(1) of the charter is "to maintain international peace and security" and "to take effective collective measures for the prevention and removal of threats to the peace, and for the suppression of acts of aggression or other breaches of the peace." Article 2(4) declares

2. *Missouri v. Holland*, 252 U.S. 416, 433 (1920).

that all members of the United Nations "shall refrain in their international relations from the threat or use of force against the territorial integrity or political independence of any state," and Article 2(7) states that the United Nations is "not authorized to intervene in matters which are essentially within the domestic jurisdiction of any state." Article 2 thus makes absolutely clear that the United Nations is founded on the cornerstone of national sovereignty and territorial integrity.

Chapter VII of the charter deals with action "with respect to threats to the peace, breaches of peace, and acts of aggression." Article 39 of Chapter VII empowers the Security Council to determine whether and when such threats, breaches, and acts exist, and to make recommendations and adopt means to maintain or restore international peace and security. Article 40 empowers the Security Council to call upon the concerned parties to comply with provisional measures deemed necessary or desirable, and Article 41 empowers the council to adopt nonmilitary measures (e.g., embargoes, diplomatic sanctions) and to call upon members to apply those measures.

Article 42 of Chapter VII provides that the Security Council "may take such action by air, sea, or land forces as may be necessary to maintain or restore international peace and security," should the council consider that lesser, nonmilitary measures would be inadequate or have hitherto failed to be adequate. This article gives the United Nations power to enforce its resolutions under Articles 39 and 40. Contrary to the view of some opponents of the Gulf War, Article 42 does not require the council to conduct a full-scale study of the likely effects of current or possible nonmilitary measures before it may undertake military action; the council need only conclude that such nonmilitary measures are unlikely to maintain or restore international peace and security.

Articles 43–45 provide for special agreements between the Security Council and member states to create standby armed forces to carry out Security Council military enforcement resolutions under Article 42. The special agreements are to be ratified by the signatory states "in accordance with their respective constitutional processes." Article 47 provides for the establishment of a Military Staff Committee, which is composed of the chiefs of staff of the five permanent members of the Security Council (China, France, Great Britain, Russia, and the United States) or their representatives, and is responsible for the direction of any armed forces placed at the disposal of the council by special agreements. No special agreements under Article 43 have ever been concluded, and the Military Staff Committee set up by Article 47 has accordingly never fulfilled its intended role.

The framers of the charter undoubtedly envisioned that armed forces made available to the Security Council by the special agreements under Article 43 would provide the means to implement enforcement action by the council under Article 42. Article 106 implies this when it permits the Big Five (the permanent members of the council) to consult with one another for the purpose of joint action on behalf of the United Nations *"pending* the coming into force of such agreements" [italics added].

On the other hand, no language in Article 42 explicitly precludes the Security Council from taking enforcement action under Article 42 to maintain peace with the armed forces that member states volunteer apart from special agreements. Indeed, Article 42 states without qualification that military action under the article may include operations by the armed forces of member states. And if the failure to implement Article 43 precludes Security Council action under Article 42, Article 106 may permit such action; the latter article permits the Big Five to take joint action to maintain international security "on behalf of the Organization" pending the conclusion of the special agreements, and Security Council resolutions taking enforcement action under Article 42 would necessarily involve the concurrence or abstention of the Big Five, the permanent members.

Article 48 states that all members of the United Nations or those members designated by the Security Council are "required to carry out the decisions of the Council for the maintenance of international peace and security." The charter thus regards the execution of mandatory Security Council resolutions as obligatory on all or specified members. The wording of the resolutions will be critical for determining whether or not the resolutions are mandatory. A resolution will be mandatory if it uses words like *demands* and *requires*; it will not be mandatory if it uses words like *recommends, requests,* or *authorizes.*

Article 51 affirms that "nothing in the Charter shall impair the inherent right of individual or collective self-defense if an armed attack occurs against a member of the United Nations, until the Security Council has taken measures necessary to maintain international peace and security." Some argue that the Article 51 right of self-defense ceases once the council exercises its jurisdiction and undertakes even nonmilitary measures under Article 41. But such an interpretation of Article 51 would punish law-abiding victims of aggression that cease military resistance, and reward law-contravening aggressors that continue to engage in military operations. Moreover, such an interpretation would be inconsistent with Article 51's description of the right of self-defense as "inherent" ("*droit naturel*" in the French text, i.e., "natural right"). The meaning of the conditional clause should rather be construed in a commonsense way, namely, that nations' individual and collective right of self-defense ceases when the Security Council has taken effective measures to maintain or restore peace, that is, measures that actually induce the aggressor to abandon its military operations and military gains, and to agree to settle the dispute by peaceful means.

Chapter VIII of the charter recognizes the right of regional arrangements or agencies to deal with matters related to the maintenance of international peace and security in particular regions, provided that the activities of the regional organizations are consistent with the principles and purposes of the United Nations (Art. 52[1]). The Security Council may utilize regional organizations for enforcement action under Article 42, and regional organizations may not undertake enforcement action without the council's authorization (Art. 53[1]). Article 53 refers to the role of regional organizations in conjunction with enforcement action by the Security Council under Article 42, not in conjunction with individual or collective self-defense under Article 51.

Article 42 and U.S. Constitutional Processes

To date, the Security Council has involved itself in two full-scale military actions, in conventional-war situations, one to repel the North Korean invasion of South Korea (1950–53),[3] the other to liberate Kuwait from Iraqi occupation (1990–91).[4] In both cases, one could interpret the council's involvement as simply endorsing the decisions of member states to come to the collective self-defense of South Korea and Kuwait, respectively, as authorized by Article 51. But nothing in the wording of the relevant Security Council resolutions or the context of the military actions precludes interpreting those military actions to be enforcement actions under Article 42.[5] Indeed, in the case of South Korea, the U.N.-sanctioned armed forces, although under American command, fought under the U.N. flag.

The word *action* in Article 42 need not be interpreted to require that participating military forces be under the control and command of the Security Council. Nor does the fact that the framers of the charter contemplated that the council would have control and command of enforcement actions by reason of the special forces to be placed at their disposal and to be commanded by the Military Staff Committee (Articles 43–47) imply that the council could not act under Article 42 with armed forces not under its direct control and command. And even if the word *action* in Article 42 refers to mandatory rather than nonmandatory action, the greater power (to mandate military action) would surely include the lesser power (to recommend or authorize military action). In any case, however one interprets the council's involvement in the Korean and Gulf wars,

3. S.C. Resolution 82 (June 25, 1950).
4. S.C. Resolution 678 (November 29, 1990).
5. Security Council Resolution 678 authorized member states to use military force, if necessary, to secure the withdrawal of Iraqi troops from Kuwait, and the word *authorizes* in the resolution suggests enforcement action. Security Council Resolution 82 recommended that member states furnish military assistance to the government of South Korea, and the word *recommends* in the resolution, though weaker than the word *authorizes*, may nonetheless indicate an endorsement functionally equivalent to authorization.

there is no a priori reason to exclude the possibility of Security Council involvement in military actions to maintain international peace and security on the basis of *both* Article 51 and Article 42.

Security Council Resolution 82 recommended that member states furnish necessary assistance to the South Korean government to repel the armed attack of North Korea and to restore international peace and security in the area. Security Council Resolution 678 authorized member states to use all necessary means to secure the withdrawal of Iraqi forces from Kuwait. Neither resolution required member states to undertake any military action, and member states were accordingly not obliged to participate, as Article 48 would have if the resolution had been mandatory. Although the resolutions appealed to the moral conscience of member states to commit armed forces to the contemplated military actions, they did not attempt to impose any legal obligation under the charter for member states to do so. Thus the legal authority of the president to commit U.S. forces to the military actions remained exactly as it would have existed had there been no Security Council resolutions recommending or authorizing member states' participation.

The more interesting question is this: If the Security Council *had* purported to mandate, that is, require, member states to commit forces to the military actions, would the council resolutions, by reason of Article VI of the U.S. Constitution making valid treaties like the United Nations Treaty the "supreme law of the land," have empowered the president to commit U.S. forces to the military actions without any further congressional approval? To answer that question, one needs to study (1) the relevant provisions of the charter; (2) the understanding, that is, the original intent, of the American government representatives who signed, and the U.S. senators who ratified, the United Nations Charter; (3) postcharter practice relevant to the question.

The framers of the charter believed that the special agreements called for in Article 43 would put enough armed forces at the disposal of the Security Council and the Military Staff Committee to carry out enforcement actions under Article 42, and Article 43 specified that the special agreements were to be ratified by the signatory states "in accordance with their respective constitutional processes." But the text of the charter does not specify how member states are to carry out enforcement obligations under Article 42 apart from special agreements. It seems reasonable to suppose that if the council were to mandate member states to contribute armed forces to enforcement actions in the absence of special agreements, the charter presumes that members should and would do so according to their own constitutional processes, as in the case of ratifying special agreements.

As indicated, the framers of the charter envisioned that special agreements with member states would put armed forces at the disposal of the Security Council for enforcement purposes, and they assumed that no further parliamentary or congressional approval of council enforcement actions would be required once the agreements themselves were approved.[6] When the U.S. Senate considered ratification of the U.N. Charter, most senators accepted the view that a valid agreement between the Security Council and the United States placing armed forces at the disposal of the Security Council, that is, an agreement approved by Congress, would be sufficient to oblige the United States to commit the forces specified in the agreement as the council directed, and to authorize the president to fulfill that obligation without further congressional approval.[7]

Members of the Senate Foreign Relations Committee arrived at a consensus that the president as commander in chief of the U.S. armed forces has a "police power" distinct from the "war power" of Congress, and that U.S. forces operating under Security Council authority by special agreement would be functioning in a police capacity.[8] The committee accordingly perceived no constitutional obstacle if the council, with the consent of the president or the president's representative on the council, had the power to deploy such

6. Secretary of State Edward R. Stettinius, *Report to the President of the Results of the San Francisco Conference* (Sen. For. Rel. Comm. Print, 1945), especially p. 95; 79th Cong., 1st Sess. Michael J. Glennon, "The Constitution and Chapter VII of the U.N. Charter," *American Journal of International Law* 85 (January 1991): 77.

7. Thomas M. Franck and Faiza Patel, "U.N. Police Action in Lieu of War: 'The Old Order Changeth,'" *American Journal of International Law* 85 (January 1991): 67–68. Glennon, "Constitution and Chapter VII," pp. 78–80.

8. Franck and Patel, "U.N. Police Action," p. 68.

forces. On the Senate floor, some senators emphasized that any special agreement concluded under Article 43 would need to be approved by the Senate, and that this would act to limit the power of the president.[9] (Actually, *both* houses of Congress would need to approve a special agreement by a legislative act.) A larger number of senators argued that the president as commander in chief already possessed the constitutional authority to deploy U.S. forces, and that the Security Council could only undertake enforcement action with the consent of the president's representative on the council.[10] A small number of senators thought that any presidential commitment of the U.S. forces to combat at the behest of the Security Council but without specific congressional approval would be contrary to the exclusive power of Congress under the Constitution to declare war.[11]

But in the absence of a special agreement, an absence neither the U.S. government nor the senators seem, inexplicably, to have envisioned, it is difficult to perceive their "mind" with respect to the required process whereby the United States would fulfill its obligation to provide armed forces for U.N. enforcement actions under Article 42. The question was simply never discussed in the hearings of the Senate Foreign Relations Committee or on the floor of the Senate, since all participants assumed that a special agreement would be concluded and approved.

A plausible argument could be made that the U.S. government and most senators presumed it to be necessary that the president obtain congressional approval for the commitment of U.S. forces to carry out even mandatory Security Council enforcement actions under Article 42 in the absence of a special agreement; since Article 43 (and presumably the U.S. Constitution) requires that Congress approve any special agreement that would allow the president to commit U.S. forces to combat at the behest of the Security Council without further congressional approval, it seems unreasonable to suppose that the president would have as much authority to commit U.S. forces in the absence of a congressionally approved special

9. Ibid.   10. Ibid.
11. Ibid.

agreement as with one. On the other hand, it can also be plausibly argued that the U.S. government and most senators would have recognized the power of the president, as the commander in chief, to commit U.S. forces to support U.N.-mandated enforcement actions apart from a special agreement, since they seem to have rested the power to commit U.S. forces to such action under a special agreement on the inherent power of the commander in chief. But even if the latter interpretation should be accepted, it remains a dubious proposition that the inherent police power is so broad as to allow the president to commit U.S. forces to unlimited, full-scale military action, and the War Powers Resolution in any case supersedes that view.

Moreover, it is a purely hypothetical question to ask whether or not the president could on his own authority commit U.S. forces to participate in U.N.-mandated military actions. It is hypothetical because most commentators recognize that the Security Council could not require member states to commit any part of their armed forces apart from special agreements[12] (assuming, of course, that the council can take action under Article 42 apart from the existence of special agreements). This means, on the one hand, that the council can only recommend or authorize member states to participate in enforcement actions, and on the other, that each member state needs to decide in accordance with its own constitutional processes whether or not to participate.

The Security Council has on several occasions approved military actions, and the United States participated prominently in each of them. In one instance, the Security Council recommended that member states furnish military assistance to the government of South Korea to repel the armed attack of North Korea.[13] President Harry S. Truman, on his own authority as commander in chief, ordered U.S. forces to assist the South Korean government before the Security Council recommended such action.[14] Some senators openly

12. Glennon, "Constitution and Chapter VII," p. 77. See also *Public Papers of the Secretary General: Trygve Lie* 1 (1969): 170.

13. See n. 3.

14. "Statement on the Situation in Korea (June 27, 1950)," *1950 Public Papers: Harry S. Truman*, p. 492.

challenged the authority of the president to commit U.S. forces to combat in Korea without congressional approval or a declaration of war, although most senators at that time voiced no objection to the merits of committing the forces.[15] Most of them seemed to accept the administration's argument that the conflict involved a "police action," and that the president accordingly possessed the constitutional authority as commander in chief to commit the forces both before and after the Security Council's recommendation.[16] The failure to seek congressional approval at the outset, which would undoubtedly have been granted, subsequently served to undermine the legitimacy of the war when the war became stalemated—and unpopular.

In another instance, the Security Council authorized member states to take all necessary means to secure the withdrawal of Iraqi troops from Kuwait.[17] President George H. W. Bush, in response to congressional and popular demands that he commit no U.S. forces to combat against Iraq to free Kuwait without first obtaining congressional approval, reluctantly sought and narrowly obtained that approval.[18] The president's recourse to Congress for its approval of the commitment of U.S. forces to combat against Iraq evidently undermines any claim that the "police action" in Korea established a precedent to legitimate presidential authority to commit U.S. forces to U.N.-sanctioned combat without such approval.

In a third instance, the Security Council "welcomed" (i.e., accepted) the offer of the United States in cooperation with other nations to undertake a military operation to create a secure environment for the delivery of humanitarian relief in Somalia.[19] President Bush, fulfilling the U.S. government's offer to the Security Council, ordered U.S. troops into Somalia without obtaining formal con-

15. Franck and Patel, "U.N. Police Action," p. 71.
16. Ibid.
17. See n. 4.
18. The House of Representatives voted 250 (164 Republicans, 86 Democrats) to 183 (179 Democrats, 3 Republicans, 1 Independent) in favor of the Gulf War Resolution. The Senate voted 52 (42 Republicans, 10 Democrats) to 47 (45 Democrats, 2 Republicans) in favor of the Gulf War Resolution. The date was January 12, 1991. See *The New York Times*, January 13, 1991, section 1, p. 1.
19. S.C. Resolution 794 (December 3, 1992).

gressional approval, but he did solicit and obtain support from congressional leaders for his action; the urgency of the situation from the humanitarian perspective may have qualified the deployment as "police action" within the president's power as commander in chief of the nation's armed forces despite the fact the deployment was evidently not designed to protect U.S. territory or citizens, or the territory or citizens of Somalia, from external attack. The deployment, however, would seem to have posed an imminent threat of involvement in hostilities and so to have triggered provisions of the War Powers Resolution requiring specific congressional authorization of the deployment beyond sixty days.

A fourth instance, that of U.N. and U.S. involvement in the Bosnian conflict, is described in the cases-and-questions section.

The United Nations, Human Rights, and Military Action

The preamble of the United Nations Charter affirms the organization's "faith in fundamental human rights, in the dignity and worth of the human person." Nonetheless, Article 2(7) disclaims any authority of the United Nations to "intervene in matters which are essentially within the domestic jurisdiction of any state" or to "require the members to submit such matters to settlement under the present Charter," and Article 2(4) pledges members to "refrain in their international relations from the threat or use of force against the territorial integrity and political independence of any state." The framers of the charter evidently did not wish to provide any legal basis for U.N. military intervention in the internal affairs of any nation even in behalf of human rights as such.

But Chapter VII authorizes the Security Council to take measures regarding threats to peace, breaches of peace, and acts of aggression, and Article 42 specifically empowers the council to undertake military action "to maintain or restore international peace and security." Accordingly, the Security Council is authorized to undertake military action even in the case of ostensibly domestic matters if the latter have negative consequences for the maintenance of international peace, as domestic matters often do. For example, if minorities declare parts of preexisting political units independent, outside nations may claim the collective right of self-defense under Article 51 to justify their military assistance to the secessionists, and the Security Council is authorized to take enforcement action under Article 42 to maintain or restore international peace. Or the Security Council may take enforcement action under Article 42 against totalitarian regimes that are threatening to breach (or have already breached) international peace and incidentally put an end to those regimes' violations of human rights. Or the fact or threat of military intervention by outside nations to protect the rights of kindred ethnic minorities in other nations may affect international peace and security and empower the Security Council to take enforcement action under Article 42. Or refugees may be using bases in neighboring nations to mount guerrilla operations against the regimes of their native lands, and the Security Council may accordingly take enforcement action under Article 42.

A prominent feature in the history of the United Nations is support for the termination of colonialism. The Security Council passed several resolutions in 1948 calling on the Netherlands to release the president of the revolutionary Republic of Indonesia and other political prisoners.[20] In connection with the administration of Southwest Africa (Namibia), the council passed several resolutions calling on the Republic of South Africa to comply fully with the Universal Declaration of Human Rights and the international status of the territory as a U.N. mandate.[21] The council repeatedly affirmed the right of the indigenous peoples of Portuguese territories in Africa to self-determination.[22] In the case of Southern Rhodesia, the council declared that the secessionist white minority regime there constituted a threat to international peace and later condemned that regime's measures of political repression because they blocked the process of majority self-determination.[23] The apartheid policy of South Africa

20. S.C. Resolutions 63 and 64 (December 28, 1948).

21. S.C. Resolution 246 (March 14, 1968).

22. S.C. Resolutions 180 (July 31, 1963), 183 (December 11, 1963), 218 (November 23, 1965), and 321 (October 23, 1972).

23. S.C. Resolutions 217 (November 20, 1965), 232 (December 16, 1966), 253 (May 29, 1968), and 277 (March 18, 1970).

moved the council to more action than any other colonial situation. The council repeatedly condemned the implications and consequences of that policy for the whole population of South Africa, and its effects on neighboring countries,[24] and imposed a mandatory arms embargo on South Africa.[25]

With regard to international armed conflicts, the Security Council has repeatedly called on occupying powers to respect the humanitarian principles of international conventions (e.g., in connection with the Indian-Pakistani conflict,[26] the Iraqi-Iranian war,[27] the Iraqi occupation of Kuwait,[28] the Israeli occupation of captured territories[29]).

The Security Council is playing an increasingly prominent role in bringing peace to countries stricken by civil wars. The council established a mission in El Salvador to monitor the agreements, including the agreement on human rights, between the government of El Salvador and the rebels.[30] The United Nations has committed itself to a full-scale peacekeeping operation in Cambodia to restore peace, to promote national reconciliation, to protect human rights, and to assure the right of self-determination.[31] The council in 1992 established a transitional authority there according to a plan with a human rights component submitted by the secretary general.[32] To combat the threat to international peace and security in the civil

24. S.C. Resolutions 134 (April 1, 1960), 190 (June 9, 1964), 191 (June 18, 1964), 392 (June 19, 1976), 417 (October 31, 1977), 418 (November 4, 1977), 473 (June 13, 1980), 556 (October 23, 1984), and 560 (March 12, 1985).

25. S.C. Resolution 418 (November 4, 1977).

26. S.C. Resolution 307 (December 21, 1971).

27. S.C. Resolutions 540 (October 31, 1983), 582 (February 24, 1986), 598 (July 20, 1987), and 612 (May 9, 1988).

28. S.C. Resolutions 664 (August 18, 1990), 666 (September 14, 1990), and 674 (October 29, 1990).

29. S.C. Resolutions 237 (June 14, 1967), 452 (July 20, 1979), 465 (March 1, 1980), 607 (January 5, 1988), 608 (January 14, 1988), 672 (October 12, 1990), and 681 (December 20, 1990).

30. S.C. Resolution 693 (May 20, 1991).

31. S.C. Resolution 745 (February 28, 1992). S.C. Resolution 783 (October 13, 1992) reaffirmed that elections would be held, and demanded that the Khmer Rouge cooperate.

32. *Report of the Secretary General on Cambodia*, U.N. Doc. S. 23613 and Add. 1.

strife in the former Yugoslavia and in Somalia, the council imposed an embargo on the delivery of all military weapons and equipment[33] and established peacekeeping forces.[34] In the case of the Somalian peacekeeping force, the secretary general and the council stressed the need for unimpeded delivery of humanitarian assistance to the affected population.

In the aftermath of the Gulf War, the council condemned the large-scale repression of the Kurds by the Iraqi army and demanded that Iraq end this repression and allow international humanitarian organizations immediate access to those in need in all parts of Iraq.[35] The council construed the repression of Iraqi civilians, in particular the Kurds, and the resulting refugee exodus across international boundaries as a threat to international peace and security in the region.

The practice of the Security Council since the collapse of the Soviet Union reveals an increased recognition that peacekeeping and peacemaking may involve a human rights component, and that large-scale violations of human rights to life may constitute a threat to the stability, peace, and security of a region and require enforcement action by the Security Council. In the case of El Salvador, the council's monitoring of the agreements between the warring powers involves the monitoring of a human rights component. In the cases of Cambodia and the former Yugoslavia, the strife there actively breaches or potentially threatens regional peace. In the case of humanitarian aid to the Kurds in Iraq, not only does the refugee exodus to Turkey, Iran, and Syria potentially threaten regional peace, but Iraq is effectively in a state of tutelage to the United Nations after the Gulf War. In this connection, it is worth noting the vast expansion of U.N. peacekeeping operations and costs from 1987 to 1993. In the former year, the United Nations had ten missions involving ten thousand peacekeepers, whereas in the latter, it had eighteen mis-

---

33. Yugoslavia: S.C. 713 (September 25, 1991); Somalia: S.C. Resolutions 733 (January 23, 1992), 746 (March 17, 1992), and 751 (April 24, 1992).

34. Yugoslavia: S.C. Resolution 743 (February 21, 1992); Somalia: 751 (April 24, 1992).

35. S.C. Resolution 688 (April 5, 1991).

sions involving seventy-five thousand peacekeepers. And the cumulative cost of the peacekeeping missions escalated from $233 million in 1987 to $3 billion in 1993.

In the case of Somalia, however, the Security Council's attempt in a single passing reference to link military intervention there to the cause of preserving international peace seems to be a fig leaf. The strife in Somalia did not seem to pose any threat to regional peace and security; the strife there was one between clans and subclans of the same tribe, and Somalis have no close blood ties to the dominant tribes of neighboring nations. (The government of Kenya was reportedly supplying arms to a warring clan in southern Somalia, but such aid would only provide a legal basis for U.N. sanctions or enforcement action against Kenya, not for military intervention in the Somali civil war.) Nor was the strife in Somalia a class war threatening to draw left-wing and right-wing partisans into the fighting. In short, the strife in Somalia seems to have been purely local, without any consequences for the maintenance of international peace.

If so, on what legal basis could the United Nations claim the right to intervene militarily? One basis might be the agreement of the warring parties to allow international forces to operate in Somalia to supervise the delivery of humanitarian aid and to help restore order. Another might be the presumed will of the people of Somalia to have humanitarian aid delivered and order restored, whatever the will of the warring parties' leaders.

As in the case of the current anarchy in Somalia, so in the case of violations of human rights without any plausible threat to regional peace, there is a problem concerning the legal basis of forcible U.N. intervention. Nazi-like persecution of an isolated minority might not pose any threat to international peace, however monstrous the local regime's crimes might be. International conventions like the U.N. Declaration of Human Rights might empower the world organization to undertake military action against signatories who are not complying with the conventions. Or if the International Court of Justice were to render a condemnatory judgment in a case over which it had jurisdiction, Article 94(2) would empower the Security Council to "decide upon measures to be taken to give effect to the judgment." Or in the case of civil wars, the United Nations might be empowered to use military force to apprehend and try war criminals. Or customary international law might empower the United Nations to intervene. Or the United Nations Charter itself might be amended to authorize intervention for specified humanitarian purposes by agreement of two thirds of the member states, including the five permanent members of the Security Council (Arts. 108, 109).

At a special meeting of the Security Council on January 31, 1992, the attending chiefs of state and government issued a notable declaration,[36] which recognized "new challenges" in the search for peace. In particular, it noted that "the nonmilitary sources of instability in the economic, social, humanitarian, and ecological fields have become threats to peace and security." The declaration clearly envisions an expanded role for the United Nations and the Security Council in the field of human rights and in the other fields mentioned, and an expanded view of the relation of human rights violations to regional and world peace.

The War Powers Resolution

The constitutional tension between the power of the president as commander in chief and the power of Congress to declare war came to a head after successive presidents, especially President Johnson, committed U.S. armed forces to combat in Vietnam without any specific authorization from Congress. The War Powers Resolution, enacted on November 7, 1973, asserted ultimate congressional authority over the president's commitment of armed forces to hostilities or to situations imminently risking hostilities.[37] The resolution became law over the veto of President Nixon, and every president from Nixon to Bush has contended that all or part of the resolution unconstitutionally infringes upon the president's power as commander in chief of the nation's armed forces. The Supreme Court has never ruled on the constitutionality of any part of the resolution.

The resolution requires that the president (1) consult with Con-

---

36. S/PV/3046.   37. 50 U.S. Code #1541–48.

gress before and after introducing U.S. forces into hostilities or imminently hostile situations[38]; (2) submit to the speaker of the House
and the president pro tempore of the Senate within forty-eight hours
a written report explaining the circumstances, legal basis, and estimated scope and duration of the deployment[39]; (3) terminate such
deployment of armed forces within sixty days unless Congress specifically authorizes the deployment, extends the period, or is unable
to meet because of an armed attack on the United States.[40] In the
absence of congressional action, the president is permitted to continue the deployment for an additional thirty days if the president
determines and certifies that military necessity so dictates,[41] but the
president is to remove the forces whenever Congress by concurrent
resolution so directs.[42]

Section 8(a) states that presidential authority to introduce U.S.
forces into hostilities or imminently hostile situations shall not be
inferred from (1) any statutory provision unless the provision specifically authorizes such deployment and does so expressly within
the meaning of the resolution[43]; (2) any treaty unless the treaty has
been implemented by legislation that specifically authorizes such deployment and does so expressly within the meaning of the resolution.[44]

Section 8(a)(1) explicates in other words what the resolution essentially requires, namely, that Congress must specifically approve
the commitment of U.S. forces to combat or the risk of combat for
longer than sixty days (or thirty additional days if the president certifies that this is militarily necessary). In addition, it leaves open the
possibility that a congressionally approved agreement between the
Security Council and the United States under Article 43 of the
United Nations Charter might specifically authorize the council, necessarily with the approval or abstention of the president's representative on the council, to deploy specified U.S. forces into hostilities
or imminently hostile situations. Section 8(a)(2) makes clear, if

38. Ibid., #1541.   39. Ibid., #1543(a).
40. Ibid., #1544(b).   41. Ibid., #1544(b).
42. Ibid., #1544(c).   43. Ibid., #1547(a)(1).
44. Ibid., #1547(a)(2).

there had hitherto been any reason to doubt, that the United Nations Charter confers no authority on the president to commit U.S. forces to U.N.-sanctioned enforcement actions in the absence of a congressionally approved special agreement to that effect.

Section 8(d)(1) declares that the resolution does not intend to alter the constitutional authority of the president or Congress, or the provisions of existing treaties.[45] The Senate Foreign Relations Committee Report indicates that the committee thought that the reference to existing treaties was consistent with Section 8(a)(2). The committee read Section 8(d)(1) to confirm the war-related obligations of the United States created by treaties like the United Nations Treaty and the North Atlantic Treaty, but not to imply that the president may implement the treaties without statutory congressional approval.[46] Put another way, the Senate Foreign Relations Committee *assumed* that no existing treaty conferred on the president the authority to execute the treaty, that is, to commit U.S. forces to combat, without antecedent or subsequent congressional approval.

Section 8(d)(2) declares that the resolution should not be construed to grant any authority to the president to deploy U.S. forces that the president would not have had in the absence of the resolution.[47] The purpose of this provision is to disavow any claim that the president has the authority to commit U.S. forces to combat or combat situations by reason of following the procedures laid down in the resolution; the provision makes clear that the president needs to have an independent constitutional or statutory basis for his action.

Conclusion

Article 42 of the United Nations Charter empowers the Security Council to undertake enforcement action to maintain international peace and security. Apart from special agreements, as provided for in Article 43, the council has no power to mandate that the armed forces of member states participate. If the council recommends or

45. Ibid., #1547(d)(1).
46. *Senate Report No. 220*, 93 Cong., 1st Sess. (1973).
47. 50 U.S. Code 1547(d)(2).

authorizes enforcement action by member states in the absence of special agreements, each nation decides according to its own constitutional processes whether or in what way it wishes to participate. In the case of the United States, this means that the Constitution and statutory law govern the legitimacy of U.S. participation in U.N. enforcement actions under Article 42. In short, the president has no more authority to commit U.S. forces to combat pursuant to a Security Council resolution calling for enforcement action under Article 42 than he would have had without such a resolution. The War Powers Resolution (assuming its constitutionality) puts the issue beyond all doubt: Section 8(a)(2) of the resolution requires that Congress explicitly authorize the commitment of U.S. forces to combat or combat situations for longer than sixty days, irrespective of any preexisting treaty, and the resolution, as the most recent sovereign act of the United States, supersedes any potentially conflicting provision of the United Nations Charter.

The present legal status of Article 42 does not necessarily preclude a contrary development. First, the United States might conclude, and Congress approve, a special agreement with the Security Council under Article 43 that would place some of the U.S. armed forces directly at the disposal of the council for enforcement action under Article 42. If so, the president through the vote of his representative on the council would have the authority to commit specified U.S. forces to combat. Second, Congress might enact a statute empowering the president to implement Security Council resolutions calling for enforcement actions under Article 42. Third, the Supreme Court might, although it is unlikely, rule that the president has inherent power as commander in chief to order U.S. forces into combat in response to Security Council resolutions, and that the War Powers Resolution unconstitutionally abridges that power.

The War Powers Resolution in practice, although not in terms, revivifies the pre–World War II distinction between the "police power" of the president and the "war power" of Congress. The resolution does require the president to consult with, and report to, Congress even when he commits U.S. forces to small-scale, short-term combat, but Section 2(c)(1) of the resolution permits the president to introduce such forces into hostile situations without congressional authorization in limited cases of national emergency, and his inherent power may extend to more cases than the resolution recognizes. Moreover, short-term success will tend to mute congressional challenges to the president's constitutional or statutory authority to have committed the forces. For larger-scale, longer-term military actions, the resolution requires the president to terminate commitment of U.S. forces to combat or combat situations within sixty days (or an additional thirty days if the president certifies that military necessity so dictates) unless Congress authorizes the commitment.

Section 8(d)(1) of the resolution avows that the resolution does not intend to take away any power that the president has as commander in chief of the armed forces. As commander in chief, the president undoubtedly has the inherent constitutional authority to order U.S. forces to defend themselves, U.S. territory and possessions, and the people of the United States against armed attack. The president also undoubtedly has the constitutional authority, prior to any congressional approval, to order U.S. forces to defend against armed attack nations with whom the United States has a mutual security treaty. The need for immediate action to defend vital national interests and unallied victim nations may also allow the president to act in such situations without first obtaining congressional approval. But the War Powers Resolution requires the president to obtain congressional approval for any such military commitments if they extend beyond sixty days.

The legitimacy of any governmental action ultimately rests on a broad public consensus about the matter, and the War Powers Resolution reflects a broad national consensus that any involvement of U.S. forces in large-scale, potentially long-term military actions should be approved by Congress. Moreover, the precedent of the Gulf War Resolution reinforces this consensus. As a practical matter, therefore, it would be folly for a president to commit U.S. forces to such hostilities, or situations imminently risking such hostilities, without obtaining prior congressional approval if time permits, or subsequent congressional approval if exigent circumstances compel the president to act immediately. Ongoing consultation with key congressional committees is critical for the legitimacy of the nation's foreign policy—and its war decisions.

Whatever the internal constitutional constraints on individual nations participating in military actions, the United Nations Charter obliges member states not to undertake military action without authorization from the United Nations except for individual or collective self-defense. World peace is a responsibility of the world community, and the United Nations was established precisely to guarantee and enforce international peace and security. Even in the case of individual or collective self-defense, members are required to submit the matter to the Security Council. The council, of course, may fail to act, and individual nations retain their moral and legal right to defend themselves. But nations should always strive to support rather than supplant the Security Council's role in legitimating just war.

Member states should for the same reason cooperate with the Security Council when it calls on them to contribute military forces to help maintain peace and security. World law makes world peace possible, and the United Nations has, quite literally, a fighting chance to make world law possible. Failure to support Security Council decisions to authorize military action against aggressors will surely undermine the rule of world law and so the cause of world peace. The Security Council is not likely to authorize military intervention lightly, and the required Security Council majority, including the concurrence or abstention of the five permanent members, is not likely to coalesce easily.

In the United States, an unusual coalition of the near-pacifist left and the neoisolationist right opposes a stronger role for the United Nations in war-related decisions. The near-pacifist left understandably fears the human and material costs of war, but it fails to realize that the credible threat of enforcement action by the United Nations is in the long run the best hope of humankind to establish and maintain international peace and security in the post–Cold War world. The neoisolationist right opposes the participation of U.S. forces in any military action, whether in conjunction with the United Nations or not, that does not involve an important, tangible American national interest. Such a view is practically and morally myopic. It is practically myopic because a world in which international law and morality are not enforced is less safe for the peace and security of the United States than a world in which international law and morality are effectively enforced by the world community; it is morally myopic because individuals and nations have a moral duty to cooperate with other individuals and nations for the common good of peace and security. (The present-day American coalition of the near-pacifist left and the neoisolationist right against expanded U.N. responsibility for peace closely replicates the coalition of the pacifist left and the nationalist right that either opposed U.S. entry into the League of Nations outright or sought to attach crippling conditions on that entry.[48])

The United Nations has to date made no attempt to establish or activate the military structures envisioned by Articles 43–47. To fulfill more effectively the role of enforcing world peace, the Security Council should seek special agreements with major powers and/or regional associations of major and minor powers to put specified armed forces at the disposal of the council, and should activate the currently moribund Military Staff Committee. In the wake of the collapse of the Soviet Union, Russia can be expected to cooperate with the Western powers (France, Great Britain, and the United States) to create those forces. China is likely to be wary of expanding the role of the United Nations in maintaining and enforcing world peace, but political and economic considerations might induce China to acquiesce, and the veto power would protect China (and the other major powers) against any enforcement action the nation opposed.

The United Nations failed to allocate the costs of the full-scale military actions that the Security Council recommended (against North Korea) or authorized (against Iraq). Nor has the United Nations to date made any attempt to devise a formula for allocating the

48. The U.S. Senate twice failed to muster the two-thirds vote required for ratification of the Treaty of Versailles, which included the Covenant on the League of Nations (November 19, 1919, and March 19, 1920).

costs of military actions that the council may undertake, recommend, or authorize in the future. The world organization needs to address this problem. Surcharges on members' dues or on the dues of those members whose per capita income exceeds a certain threshold might be an acceptable formula. Moreover, there should be penalties (e.g., suspension of U.N. voting rights) to induce member states to pay such surcharges, and indeed all U.N. dues and assessments.

The Security Council and the Secretariat are the chief organs of the United Nations, and each has structural problems. The Security Council, originally eleven members, currently has fifteen members, and there are proposals to enlarge it further. The larger the council, the more difficult it is to mobilize a majority. The original membership reflected a delicate balance between the major powers (the five permanent members with the power to veto resolutions) and the minor powers (the six members elected by the General Assembly). That balance no longer exists, both because some of the permanent members are no longer major powers, and because minor powers now compose two thirds of the membership of the council. From the point of view of effectiveness, it would seem to make more sense to shrink than to enlarge the council. Even apart from the size of the council, the present council's decisions require the concurrence or abstention of the permanent members, and the affirmative vote of at least three other members. This collective decision-making process often leads to ineffectual compromises.

The Secretariat is the administrative arm of the United Nations. Like any bureaucracy, it tends to develop its own agenda. In particular, the secretary general and his lieutenants are in a strong position to shape the policies of the United Nations in the course of administratively implementing Security Council resolutions.

There are no easy solutions to these problems. But there is reason to hope that, with the collapse of the Soviet Union, China's need for international trade, and appreciation of common interest, the council may be able to function effectively for world peace. Second, the deliberation and compromise involved in the council's process of collective decision making may be creative. Third, the council could provide more exacting guidelines for the Secretariat. In any case, whatever its limitations, the United Nations represents the best and perhaps the only hope in an imperfect world for legitimating effective maintenance of world peace both between and within nations.

3

THE JUST WAR DECISION
Traditional Just-Cause Considerations

Just-war theory requires that nations resort to war only for just causes.[1] The justice of the cause of waging war involves two elements. First, the aim of a nation waging war should be to prevent or rectify wrongful, that is, unjust, action by another nation against itself or a third nation. Second, there should be a due, that is, just, proportion between the wrong to be prevented or rectified and the human and material destruction that the war can be reasonably expected to entail. Not every wrong suffered at the hands of another nation will proportionally justify the injured nation's waging war, or other nations' waging war on its behalf; the wrong threatened or suffered should equal or surpass the destructive human and material costs of waging war.

Defense of National Territory and International Space

Nations have a prima facie just cause to defend their territory and citizens against armed attacks. Reason and international law recognize the right of human persons to organize themselves into political communities and the right of political communities to defend themselves against armed attacks. This right of national self-defense

---

1. Cf. Thomas Aquinas, *Summa theologiae*, I–II, Q. 40, A. 1.

includes a right to defend colonial dependencies as long as the indigenous peoples accept colonial status or at least prefer it to another nation's rule. The justice of nations' defending themselves against armed attacks, of course, presupposes that the attacked nation has at least a prescriptive right to rule the territory attacked, and that the attacking nation has no just cause to attack (e.g., to prevent an imminent attack on itself or a third nation). It also presupposes a reasonable expectation that the defense will be successful,[2] and that the destructive human and material costs of war will be duly proportional to the cause.

On the other hand, justice requires that nations be willing to negotiate or arbitrate genuine territorial disputes, that is, disputes that are not subterfuges for aggression. Boundary disputes can be settled by arbitration, and even regional disputes might be resolved by the parties' accepting a compromise (e.g., greater regional autonomy, binational consultation on regional problems). Both possessor nations and rival claimants should negotiate in good faith and be open to compromise. The failure of the possessor nation to enter into meaningful negotiation of genuine territorial disputes, however, is not sufficient to give a rival claimant just cause to wage war against the possessor nation to vindicate the claim, as we shall argue later in this chapter.

Whereas defense of national territory is a generally accepted cause justifying military resistance and counterattack, application of the principle is not always so simple. Aggressors may, and most often do, appeal to some cause that they argue justifies their invasion of another nation. For example, when Hitler invaded Poland on September 1, 1939, he claimed that part of Poland (the Polish Corridor) rightfully belonged to Germany. Similarly, when Iraq invaded Kuwait on August 2, 1990, Iraq claimed that Kuwait was exceeding its allotment from the jointly owned Rumalian oil fields. To determine whether an alleged cause actually justifies one nation's attack

---

2. A nation without reasonable expectation of successful military defense in the short run may nevertheless reasonably hope that its unsuccessful short-term defense will rally the world community against the aggressor nation and so bring about the victim nation's ultimate victory.

against another, one needs to assess (1) whether the asserted cause as such should justify one nation's initiating war against another; (2) whether, if the asserted cause might do so, the facts substantiate the cause in the particular case.

As indicated, the very matter at issue in territorial wars may be the status of the territory attacked. In other words, both warring nations may be asserting claims to the same territory. I am not here referring to claims by one party to "lost" territories, which issue we shall consider later in this chapter, but rather to disputes about borders. The Mexican-American War (1846–48) represents a classic case of a war provoked, at least as regards its immediate casus belli, by rival claims to border territory between the Nueces and Rio Grande rivers in what is now southeastern Texas. That territory was then sparsely populated, and there had been no American settlers there prior to 1845. Such boundary questions seem readily amenable to negotiation and arbitration.

Nations have a prima facie just cause to use military force against those who attack their vessels in international waters or their aircraft in international airspace. This right of self-defense presupposes that the waters or airspace in question is commonly recognized in international law or treaties or convention to be extranational, that the attacking nation's forces have no just cause to attack, and that the human and material costs of military engagement are duly proportional to the cause.

Nations claiming disputable rights of passage should, of course, avoid provocative actions. They should negotiate the claims, submit them to arbitration, or seek a declaratory judgment from the International Court of Justice. But if international law publicists (specialists) commonly recognize waters or space to be extranational, nations may actively assert their rights of passage if they give adequate notice to the other party of their intention to do so.

As in the case of defense of national territory, so the very matter at issue in defense of asserted rights to use open waters may be the national or international status of the waters. The Gulf of Sidra incident (1986) illustrates this point. Libya had proclaimed the Gulf up to 150 miles from the Libyan coast to be territorial waters and warned foreign nations not to breach what it called the "line of death." The United States, relying on international law and practice, sent warships across the line. Libya fired missiles at U.S. jet fighters in the Gulf, and the jets then sank two Libyan patrol boats and damaged two missile sites on the Libyan coast. Since Libya's claim was so patently contrary to existing international law and practice, there seems to be no good reason why the United States should have submitted the issue to arbitration or the International Court of Justice. But there might be good reason to do so in cases involving more plausible claims to territorial waters.

Nations also have a prima facie just cause to help other nations defend themselves against armed attack. The justice of outside nations' helping nations defend themselves against attack presupposes that the assisted nation has been unjustly attacked, and that the costs of war are duly proportional to the cause. The justice of third-party intervention, however, need not presuppose that the assisted nation is blameless; it need only presuppose that the assisted nation was unjustly attacked.

Article 51 of the United Nations Charter recognizes the right of nations to both individual and collective self-defense, but this right remains subject to the authority and responsibility of the Security Council to take whatever means the council deems necessary to maintain international peace and security.

Preventive Attack

A nation need not wait until it is attacked to have just cause to use military force against a would-be aggressor; it is as much an act of self-defense to initiate hostilities to prevent imminent attack as it is to respond to hostilities already initiated by an aggressor. Nor need a would-be victim nation wait until a would-be aggressor nation is immediately poised to attack before the would-be victim nation has just cause to strike preemptively against the would-be aggressor nation, although the more remote the threat, the more the opportunity to seek redress by means short of war (e.g., diplomacy, economic sanctions). Nor need a would-be victim nation wait until a would-be aggressor nation has stockpiled nuclear or chemical weapons be-

fore the potential victim nation has just cause to strike plants producing such weapons of destruction.

But the justice of a preemptive strike requires that the would-be
victim nation have moral certitude about the hostile intentions of
the putative would-be aggressor nation, and that the targets of the
preemptive strike pose a credible threat to the would-be victim nation's security. Since preemptive strikes evidently destabilize international peace as much as overtly aggressive attacks, it is not enough
for would-be victim nations to have merely probable cause (more
than 50 percent probability) to believe that potential aggressor nations are planning to attack. Because preemptive strikes themselves
break international peace, would-be victim nations should have as
much certitude about the hostile intentions of would-be aggressor
nations as human affairs allow, that is, practical certainty, no reasonable doubt (better than 90 percent probability).

Rescue of Nationals

Nations may have just cause to mount military expeditions to rescue nationals seized by foreign governments or their surrogates. It
is contrary to both reason and international law to detain the nationals of another country for policy reasons, that is, to retaliate
against another nation's policies or to gain policy concessions from
another nation. But military action to rescue nationals can only be
justified if the rescuing nation has moral certainty, practical certainty
excluding reasonable doubt, that a foreign government is responsible
for or supporting the detention, and that negotiations and mediation
will not obtain the nationals' expeditious release. The rescuing nation also needs to have probable cause to believe that the release
attempt will be successful and not likely to lead to the nationals'
death if the attempt is prematurely discovered or fails.

In the spring of 1980, the United States made an ill-fated attempt
to rescue American personnel held hostage in Teheran by surrogates
of the Iranian government, and its failure illustrates the practical
difficulties of such missions. Helicopters landed a small commando
team and equipment in a relatively remote desert area. A technical
problem connected with operating the helicopters in the desert

caused the mission to be aborted before any attempt could be made to rescue the hostages. That may have been rather fortuitous for the commandos and the hostages, since the commandos would have had to defy heavy odds to carry out the mission, and the hostages might have been killed by their captors during the rescue attempt. All in all, military rescue attempts are risky business.

If the seizure of the nationals by foreign governments or their surrogates results in the nationals' death, the wronged nation has no moral or legal right to take offensive military action to punish the guilty nation. Just-war theorists once recognized the justice of individual nations' using military force to punish guilty nations for wrongs suffered (reprisals) and to vindicate international law, but this is no longer the case.[3] The United Nations Charter recognizes the right of individual nations to use military force only in individual or collective self-defense (Arts. 2.4 and 51) and reserves to the Security Council the right to punish guilty nations in connection with enforcement action (Art. 42). The reasons for the modern view are evident: nations all too readily assume themselves to have been wronged in doubtful cases, and legitimating the use of military force by individual nations to punish other nations for alleged wrongs would undermine international peace and invite retaliation, larger hostilities, and possibly the intervention of third parties.

Terrorism

Terrorism is a major international problem, and one of its dimensions is the support that certain nations lend terrorist groups. Nations whose citizens are targets of terrorists at home and abroad may have just cause to use military force to prevent or deter foreign gov-

3. On the older, favorable view of certain offensive wars, see Alfred Vanderpol, *La doctrine scholastique du droit de guerre* (Paris: Pedone, 1919), pp. 32–38. On the newer, unfavorable view, see Joseph C. McKenna, "Ethics and War: A Catholic View," *American Political Science Review* 54 (September 1960): 650; Joseph C. Murray, *Morality and Modern War* (New York: Church Peace Union, 1959), pp. 9, 12; Richard J. Regan, *The Moral Dimensions of Politics* (New York: Oxford University Press, 1986), pp. 150–51. The latter position is also that of recent Popes. See Pius XII, "Già per la sesta volta," *Acta Apostolicae Sedis* 37 (1944): 18; John XXIII, "Pacem in terris," *Acta Apostolicae Sedis* 55 (1963): 291.

ernments from lending such support and to destroy terrorist bases in foreign countries. As in the case of resisting armed attacks by aggressor nations, victim nations need not wait until foreign-based or foreign-supported terrorists actually attack nationals before they have just cause to use military force against nations harboring or supporting terrorist organizations and activities. But victim nations taking military action against nations abetting terrorists need to have moral certitude that the latter nations are in fact linked to terrorist acts against the victim nation's nationals. Such military action would be defensive insofar as its purpose is to destroy terrorist bases and to deter guilty nations from continuing to harbor or lend support to the terrorists. The principle of proportionality should also be observed.

As individual nations have no right to retaliate against or punish nations responsible for the death of their nationals, so individual nations have no right to retaliate against or punish nations responsible for terrorist acts against their nationals. Using military force to punish errant nations is offensive action, and such action is reserved to the Security Council under Article 42. Moreover, the United Nations alone would be competent to try national leaders for international war crimes related to terrorism, although individual nations may try to convict terrorists for crimes within the nations' domestic competence.

The distinction between punitive and deterrent military action against the sanctuaries and sponsors of terrorists, of course, concerns the intentions of those responsible for such action, and the very same military action might be morally and legally (in terms of the U.N. Charter) unacceptable as punitive, and morally and legally acceptable as deterrent. But strict observance of the distinction will often serve to limit the legitimate scope of military action. Were punishment an acceptable cause for waging war, retributive justice would be the professed aim, and human passion for vengeance would be likely to dominate. On the other hand, if defense or deterrence is the only acceptable norm for initiating military action against another nation, the security of a nation and its nationals will be the aim, and war measures will be considered only insofar as they are likely to conduce to that end. Nonetheless, statesmen will find it difficult to exclude passion from their deliberations about military actions to deter terrorists and the sponsors of terrorists.

Several examples may help to illustrate applications of the deterrence principle, and problems connected therewith. One example is the U.S. air raid on Libyan bases on April 14, 1986. President Ronald W. Reagan said that he ordered the attacks because the United States had "solid evidence" that the Libyan government was responsible for the bombing of a West Berlin discothèque that resulted in the death of one U.S. serviceman and the wounding of fifty others. The bombing of the discothèque was not the only contemporaneous incident of Arab terrorism affecting Americans abroad. In January 1985, Arab terrorists hijacked the Italian cruise ship *Achille Lauro* and killed an American passenger; on April 2, 1986, a bomb aboard a TWA passenger jet flying over Greece exploded and killed four people. If there was the "solid evidence" that President Reagan claimed, then it seems reasonable for the U.S. government to have concluded that the air raid was likely to deter future Libyan support for terrorists threatening the lives of Americans in Europe.

More complicated is the situation that confronted Israel with respect to Palestine Liberation Organization (P.L.O.) terrorist attacks against Israeli settlements from bases in southern Lebanon.[4] In response to several such assaults on settlements in northern Israel, Israeli tanks and infantry invaded Lebanon on June 6, 1982. The Israeli government declared that its intention was to clear out P.L.O. bases in a twenty-five-mile zone north of the Israeli-Lebanese border. Prior to that date, Israeli forces had executed tit-for-tat military actions against P.L.O. bases in southern Lebanon in response to assaults on Israeli settlements. The questions to be asked about both the tit-for-tat actions and the initial invasion of Lebanon concern the relative necessity for such actions as deterrents, and the reasonableness of an expectation that they would deter. On the face of it, there was an evident need to deter the P.L.O. attacks on Israeli settlements,

---

4. See Benny Morris, *Israel's Border Wars, 1949–1956* (New York: Oxford University Press, 1994); William V. O'Brien, *Law and Morality in Israel's War with the P.L.O.* (New York: Routledge, 1991).

there seemed to be no other way to do so, there was a reasonable chance that the tit-for-tat military actions would deter the P.L.O., and there was certainty that the destruction of P.L.O. bases in southern Lebanon would prevent or radically inhibit future attacks on Israeli settlements.

The moral propriety of Israeli war conduct during the invasion of Lebanon, of course, is another question. Moreover, the subsequent advance of Israeli forces from southern Lebanon to the environs of Beirut, with the newly declared intention of forcing the evacuation of P.L.O. cadres, resulted in the death of eighteen thousand Arabs and the wounding of thirty thousand, according to Lebanese government estimates (which may be exaggerated). To the extent that the casualties were civilians, and they were mostly such, the expansion of the invasion beyond southern Lebanon may for that and other reasons have lacked the requisite proportionality.

Although nations whose citizens are actual or potential victims of terrorism may be justified in taking defensive military action to prevent or deter nations abetting terrorists, the Security Council retains ultimate authority and responsibility even in military self-defense, as Article 51 makes clear. The United Nations could establish rules of international conduct relating to terrorism, but the efficacy of the rules would depend on the ability and willingness of the Security Council, with the support of the major powers, to take enforcement action under Article 42.

Rectifying Economic Injury

For a government to repudiate debts and interest owed to foreign governments or foreign nationals, or to confiscate the property of foreign nationals without compensation, would be prima facie unjust. Injured nations might accordingly have just cause to impose, and mobilize other nations to impose, economic sanctions on the offending nation, and the resulting economic harm to the citizens of the offending nation could be proportional to the economic harm inflicted on the victim nation or its citizens. But no due proportion seems possible between the killing involved in war and the economic harm involved in violation of contractual or property rights. Moreover, such economic harm can be and normally is indemnified in whole or in part at a future date. There might be due proportion between the killing in war and the vindication of international law, but no individual nation has the authority or responsibility to vindicate international law. Only the Security Council has the authority to do so, and it has that authority only in connection with maintaining international peace and security (cf. Art. 42).

Moreover, economic sanctions are likely to be highly effective in rectifying and deterring violations of international contractual or property rights. This is because creditor nations are almost necessarily major economic powers, and private parties with economic assets or credits in foreign countries will almost certainly be nationals of major economic powers. Developed nations have vast economic leverage, especially the denial of fresh public and private capital, to bring to bear against offending, presumably developing, nations.

An international cartel of oil-producing nations might attempt to set prohibitively high oil prices and/or excessively low export quotas and thereby wreak worldwide economic havoc. This is unlikely to occur for two reasons: (1) some oil-producing nations would be likely to undercut prices or exceed quotas if the cartel sets prices too much higher than the market prices or sets quotas too much lower than the market demand; (2) oil-importing nations could and would reduce their oil consumption, develop alternate energy sources, and/ or spend less on other goods. Voluntarily established oil-production quotas and prices are unlikely to result in more than limited, short-term dislocations in the economies of oil-importing nations, and it is not obvious why such quotas and prices would be unjust to the consumers of oil-importing nations in the absence of conventions banning cartels.

But if a cartel of oil-producing nations were successfully to use threats of military force or political subversion to compel reluctant oil-producing nations to comply with the quotas and prices set by the cartel, the long-term consequences for the economies of oil-importing nations might well be disastrous. The world community might then be justified in considering such coercive activities to be the functional equivalent of aggression, and the U.N. Security Council might be justified in taking measures, including enforcement action under Article 42, to counter such activities.

Military intervention to rectify economic injury is prominently associated with the "Big Stick" policy of the United States regarding Caribbean nations in the early decades of the twentieth century. In 1901, for example, the U.S. Congress passed the Platt Amendment, which, among other things, claimed the right of the United States to intervene in Cuba to oversee the latter's fulfillment of its international financial commitments, and the U.S. government successfully insisted that the Cubans incorporate the amendment into their new constitution. And in 1904, President Theodore Roosevelt warned Caribbean nations that the United States would intervene to restore order and force them to live up to their international financial obligations.

To forestall the possibility of European nations' using military force against the Dominican Republic to secure repayment of debts to their nationals, the U.S. government in 1905 took over the republic's customshouses and earmarked custom receipts for repayment of the debts. Native opposition led later to the stationing of U.S. marines in the republic from 1916 to 1924.

For similar reasons, the United States took over the customshouses of Haiti in 1905 and occupied the country from 1915 to 1934. After the end of the occupation in 1934, the United States continued to exercise direct fiscal control over Haiti until 1941.

In 1912, the U.S. government sent a detachment of marines to Nicaragua, and Nicaraguan customs receipts were placed under U.S. control to ensure the repayment of loans to American and European bankers. The marines were withdrawn in 1925 but returned in 1927 and remained there until 1933.

This "Big Stick" policy not only risked war in part to vindicate economic claims but also led to deep-seated Latin American resentment against the United States. But the perceived necessity to prevent European military intervention in the Western Hemisphere to secure repayment of debts might arguably have justified some of the U.S. government's actions in the Caribbean up to the outbreak of World War I.

Vindicating Territorial Claims

The aim of using military force to resist actual or imminent military action by another nation, to recover territory recently seized by another nation, to rescue nationals held by another nation, or to prevent or deter terrorists operating from foreign bases is avowedly defensive and may be justified if the requisite conditions are satisfied. But the use of military force to vindicate territorial claims unconnected with other nations' current or recent aggression is offensive action. Although the aim of military action to vindicate long-standing territorial claims may be to right a putative wrong, and the cause may be "just" in that sense, the human and material destruction of modern warfare and the destabilizing effect of such wars on world peace are vastly disproportionate to the cause.

Perhaps no other cause in recorded history has been invoked as often as that of vindicating territorial claims. Up to World War I, just-war theorists and international-law publicists held that such wars might be justified.[5] After World War I and the overwhelming popular revulsion at its ghastly toll of more than 36 million dead, most nations of the world became signatories of the Kellogg-Briand Pact, which explicitly renounced war as an instrument of national policy and implicitly repudiated offensive wars, that is, wars initiated to force recognition of a nation's putative rights or territorial claims, or to punish putative violations of international law or national rights. And Article 2.4 of the United Nations Charter requires members to refrain from the use of force against the territorial integrity or independence of any state.

The reasons for the contemporary consensus against initiating wars to acquire or recover disputed territories are not difficult to understand. From the development of the machine gun in the second half of the nineteenth century, modern technology has made warfare vastly more deadly for combatants and civilians alike. Second, unprovoked attacks on other nations to vindicate territorial claims are likely to draw allies of the two principals into the hostilities and so transform a local conflict into a regional or worldwide conflict.

---

5. See n. 3.

Third, to admit that nations might have just cause to initiate hostilities to vindicate territorial claims would encourage war and endlessly imperil international peace and security. Indeed, because wars to vindicate territorial claims inevitably have the latter effect, it is difficult to understand how such wars could ever have been thought to be justifiable.

There is scarcely a region in the world where one nation could not lay claim to a territory presently incorporated in another nation. On the basis of prior occupancy, for example, many Palestinians lay claim to the whole of Israel, and France could on the basis of prior occupancy lay claim to Quebec, Germany to Silesia, the Republic of Ireland to Ulster, Colombia to Panama, and Mexico to the southwestern United States. Nor would treaties between the affected parties necessarily preclude such claims, since nations seeking to vindicate territorial claims relinquished by treaty might argue, in some cases plausibly, that they were coerced into signing the treaties that recognize other nations' title to disputed territories. Moreover, aggressors have used territorial claims as a pretext to attack and conquer whole nations. Hitler, for example, in 1939 used a German claim to the Polish Corridor as a pretext to occupy the whole of Poland (in consort with the Soviet Union), and Saddam Hussein in 1990 used an Iraqi claim to certain oil fields in Kuwait as a pretext to occupy the whole of Kuwait.

To argue that nations may not justly initiate hostilities to vindicate claims to lost territories is not to argue that nations may not justly resort to military action to recover territory recently occupied by an aggressor. But when should territory be considered "lost" and no just cause for waging war for its recovery, and when should territory be considered "recently occupied" and a just cause for waging war? How long does a nation need to occupy or possess a territory before that nation should be presumed to have acquired at least a prescriptive right to it?

The situation is analogous to the acquisition of private property by prescription (adverse possession) in domestic law. As nations in their domestic law recognize adverse possessors' right to private property after a specified period, so the world community recognizes occupying nations' right to territory after some time. Unfortunately, there is no agreement about the length of that period. A generation would certainly seem long enough, but a single year might be a preferable limit from the viewpoint of international peace and security. That would give the victim nation and supporting nations, ideally with the approval of the Security Council, sufficient time to mobilize military forces to expel the occupying power without encouraging wars to reclaim longer-lost territories. It is also important to note that the right of possessor nations to retain sovereignty over disputed territories after some period in no way affects the rights of individual owners to compensation for private property forcibly taken from them by the possessor nations or their irregular surrogates, or the human rights of ethnic minorities.

Two examples will illustrate the chief reasons why the U.N. Charter and contemporary commentators disallow the legitimacy of waging war to vindicate claims to "lost" territory. The first, the brief Falklands War, represents a classic case: a war between rival claimants to territory long in possession of one of them. One claimant, Argentina, had declared its sovereignty over the Falklands in 1820, and Argentine colonists settled there in 1829. The other claimant, Great Britain, ejected the handful of Argentine colonists in 1833 and resettled the islands. The British held unchallenged possession of the islands from 1833 to 1982, by which time the mainly British-stock inhabitants numbered close to two thousand persons. After seventeen years of fruitless talks under U.N. sponsorship about the status of the islands, Argentine armed forces occupied the Falklands on April 2, 1982. The British mounted a successful campaign to recover the islands, and Argentine forces there surrendered on June 14. Whatever the abstract merits of the Argentine claim, the British had been in possession of the Falklands for 149 years, and the residents evidently had no desire to be under Argentine sovereignty. Moreover, close to one thousand combatants lost their lives in the war, and the war's financial costs, especially for the British, were substantial. (For further details, references, and questions, see the case study on the war.)

The second example is more complicated. The state of Israel proclaimed its independence on May 14, 1948. Prior to that date, Zionist militias had achieved control of a sizable part of Palestine, and terrorist acts, especially the massacre at Deir Yasin, had resulted in a mass exodus of hundreds of thousands of Arabs from Zionist-controlled territory. In the ensuing war between the new state of Israel and its Arab neighbors, Israel acquired significantly more territory. Refugee Arabs and Arabs in neighboring Middle Eastern states refused to accept the legitimacy of Israel and vowed to restore Israeli territory to Arab control. There were sporadic guerrilla attacks against Israel from neighboring countries. The rise of Gamel Abdel Nasser to power in 1954 led Israel to perceive Egypt under his leadership as a major threat to its existence, and so Israel cooperated with the 1956 Anglo-French invasion of Egypt and attacked Egypt preemptively in 1967. As a result of the latter war, in which Syria and Jordan participated as allies of Egypt, Israel occupied the rest of Palestine, and the Gaza strip, areas heavily populated by Arab refugees from Israeli territory before and after Israel's declaration of independence. In 1973, Israeli forces successfully repulsed an attack by Egypt (and Syria), crossed the Suez Canal, and were poised to attack Cairo. At this point, the Soviet Union threatened to intervene, and there was a serious risk of war between the United States and the Soviet Union. Pressured by the United States, Israel agreed to withdraw its forces from Egyptian territory.

In a dramatic break with the Arab coalition against Israel, Egypt concluded a peace treaty with Israel on March 26, 1979. But the détente induced Palestinians to rely on their own efforts rather than on help from neighboring Arab states for the restoration of Arab rule in Palestine. Palestinian attacks on Israeli settlements and settlers from bases in southern Lebanon precipitated an Israeli invasion of Lebanon. The Israeli forces, though suffering relatively high casualties, forced the evacuation of P.L.O. militias from Lebanon to other Arab states, after which Israeli forces withdrew to territory in southern Lebanon that the Israeli government designated a security zone. The focus of the Arab-Israeli conflict then shifted to the occupied Palestinian territories. On December 8, 1987, Palestinian Arabs in those territories began a series of boycotts, demonstrations, and attacks on Israeli settlers. Some three hundred Palestinians were killed in the first year of the uprising (the *intifada*).

Palestinian Arabs may have reasonable claims against some of the means Zionists employed at the creation of the state of Israel. They may have reasonable claims to restitution or compensation for property taken by the Israelis in the course of the events leading to, and consequent upon, the formation of Israel. Those living on the West Bank or in the Gaza strip have reasonable claims to an autonomy consistent with the security of Israel. But more than forty-six years of possession of the pre-1967 territory gives Israel a prescriptive right to exist in that territory. The casualties of the conventional wars and unconventional warfare since 1948 demonstrate the moral irresponsibility of attempting by force to destroy the state of Israel, not least because the Arabs themselves suffered most of the casualties. This is not, of course, to deny that many of Israel's post-1948 military and police actions, Israel's treatment of the inhabitants of the occupied territories, and Israel's invasion of Lebanon beyond a security zone may also have been morally irresponsible. Nor is it to deny that the occupied territories should be granted autonomy with due regard for the security of Israel.

Proportionality

The decision to wage war will be justified only if the wrong to be prevented or rectified equals or surpasses the reasonably anticipated human and material costs of the war. Such due proportion involves three elements: (1) a value judgment about the worth of the cause that purports to justify recourse to war; (2) factual judgments about the war's likely casualties and costs; (3) a value judgment about the proportional worth of the war's cause in relation to its likely casualties and costs.

Judgments about the worth of a war's cause are undoubtedly subjective insofar as the human subjects making them have values that influence their evaluations, but the judgments have an objective reference point: the cause's real worth in the scale of human values.

Estimates of a war's likely casualties and costs will necessarily involve hypothetical projections of the war's likely course, and the estimates have no higher probability than the probability of the war's projected course. Moreover, experts often reach different conclusions about a war's likely course, and experts' values and attitudes undoubtedly incline them to be either optimistic or pessimistic about the war's likely course, and so to minimize or maximize its potential casualties and costs. Nevertheless, these estimates have an objective point of reference: the empirical context of the contemplated war.

Third, practical reason needs to compare the value of a war's cause to its likely casualties and costs, and to judge whether or not there is due proportion between them. It is not enough for reason to estimate in absolute terms the war's likely casualties and costs; if reason fails to weigh the proportionality of the casualties and costs to the cause, no war (or no war beyond an unspecified threshold) could be justified. These comparative judgments also have an objective point of reference: the real worth of the contemplated war's cause and the evidence and logic supporting estimates of the war's anticipated casualties and costs.

Despite the indemonstrable values and the factual uncertainties involved, it is the function of practical reason to make such judgments, and statesmen need to make these judgments if they are to ascertain that they have a proportionate just cause to wage war.

Last Resort

Nations are not justified in resorting to war as long as they have reasonable hope that means short of war can prevent or rectify wrong. In the case of direct military attack, of course, the nation attacked has no short-term choice other than to resist or capitulate. In other situations, however, negotiations may offer a reasonable alternative to war. The key word is *reasonable,* and negotiations will be a reasonable alternative to war only if nations wronged or about to be wronged have probable cause to believe that negotiations will lead to the prevention or rectification of wrong, not merely that negotiations may do so. Offers to negotiate by aggressor nations in possession of the fruits of their aggression, for example, may be only ploys to delay or escape retribution, and it would be unreasonable for victim nations and their allies to take such offers seriously without tangible evidence that the guilty nation intends to withdraw and indemnify the victim nation. (The guilty nation may be using the ploy of negotiations to gain time for military advantage or to undermine the political will of democratic countries to take military action against it.) And the victims of aggression (e.g., citizens of occupied territories, hostages) pay the price of lost liberty for any delay.

Third parties may be able to facilitate negotiations between nations in disputes that threaten to lead to war. Regional associations (e.g., the Organization of American States, the European Community) or the U.N. secretary general may be able to mediate disputes and suggest ways to resolve them. As in the case of direct negotiations, mediation will be a reasonable alternative to war only if nations wronged or about to be wronged have a reasonable, not merely a possible, hope that mediation will result in preventing or rectifying wrong, and the reasonableness of such a hope will depend on clear evidence that the other nation intends to do so. Moreover, once hostilities have commenced, the chance of mediation's being successful will be slight until military events dictate the outcome or induce the parties to negotiate.

Economic sanctions are the other possible alternative to war. But to be a reasonable alternative to war, economic sanctions need first of all to be appropriate to the wrong to be rectified. Economic sanctions are appropriate remedies to rectify economic wrongs, since, no matter how long the sanctions take to have a significant effect, the wrongs can be adequately compensated at a later date. On the other hand, noneconomic wrongs (e.g., depriving whole peoples or innocent individuals of their liberty) cannot be later adequately compensated by money, and economic sanctions necessarily take time to produce a significant enough impact to cause the guilty nation to yield.

Moreover, to be a reasonable alternative to war, economic sanctions need to have a reasonable, that is, a solidly probable and not merely a possible, hope of bringing about the desired rectification of wrong. There are several reasons why economic sanctions alone may often not prove ultimately effective. First, economic sanctions may be difficult to enforce. The ingenuity of private entrepreneurs, the disinclination of some nations to cooperate, and inadequate means of enforcement may limit the effectiveness of economic sanctions. Second, interdiction of food supplies is particularly unlikely to be effective, since the target nation will probably be able to increase its domestic production of vegetables and poultry in a matter of months.[6] Third, and most important, economic costs alone, however severe, may and probably will not induce authoritarian rulers to desist, since such rulers are not responsible to their citizens.[7]

Cessation of Just Cause

The causes justifying war may cease to do so. If and when the belligerent that unjustly caused a war calls for a truce, the other belligerent and its allies may no longer have any just cause to wage war. The other belligerent and its allies will have no just cause for continuing the war if the guilty nation is seriously willing to rectify wrong and to accept just conditions that the wronged nation and its allies require to ensure rectification of wrong. Any serious violation of the truce or any serious failure to abide by its conditions will justify resumption of hostilities.

Economic sanctions after a truce may be justified to guarantee that guilty nations carry out the just conditions that the wronged nation and its allies have imposed. Although some conditions can be carried out promptly (e.g., withdrawal from occupied territory, release of hostages, exchange of prisoners), other conditions may require time to fulfill (e.g., destruction of offensive weapons or nuclear materials). Continued economic sanctions may accordingly be justified to assure that the latter type of conditions are fulfilled, especially if there is good reason to fear deception. But economic sanctions should not be continued if and when the guilty nation has substantially carried out the conditions.[8]

6. Interdiction of food supplies also raises a serious moral question, since enemy civilian populations would be the chief targets. This would seem to be functionally equivalent to making ordinary civilians military targets and so contrary to the principle of discrimination. See chapter 5.

7. The ability of Iraq during and after the Gulf War to sustain the effects of economic sanctions is a case in point. If the regime in Iraq was able to survive economically after its defeat in that war, it is hardly likely that economic sanctions alone would have induced that regime to withdraw from Kuwait.

8. The same principle would apply to the continuance of economic sanctions

It is prima facie just for victors to demand that guilty nations pay reparations to the latter's victims. But it would not be just for victor nations to demand that guilty nations pay reparations in such an amount or at such a pace as to leave the guilty nation's citizens destitute or seriously to impair the health of the guilty nation's citizens. Moreover, it will be imprudent for victor nations to impose severe reparations on the guilty nation, however just the reparations may be in principle, since severe reparations sow seeds of resentment that may yield a harvest of future war.

---

against a decisively defeated enemy without any real possibility of resuming hostilities. Such was the case when the Allies continued blockading food imports to Germany after the armistice until the signing of the Treaty of Versailles. Since Germany was for many reasons incapable of resuming hostilities, continuance of the Allied blockade seems to have been purely vindictive and to have inflicted indiscriminate hardship on German civilians.

4

THE JUST WAR DECISION
Just Cause and Interventionist Wars

Traditional just-cause considerations focus on the putative rights of one nation to wage war against another. But other kinds of war situations involve the putative rights of one nation to intervene in conflicts within another. Dependent regions often seek either to become independent sovereignties or to shift political allegiance to other sovereignties. Wars of secession result if the preexisting sovereignties resist, or if the two parties fail to reach agreement on the terms of divorce. Such wars are sometimes included in the category of civil wars, but the former wars differ from the latter wars in one very important respect: wars of secession are those in which regional parts of preexisting political units seek to secede from the latter, whereas civil wars are those in which particular individuals and/or groups seek to gain or retain control of the whole of existing political units. There are accordingly different kinds of moral issues at stake in the two kinds of wars, and different kinds of moral issues with respect to outside military intervention in the wars.

Intervention in Other Nations' Internal Affairs and Civil Wars

Each political community has a prima facie right to determine its form of government and the domestic policies it wishes to pursue.

68

Nations, therefore, have a prima facie duty not to interfere in the internal affairs of other nations, least of all by fomenting or supporting revolutions against other nations' governments.

But nations waging just wars against unjust enemies may justly foment or support revolutions against enemy governments. And nations may in self-defense or defense of other nations foment or support revolutions against the governments of potential enemies that credibly threaten aggression. The threat of aggression should not be fanciful: the potential enemy should pose a credible military threat, whether alone or in concert with its allies, and have adequately demonstrated its intention to attack. If a potential victim nation and its allies have moral certitude that these conditions are fulfilled, they will have the just cause of self-defense to support revolutionaries against the potential enemy's government. By the same token, if a potential victim nation and its allies have moral certitude that foreign revolutionaries, if victorious, would possess a credible military potential for aggression, and that the foreign revolutionaries have adequately demonstrated their intention to attack, the potential victim nation and its allies will have the just cause of self-defense to support the foreign government against the revolutionaries.

Nations may also have humanitarian reasons for intervening militarily in the internal affairs and civil wars of other nations. Foreign governments may be totalitarian or authoritarian, oppressing ethnic or religious minorities, or even practicing genocide. Or foreign revolutionaries may be seeking to impose a totalitarian regime. Or foreign nations may be sinking or have already sunk into a state of anarchy. Such humanitarian reasons have not traditionally been considered just causes for outside nations or the world community to intervene militarily, although they would in the case of actual or impending anarchy if the nominal government invited outside nations to do so. But world opinion is changing in this regard, and humanitarian reasons are prima facie just causes for intervention. Whether or not it is proportionately just for outside nations or the world community to intervene militarily is another question.

There are powerful systemic reasons why outside nations and the world community should be reluctant to intervene militarily in a nation's internal affairs or civil war for humanitarian reasons. First, there may be fundamental international disagreement about the standard of justice to be applied. Second, there may be fundamental international disagreement about the application of a universally accepted standard of justice to particular cases. Third, intervention may prove very costly in human lives if the dominant local or regional population perceives it to be politically, economically, or ethnically motivated. Fourth, assuming that individual nations and the world community would be unable or unwilling to prevent or remedy every violation of human rights, on what basis could they or should they choose to intervene in particular cases? Fifth, interventions avowedly to prevent or remedy human rights violations could easily mask, or be transformed into, intervention to annex territory or dismember the affected nation. Sixth, nations might seek to manipulate U.N.-sanctioned intervention for their own political, economic, or ethnic advantage rather than to alleviate human suffering. Lastly, intervention for humanitarian reasons in the internal affairs or civil war of a major power might provoke a major war.

The United States cited the humanitarian goal of protecting the people of South Vietnam from Communist rule as one justification for U.S. military intervention there from 1965 to 1973. Assuming that the rebels, if victorious, would establish a radically unjust regime, and that the humanitarian goal of preventing the establishment of such a regime was a cause that might justify intervention, the United States had to weigh the feasibility of committing its combat forces to the defense of the Saigon government, that is, whether the war would be "winnable," and whether it would be "winnable" at acceptable political, military, and economic costs. U.S. leaders evidently underestimated the capacity and will of the Viet Cong and the Hanoi government to wage war, as well as the resulting military and economic costs to the United States. U.S. leaders also overestimated the willingness of the American public to support a casualty-intensive and economically costly war of indeterminate duration. Moreover, the corruption and autocratic character of the Saigon regime undercut the humanitarian premise of U.S. intervention. (For further details, references, and questions, see the case study on the war.)

Although the United States cited, in part, humanitarian reasons for its invasions of Grenada (1983) and Panama (1989), those actions involved no long-term commitment of armed forces. Victory was swift, and U.S. involvement short. The same cannot be said about the operation in Somalia. There the United States and associated nations, with the approval of the U.N. Security Council (S.C. Resolution 794), landed troops on December 9, 1992. The primary declared purpose of the military mission was to secure the delivery of relief supplies to starving Somalis, and President George H. W. Bush had assured the American people on December 4 that the United States would not dictate a political settlement to the Somali people. The U.S.-led forces met no organized opposition and suffered very few casualties. In the ensuing months, the forces successfully secured the delivery of relief supplies to the countryside. The transfer of command to the United Nations on May 4, 1993, however, led to attempts to disarm the forces of one of the two factions in Mogadishu, those of Mohammed Farah Aidid, and U.N. peacekeepers and U.S. forces began to suffer casualties. When a raid on an Aidid compound on October 5 resulted in the death of eighteen U.S. soldiers and the wounding of more than seventy-five, the United States declared its intention on October 7 to withdraw its forces from Somalia by March 31, 1994. Other nations followed suit.

The first phase of the Somali operation (December 8, 1992–May 4, 1993) was successful both in terms of accomplishing its primary aim of securing the delivery of relief supplies, and in terms of suffering almost no casualties. The second phase of the operation (May 4–October 7, 1993) transformed the mission to one of reconstructing the Somali political structure. Not only did the second phase fail to achieve its military and political goals, but the resulting casualties became unacceptable to Western leaders and electorates. (For further details, references, and questions, see the case study on the war.)

The transformation of the Somali mission and the consequences thereof illustrate the dangers of outside nations' trying to be too good Samaritans. Interventionist military operations for humanitarian purposes work best when they have narrowly defined, limited objectives that enjoy the broad support or tolerance of native parties and factions; they work worst when they have broadly defined, virtually indeterminate objectives that risk confrontation with one or more native party or faction. The lesson of the Somali operation is clear: intervening nations should limit their objectives to humanitarian relief unless they—and their electorates—are prepared to accept a long-term commitment and appreciable casualties, not to mention economic costs.

The United Nations in 1992 established a full-scale peacekeeping operation in Cambodia to restore peace among three warring factions in that country (S.C. Resolution 745). The United Nations did so only after receiving assurances that the parties would support or tolerate the intervention, although the United Nations needed to threaten one of the parties (the Khmer Rouge) in order to secure its cooperation with the agreed-upon elections (see S.C. Resolution 783). And the transitional peacekeeping operation had a human-rights component (U.N. Doc. s/23613). The United Nations thus moved actively but circumspectly in its efforts to reconstruct Cambodia. In the one instance when, by threatening one of the warring parties, it had arguably crossed the line between peacekeeping and peacemaking, the support of the other two parties enhanced its position.

A policy of legitimating outside intervention in a nation's internal affairs or civil war for humanitarian reasons poses many risks and uncertainties over the long run. On the other hand, just as the world community has a moral duty to help alleviate the human suffering resulting from natural disasters, so it has a general moral duty to help alleviate the human suffering resulting from human activity. A commonsense approach might be to legitimate external humanitarian intervention only in worst-case scenarios (e.g., to prevent genocide). The world community should move slowly down the unchartered path of intervention in nations' internal affairs and civil wars, and resist the Messianic temptation to right every wrong without regard to short- and long-term consequences.

In worst-case scenarios of human rights violations or anarchy, the world community would have ample just cause to intervene. But the United Nations, not an individual nation or group of nations, has the primary responsibility for the well-being of the world community.

The U.N. Security Council should authorize any intervention before the fact if possible, and after the fact if not antecedently feasible. The multinational composition of the council and the likely reluctance of nations to undertake military actions unrelated to their paramount interests should be sufficient to preclude intervention's being a pretext for political, economic, or ethnic imperialism.

Secession and Intervention in Secessionist Wars

Just-war theorists recognize the general right of a people of a given territory to decide how they will organize themselves as a community. This right derives from the rational and free nature of human beings; human beings, because they are rational, need to form a political community for their mutual benefit, and human beings, because they are endowed with free will, should decide how that community will be organized. There are many reasons why peoples in dependent regions may seek independence (e.g., political, economic, sectional, ethnic, religious reasons), but ethnicity and religion stand out as the most important causes of secession in many parts of Eastern Europe in the aftermath of the collapse of the Soviet Union, and as the primary cause of the descent into violence of the former nation of Yugoslavia and the would-be nation of Bosnia. Indeed, minority ethnic groups in the former Soviet Union and the former Yugoslavia had little or no choice in the creation of the multi-ethnic units from which they seek to secede.

The present condition of the former Yugoslav federation illustrates the problems connected with the principle of self-determination. The central problem posed by the principle is that its consistent application would justify minorities within a secessionist state in demanding independence from that state, and especially demanding reunion with fellow ethnics of the remainder state. For example, if the people of Ireland have a right to independence from Great Britain, cannot the people of Northern Ireland claim the right to affiliate with the United Kingdom? And if the people of Northern Ireland have a right to affiliate with the United Kingdom, cannot the people in Catholic areas of Northern Ireland claim the right to affiliate with the Republic of Ireland? And if the people of the Catholic areas of

Northern Ireland have a right to affiliate with the Republic of Ireland, cannot the people in Protestant enclaves in Catholic areas of Northern Ireland claim the right to dissociate themselves from those areas and to affiliate with the United Kingdom? This problem is most acute when the two ethnic groups claiming a right of self-determination live in a checkerboard pattern of close proximity, as in Bosnia.

A further question concerns the right of component states in a federal union to secede from the union to which they have previously given free consent. Do communities that have previously consented to a federal union lose the right to alter their political status when they disagree with the federal union's policies, presupposing that the previously agreed-upon constitution is being fully observed? This, of course, was the issue posed by the secession of the Confederate States from the United States in 1861.

The right to self-determination, then, needs to be qualified in important ways. At a minimum, the secessionist state and the remainder state should settle boundary disputes by negotiation or arbitration; they should do so because of practical considerations (e.g., peaceful coexistence, political stability, economic development) and because their rival claims to particular territory are often incapable of being resolved on any principled moral or legal basis. Second, the secessionist state should recognize and protect the civil rights of ethnic minorities, and the remainder state should do likewise with respect to its ethnic minorities. Third, the secessionist and remainder states should compensate individuals for official or officially condoned violence and the destruction or confiscation of private property. Fourth, the secessionist and remainder states should negotiate or agree to arbitrate apportionment of the preexisting national debt and nonterritorial assets (e.g., national airlines).

Secessionist states necessarily rely on, and expressly appeal to, the moral right of indigenous peoples to determine how their communities will be organized; they are less likely to appreciate the correlative principle that peoples organized in separate political communities have a practical need and a moral obligation to cooperate with one another. This cooperation is a practical necessity because separate political communities, especially small ones, cannot enjoy physical security and enhance their economic development without such cooperation; it is a moral obligation because reason dictates that peoples, like individuals, should cooperate for their mutual benefit and self-development. Where a federal union previously existed, a looser federation of the member states, or a confederal association, might be constituted. Both the secessionist and remainder states might be incorporated into a larger, regional association like the European Community. Only a world federation in which member states relinquish their right to wage war and to exercise independent control over their economies could fully achieve the objectives of peace, security, and economic development, but regional associations are probably a necessary first step in modifying the existing nation-state system and creating a more integrated world order.

In a secessionist conflict, the initial aim of outside nations should be to bring the parties to reconcile their differences and reconstitute the distribution of power between the central government and regional divisions. Neither of these objectives may be possible, at least in the short run. If so, outside nations should accept that reality and work to mediate the terms and conditions of divorce.[1] If mediation fails, and one party resorts to military force to acquire territory, outside nations may have proportionate just cause to provide direct or indirect military assistance to the victim party. As indicated in the previous chapter, Article 51 of the United Nations Charter recognizes the right of individual and collective self-defense, subject to the authority of the Security Council.

But the only just aim of an outside nation's assisting secessionists is to support the secessionists' right of self-determination, not to vindicate the assisting nation's territorial claims or to further the assisting nation's regional hegemony. Moreover, outside nations should condition any military assistance to secessionists on the latter's agreeing to negotiate or arbitrate boundaries, to protect the lives and

---

1. Professional foreign-service personnel are often slow to recognize the fact that a preexisting political unit has irreparably dissolved. The United States, for example, was slow to perceive the irreparable dissolution of the political unity of the republics of the former Soviet Union after Communist rule collapsed in 1991.

property of ethnic minorities, and to observe the rules of just war. (If outside nations have just cause to assist the remainder state to defend itself or the rights of fellow ethnics within the secessionist state, outside nations should impose similar conditions on the remainder state, namely, recognition of the secessionists' right of self-determination, negotiation or arbitration of boundaries, protection of ethnic minorities, and just-war conduct.) Third, intervention will not be just if it raises casualties and costs beyond due proportion, and the intervention of one or more nations in behalf of secessionists may do so, especially if the intervention provokes one or more nations to intervene in behalf of the remainder state—or vice versa. Fourth, regional assistance or U.N. action is preferable to intervention by a single nation or an ad hoc coalition of nations, since regional assistance or U.N. action would not only shoulder the burdens of intervention more effectively but also enhance the legitimacy of the intervention.

Given the emotional intensity of ethnic conflicts, it is almost inevitable that one or both sides will commit atrocities. Moreover, ethnic conflicts are likely to spawn irregular forces, that is, forces under a local warlord, and these forces may be more disposed to commit atrocities than the regular forces, that is, forces under the official leadership of the group. A consistent pattern of war atrocities with or without the official leadership's overt complicity would vitiate the group's claim to be fighting for a just cause, and outside nations would accordingly have no just cause to intervene in the group's behalf. And it is indeed possible that both sides will be guilty of pervasive, unpunished atrocities, in which case outside nations would have no just cause to intervene in behalf of either side.

Intervention to provide humanitarian aid to the minority victims of ethnic majorities seems at first glance to promise relief to the victims and to avoid heavier costs. But provision of humanitarian aid, even if successively delivered, would neither end the victim's plight nor pacify the region. And the prospects of outside humanitarian aid's being effectively delivered without involving the use of outside military force are poor unless the dominant ethnic faction in an area agrees to allow the aid to be delivered. If the dominant ethnic faction in the area does not, outside nations will need to use military force to escort personnel and supplies to the stricken area and to pacify the area in order to deliver aid to the victims. Effective humanitarian aid is likely to involve the use of considerable military force and so to incur high human and material costs.

The world community might also ban the shipment of military or war-related supplies (e.g., oil) to the belligerents or their patrons. But such a ban, even if effective, would leave the dominant faction in control of disputed territory and the ethnic minority and do nothing in the short run to stop the dominant ethnic group from victimizing the ethnic minority. Moreover, the dominant ethnic faction may already have in its possession enough heavy weapons and ammunition to wage large-scale war, as ethnic Serbs in Bosnia did with the equipment and ammunition bequeathed them by the former Yugoslav army when it withdrew to Serbia. Third, notwithstanding a ban on the shipment of military supplies to belligerents, dominant ethnics and their kindred patrons will probably be able to import arms, ammunition, parts, and oil by air, sea and inland waterways, or land. Fourth, the embargo will in any case take time to affect the ability of the dominant ethnic faction to wage large-scale war and to victimize the ethnic minority. Lastly, the result of the ban, if and when it is effective, will be limited to transforming a heavy-weapons war into a small-arms war.

Some, like Baroness Margaret Thatcher in the case of Bosnia, have proposed that outside nations arm the victim minority. That might help the victim minority resist encroachment by the military forces of the dominant ethnic faction, but it certainly would not pacify the region; it would in fact have exactly the opposite effect, increasing war casualties without resolving the conflict. Moreover, the international community would thereby lose any ability to control the behavior of the victim minority provided with military arms, unless the international community were to impose conditions on the assistance and were able to enforce the conditions.

It has also been suggested that regional associations or nations acting under the authority of the Security Council lend air support, and naval support where practicable, to assist victim minorities in secessionist wars. Such direct intervention might inflict considerable damage on the military forces of the dominant ethnic faction, reduce its capacity to wage conventional war, and expose intervening nations to low risk of casualties. But air power alone might and probably would be insufficient to alter the military situation on the ground significantly, relieve the plight of the victim minority, or pacify the region. The U.S. experience in Vietnam seems to have demonstrated that control of the air will not by itself bring military victory on the ground against a determined enemy. The most that air power alone may be able to accomplish is to induce the enemy forces to wage covert, guerrilla warfare in place of open, conventional war.

Intervening nations may seek to win a decisive victory by committing large-scale ground forces to the war. But the casualties of doing so might be very high, the conventional war might be transformed into a guerrilla war, and the war might become intractable. Casualties would mount, the war would drag on, and the political will of the intervening nations might erode without decisively weakening the political will of the enemy. Second, maintaining operational ground forces in remote areas over time would be expensive. Third, there may be several concurrent secessionist wars in which ethnic minorities are being victimized, and there will certainly be many successive secessionist wars involving victimized ethnic minorities. The cumulative casualties and costs of outside interventions would be high, and intervening nations would probably be unwilling or unable to sustain all such casualties and costs. On what principle should outside nations or the world community ration large-scale military interventions?

On the other hand, outside ground-force intervention in ethnic secessionist wars would for several reasons probably be more manageable than U.S. intervention in Vietnam was. First, the civil war in South Vietnam was between warring factions fighting either to unite the whole of South Vietnam with North Vietnam or to maintain the whole of South Vietnam as an independent, non-Communist political unit, whereas ethnic secessionist wars are between groups fighting for control of parts of the preexisting political unit. Second, warring factions in South Vietnam were not readily identifiable as friendly or hostile and did not live in different communities, whereas ethnic secessionists are generally identifiable, at least by locals, and may live in relatively discrete territories, albeit often in checkerboard patterns of close proximity. It will accordingly be easier to wage conventional war in the latter context than in the former. Third, the war in Vietnam did not involve specific territory and boundaries within a larger territory; an ethnic secessionist war does. Despite these differences, however, large-scale outside intervention might very well still involve ultimately disproportionate and politically unacceptable casualties and costs.

The world community and the United Nations are at an important crossroad. The East-West Cold War dominated world concerns from the end of World War II to August 1991. That "war" abruptly ended when the Soviet Union collapsed. With its demise and the almost simultaneous disintegration of Titoist Yugoslavia, ethnic nationalism has induced secessionist wars in Eastern Europe. Should the world community and the United Nations intervene in these wars, or should they restrict their efforts to mediation? The United Nations Charter did not envision such an interventionist role for the world organization, since the charter, echoing the traditional concerns of international law, was designed to prevent war and enforce peace among existing nations with defined boundaries. The world community and the United Nations must now decide whether and to what extent they wish to intervene in secessionist wars to determine and enforce rights of self-determination and rights of ethnic minorities in both secessionist and remainder states.

Outside intervention in secessionist wars might promote both the short-term goal of restoring justice and peace in particular regions and the longer-term goal of worldwide peace and security. But what kind of intervention and for what objectives? Humanitarian aid has the limited objective of relieving the suffering of victims, but even this objective may not be achievable without the use of military force. Sanctions have the broader objective of denying to belligerents the ability to wage war, or of weakening the military or economic base of aggressor belligerents, and they are as such not likely to lead to large-scale external military involvement, but they alone are also not likely to bring any quick peace to the region. External air support in behalf of victim minorities might reduce the capacity of a dominant faction to wage conventional war, but air support alone is unlikely to alter the dominant faction's local control. The purpose of introducing outside ground forces would be to win a decisive victory over the dominant ethnic faction, but the quest for such a decisive victory may result in an open-ended, quasi-permanent commitment of the forces.

Opponents of large-scale outside military intervention in secessionist wars argue that there will be over time and even concurrently many calls on outside nations to intervene in behalf of victim minorities, and that the military and economic resources of Western nations and the political will of their publics are too limited to sustain multiple interventions. There is, moreover, they argue, no principled way to determine whether to aid one victim ethnic minority rather than another. Nor does it seem possible to maintain that one or a few successful large-scale military interventions will induce ethnic factions to behave rationally in the future, as the successful Gulf War may well discourage would-be aggressor nations from invading their neighbors; rational calculation is not a prominent characteristic of ethnic disputes.

The basic causes of ethnic conflicts are political in the most fundamental sense, that is, radical disagreement about the composition and structure of the community, and there will be no political solution until the conflicting parties agree on the boundaries of their territories, or on a federal union. The ultimate aim of outside military intervention, if such action is undertaken, should be to pressure one or both parties to seek a political rather than a military solution to their problem. For outside nations to impose a purely military solution on the parties would involve those nations in either a quasi-permanent occupation or in an "ethnic-cleansing" operation. Complicating the quest for a political solution is the fact that ethnic irregulars may, and some almost inevitably will, resist any attempt by their official leadership to compromise.

The justice of the cause of minority victims in a secessionist war may be clear, but the proportional justice of outside nations' intervening militarily, especially by committing ground forces, is more complicated. Due proportionality is a matter of prudence, practical wisdom. Prudence demands that statesmen weigh the likely benefits of various levels of military intervention against the likely casualties and costs of intervention in a particular case and as a precedent for other cases. Prudence also requires statesmen to establish the technical means of intervention, and this may call for permanent standby forces if the world community decides to become involved in defending victim minorities in secessionist wars.

The war in Bosnia, described more fully in the case study, illustrates the problems confronting the world community in the matter of ethnic secessionist conflicts. The response of the world community until late summer 1995 was ineffective. With the vantage point of hindsight, the United States made a disastrous mistake when it pressed Bosnian Muslims to repudiate an agreement with Bosnian Croats and Bosnian Serbs (February 23, 1992) to form a partitioned, confederated Bosnia. On the level of principle, there seems to be no consistent way to accept the legitimacy of Bosnian-Croat and Bosnian-Muslim secession from Serb-dominated Yugoslavia, on the one hand, and to deny the legitimacy of Bosnian-Serb secession from the prospect of a Croat- and Muslim-dominated Bosnia. On the level of practical consequences, had such a confederated Bosnia been agreed to at that time, the parties might have negotiated or arbitrated the boundaries of the component ethnic units, Yugoslavia might have fully withdrawn its military equipment rather than bequeathed it to Bosnian Serbs, and dominant ethnic majorities in the units might have respected the rights of ethnic minorities. There is, of course, no certainty that such would have been the case, but the consequences of *not* establishing a partitioned, confederated Bosnia are tragically obvious.

From the spring of 1992, when the war in Bosnia erupted, to the spring of 1993, the United Nations and the world community responded with condemnations of, and economic sanctions against, Yugoslavia and with attempts to deliver relief supplies to the residents of Sarajevo. From the spring of 1993 to the winter of 1994, the United Nations and the world community expanded relief efforts to include other Bosnian-government enclaves created by Bosnian-Serb forces. In the winter of 1994, the threat of N.A.T.O. air strikes induced Bosnian Serbs to agree to a ceasefire in the Sarajevo area on February 9, and to remove their heavy weapons from striking range of the city by February 21. A similar threat in the spring induced Bosnian Serbs largely to withdraw their militias three kilometers from the center of Gorazde by April 23, and to withdraw their heavy weapons from striking range of the town by April 26. But Bosnian Serb forces continued to besiege, and block at will the passage of relief convoys to, the Bosnian-government enclaves. In short, the United Nations and the world community had opted for very limited military involvement. That may have been a prudent decision for political, military, and economic reasons, but it brought the Bosnian tragedy no closer to a solution, and the relief and peacekeeping operations were themselves economically costly and ever at risk of provoking a military confrontation. Only N.A.T.O. action in late summer 1995 changed the situation.

The problem of ethnic conflict is not unique to Bosnia or even to other parts of the former Yugoslavia (Albanians in Serbia's Kosovo province and Macedonia). For example, the breakup of the former Soviet Union has unleashed ethnic passions in the newly independent republics that were constituent parts of that union. Russian ethnics anxious for at least autonomy and perhaps incorporation into Russia dominate the Crimean peninsula of Ukraine. Russian ethnics in the northern section of Georgia are anxious to secede and join Russia. Armenian ethnics populate a western pocket of Azerbaijan, and Armenia is fighting to annex the pocket and the corridor linking it to Armenia. These ethnic problems are partially the result of the boundaries that the Soviets often arbitrarily decreed for their constituent republics. Some of the ethnic problems are a by-product of the Soviet policy of settling Russians in the constituent republics. Leaders of the concerned ethnics—and the world community—will be sorely taxed to find peaceful ways to resolve such problems. Any one of the problems has the potential to become another Bosnia, and some of the areas have greater risk of external intervention (Russia to aid fellow ethnics in the Crimea and Georgia, Turkey to aid fellow Muslims in Azerbaijan).

Nor is the problem of ethnic conflicts restricted to Eastern Europe. There is a persistent threat of ethnic conflict between Hindus and Muslims in Kashmir, a conflict that could easily escalate into a war between India and Pakistan. And there is an ongoing conflict in the Sudan between Muslim Arabs of the north and animist and Christian blacks of the south.

5

THE JUST WAR DECISION
Right Intention

Just-war theory requires that those who make decisions to wage war should be constitutionally and legally authorized to do so, and that wars should be waged only for proportionately just causes, as chapters 2 and 3 explain. Legitimate authority and just cause are objective criteria about the morality of waging war, objective criteria about the institutions and personnel authorized to make the decisions to wage war. Just-war theory also involves a subjective criterion, right intention, and right intention concerns the subjective intentions of war-decision makers.[1] War-decision makers have right intention if—and only if—they aim to conform their decisions to the objective criteria of just war. In other words, statesmen are just warriors if and only if they strive to reason rightly about war and warfare, and act accordingly. Right moral reasoning about war and warfare concerns several key issues.

Right reason understands that war, unless decided upon by proper authority and proportionately justified, is a moral evil to be avoided, and so right intention requires first of all that statesmen strive to avoid war by all reasonable means.

Second, right reason understands that only properly constituted authority should make the decision to wage war, and so right inten-

1. Cf. Thomas Aquinas, *Summa theologiae*, I–II, Q. 40, A. 1.

tion requires that statesmen have at least solidly probable cause to conclude that they have such authority. In particular, right intention requires that American presidents carefully and dispassionately assess their authority to commit armed forces to combat in the context of the U.S. Constitution, the War Powers Resolution, the U.N. Charter, and relevant Security Council resolutions.

Third, right reason understands that war should be waged only for proportionate just cause, and so right intention requires that statesmen resort to war only for just cause and limit war objectives to vindicating the just cause. A war will not necessarily be unjust if it results, and is foreseen to result, in some benefits that of themselves would not justify the war; right intention requires only that war should not be waged for the sake of such benefits.

Fourth, right reason understands that war should be conducted justly. As we shall explain in the next chapter, right reason concludes that just warriors should not directly target any portion of the enemy population not involved in the enemy war effort, and that just warriors should observe due proportion between the military importance of targets and the unintended but inevitable civilian casualties in warfare. Right intention, therefore, requires that just warriors strive to conform their behavior to these principles of just war conduct. Political leaders and military commanders have the chief responsibility to see that war is waged justly, but citizens have a responsibility to hold leaders and commanders accountable for the justice of their nation's war conduct. This responsibility will be difficult to achieve in the heated emotions of war, but it is what right reason demands, and what just warriors should intend and do.

Fifth, right reason understands that war should cease when its just cause has been vindicated, and that no more than just peace terms should be exacted from the defeated enemy. Right intention, therefore, requires that statesmen aim to conclude war according to the norms of justice. This, like restraint in war conduct, will not be easy to achieve. Since political leaders are likely to reflect the will of a vindictive public, it is particularly important that the public neither encourage their leaders to pursue vindictive policies nor support them if they do.

Political leaders will find it difficult to reconcile the need to mobilize public support for war, on the one hand, and the moral duty to wage war and conclude peace justly, on the other. During the war, political leaders will need to stimulate the public's war spirit because modern warriors are drawn from rank-and-file citizens, and because modern war requires sacrifices from citizens, at least if it is protracted. But the public's war spirit, once aroused, can and often will overwhelm the public's ability or willingness to reason rightly about war conduct and the terms of a peace settlement. The history of modern war indicates that it is easier to arouse the public's war spirit than it is to damper that spirit after the successful conclusion of a war, especially if the war has been protracted and has cost heavy casualties.

6

JUST WAR CONDUCT

The Principle of Discrimination

Just-war theorists have developed two central principles to govern just war conduct. The first is the principle of discrimination: just warriors may directly target personnel participating in the enemy nation's wrongdoing but should not directly target other enemy nationals. The reasoning behind the principle is twofold: On the one hand, the enemy nation's wrongdoing justifies the victim nation's use of military force to prevent or rectify wrongdoing, and the victim nation's use of military force will necessarily involve targeting enemy personnel engaged in the wrongdoing. On the other hand, enemy nationals not engaged in the war or contributing to waging it are committing no wrong against the victim nation, and so the victim nation has no just cause to target such nationals.

It is the wrong that enemy personnel are committing, not their individual moral responsibility for it, that justifies the victim nation's use of killing force against them. Whether or not enemy military and war-related personnel are conscious of the wrong they are committing against the victim nation, they are nonetheless committing the wrong, and the victim nation is accordingly justified in authorizing its military forces to kill them in order to prevent or remedy the wrong. This is similar to the case of individuals' using killing force in self-defense against life-threatening assailants who are not morally culpable for their actions (e.g., homicidal maniacs).

An unjust enemy's armed forces may be justly targeted because they are evidently participating in the enemy's wrongdoing against the victim nation. When enemy military personnel surrender, however, they are no longer participating in the enemy's wrongdoing, nor do they have any potential to do so once they are disarmed and imprisoned. Accordingly, the law of nations and international conventions require that belligerents not kill nonresisting prisoners of war, and that belligerents treat prisoners of war humanely. Out-of-uniform military infiltrators, and civilian or military spies operating in enemy territory, are likewise evidently war participants, and the law of nations even allows belligerents to execute them; nations have traditionally regarded such activities as criminal war conduct punishable by death.[1]

A victim nation may also justly target an enemy's political leadership, since that leadership bears the primary responsibility for the war. Only in relatively recent times has the capability of aircraft and missiles made the targeting of an enemy's political leadership militarily feasible. The likelihood that ordinary enemy civilians will be killed as a result of targeting enemy political leaders would raise a problem of proportionality but not a problem of discrimination.

In principle, recourse to assassination to eliminate an unjust enemy's political leaders would seem to be no more morally objectionable than killing them by conventional military means. But belligerents in conventional wars have traditionally refrained from attempting to assassinate their enemies' political leaders. Prior to World War I, the prevailing European aristocratic code precluded the legitimacy of assassinating enemy political leaders. (The ruling classes of each nation regarded the ruling classes of other nations almost as kin, and the crowned heads of Europe in fact were.) Moreover, then and now, practical considerations militate against a policy

---

1. Since infiltrators and spies, once captured, are no longer any threat to the affected belligerent, it seems to this writer that there is no more moral justification for executing them after their capture than there is for executing prisoners of war. Moreover, nations paradoxically regard the activities of enemy nations' infiltrators and spies operating in their territory as criminal, but they do not so regard the activities of their own infiltrators and spies operating in enemy nations' territories.

of assassinating enemy political leaders. Such a policy would beget a cycle of reprisal assassinations, and so putatively just leaders would be as vulnerable to assassination as putatively unjust leaders. Assassinating one enemy political leader also might not affect the leadership's determination to wage war, might stiffen the enemy public's war spirit, and might alienate the political leaders and publics of other nations.

Not every member of an unjust enemy's military forces is a wrongdoer against the victim nation. Medical corps, for example, engage neither in combat nor in war-related activity. Accordingly, the law of nations and international conventions prohibit attacks on medical military personnel, vehicles, or hospital units if they are designated as medical by the Red Cross symbol.[2] Revolutionaries frequently do not recognize or observe the distinction between combat-related and non-combat-related military personnel. The Irish Republican Army (I.R.A.), for example, claimed responsibility for targeting and killing members of a British military band in Regent's Park, London. Targeting off-duty, combat-related military personnel, however, would not violate the principle of discrimination, since such personnel are combat-related whether they are on duty or off duty, whether they are in or out of uniform, whether they are awake or asleep.

Prior to World War I, Western belligerents intent to observe the principle of discrimination in their war conduct had little difficulty distinguishing the guilty enemy, the enemy participating in war, from the innocent enemy, the enemy not participating in war; enemy combatants were the active wrongdoers, and enemy civilians (apart from spies and political leaders) were not. But modern war involves many civilians, and so the rigid distinction between military combatants as the guilty enemy and civilian noncombatants as the innocent enemy has become obsolete. Civilians produce the weapons and equipment integral to the waging of modern war, and civilians maintain a modern belligerent's industrial infrastructure (its rail-

2. See Protocol I, Article 12, and Protocol II, Article 12, of the 1977 Protocols to the 1949 Geneva Convention on amelioration of the condition of wounded and sick in armed forces in the field, Articles 24 and 28.

roads, roads, communications systems, and electric power), which is also integral to the waging of modern war. In the context of modern war, therefore, the concept of the guilty enemy, the enemy participating in an unjust war, is much more inclusive than it was in premodern times.

There is a rather broad consensus among just-war theorists that a victim nation, in the context of modern war, may justly target an unjust enemy's war-production centers and industrial infrastructure.[3] This necessarily involves targeting the civilians working in those facilities, and targeting such civilians in their war-related workplaces would not violate the principle of discrimination. But targeting such civilians at their homes, or on their way to or from their war-related workplaces, would. Such civilians are part of an enemy's war effort only insofar as they are actively engaged in war-related work; whereas most military personnel can at any time be ordered into combat or combat-support duties, civilians cannot. Nonetheless, even targeting civilians in their war-related workplaces might cause disproportional death and injury to other, non-war-related civilians and so violate the principle of proportionality.

How related to an enemy's unjust-war effort does civilian work have to be to make the civilians' workplace a legitimate military target of just warriors? Michael Walzer argues that it is not morally legitimate to target factories producing shoes, or farms producing food, for an enemy's armed forces.[4] Unlike the production of weapons and water materials, he argues, manufacture of shoes and food does not produce instruments of war. But it is in my opinion more plausible to argue that shoes enable an enemy army to march, and food sustains an enemy army's ability to fight; therefore, those who produce shoes or food for an unjust enemy's armed forces may be justly targeted at their factories or farms. Even the latter analysis,

3. See, for example, Joseph C. McKenna, "Ethics and War: A Catholic View," *American Political Science Review* 54 (September 1960): 656; Richard J. Regan, *The Moral Dimensions of Politics* (New York: Oxford University Press, 1986), p. 154; Michael Walzer, *Just and Unjust Wars* (Harmondsworth, England: Penguin, 1980), p. 146.

4. Walzer, *Just and Unjust*, p. 146.

however, would only permit belligerents to target factories and farms whose products are destined for the enemy's armed forces; to bomb factories and workers producing baby shoes, or farms and farmers producing food for the general population, would violate the principle of discrimination even if that principle permits the bombing of nonmilitary supplies destined for an enemy's armed forces.

However many enemy civilians may be considered participants in the waging of modern war and so legitimate military targets of just warriors, many others by no stretch of the imagination may be so considered. Housewives, children, and the elderly, as such, for example, are not participants in the enemy's war effort, nor are civilians performing purely civilian tasks (e.g., shopkeepers, clerks, teachers, bus drivers). Although ordinary civilians contribute indirectly to the enemy war effort insofar as they help sustain morale on the homefront and the warfront, they do not participate in waging war, producing instruments of war, maintaining the industrial infrastructure, or supplying the needs of armed forces. Ordinary citizens, of course, may justly be considered war participants if they engage in war-related activities. Such would be the case if civilians in occupied countries participate in resistance movements, or civilians in revolutionary wars covertly support the revolutionaries.

Few Westerners would disagree with the principle of discrimination as a general proposition: that is, they would agree that ordinary enemy civilians should not be targeted under ordinary circumstances. But some Western statesmen have argued that ordinary civilians may be targeted if doing so promises to save a greater number of lives, or at least an overwhelmingly greater number of lives. This was the argument that then–secretary of war Henry L. Stimson advanced to justify the U.S. decision to drop atomic bombs on the Japanese civilian population of Hiroshima and Nagasaki in the last weeks of World War II.[5] Stimson argued that dropping the bombs shortened the war and saved one million potential Allied casualties that would have resulted had the Allies been forced to invade the

5. Henry L. Stimson, "The Decision to Use the Atom Bomb," *Harper's Magazine* 94 (February 1947): 100–101, 106–7.

Japanese mainland. Along similar lines, some defended the Allied firebombing of residential areas of Cologne and Dresden, Germany, in the last year of World War II in Europe.[6]

The central question at issue in these arguments is whether or not it is ever morally permissible to aim to kill any innocent person. The question itself reflects broader, fundamental ethical questions: Are any moral principles absolute? If so, on the basis of what argument?

There are two basic approaches to answering these questions. One is the so-called deontological approach, that is, the attempt to discern the intrinsic nature of actions and to draw conclusions therefrom; the other is the so-called teleological approach, that is, the attempt to discern the extrinsic consequences of actions and to draw conclusions therefrom. Deontologists argue that no one should ever aim to kill or directly target an innocent human being. Human beings have rights to their lives, and they may be justly killed only if they commit proportionately serious wrongs against the community or any of its members.[7] In other words, only proportionately serious wrongdoing against the community or any of its members can justify the killing of a human being. Many teleologists reach the same conclusion but by a different line of argument. They argue consequentially that the life of every innocent human being would be at risk if any exception were allowed to permit the direct killing of any. Thus deontologists and many teleologists reach the same conclusion, that just warriors may never directly aim to kill innocent enemy civilians.

The principle of discrimination governs the subjective intention of those proximately and ultimately responsible for military actions.

---

6. It should be noted, however, that the Germans in the last years of World War II in Europe, in order to prevent the destruction of war-production plants by Allied bombing, dispersed much war production to residential areas. The firebombing of residential areas of Cologne might accordingly have satisfied the principle of discrimination. The same cannot be said about the firebombings of Dresden. General Sir Arthur Harris, the commander in chief of the R.A.F. Bomber Command, which was responsible for the firebombings of Dresden, explicitly declared that it was better to bomb any target in Germany than to bomb nothing. Obviously, such a view disavows any aim to discriminate between the guilty enemy and the innocent enemy.

7. Cf. St. Thomas Aquinas, *Summa theologiae*, II–II, Q. 64, A. 6.

But the principle involves an objective component, namely, the projected target of military actions, and human agents in the full possession of their conscious faculties presumably intend the object of their actions. Therefore, the underlying focus of the principle of discrimination is on the nature of the target. A just warrior satisfies the principle of discrimination if the warrior aims to target the guilty enemy, and the warrior does not satisfy the principle if the warrior aims to target the innocent enemy. And the objective character of a target will test the sincerity of a belligerent's professed intention to discriminate between the guilty enemy and the innocent enemy.

William V. O'Brien argues that the principle of discrimination, as traditionally formulated, is obsolete in the context of modern war[8]; modern war necessarily involves the death of ordinary civilians, and so O'Brien argues that those waging modern war necessarily intend to kill such civilians. But O'Brien disapproves targeting civilians apart from military necessity, and he would accordingly reformulate the principle of discrimination in terms of military necessity without regard to the subjective intention of military combatants. The difference between the traditional formulation of the principle of discrimination and O'Brien's may be largely one of terminology. Modern war does necessarily involve the killing of ordinary civilians, but that does not mean that ordinary civilians are necessarily the intended target. If there is a real military target, which would seem to be a "military necessity" in O'Brien's terminology, and the belligerent intends to destroy that target, the belligerent does not intend the concomitant, even the necessarily concomitant, deaths of ordinary civilians. As indicated, the objective test of right intention with respect to discrimination is the target. O'Brien's emphasis on military necessity captures the essence of the principle of discrimination,

---

8. William V. O'Brien. *The Conduct of Just and Limited Wars* (New York: Praeger, 1981), pp. 44–47, 338–41. The principle of discrimination has traditionally been formulated to require that just warriors not intend to kill civilians unrelated to an unjust enemy's war effort. Unlike O'Brien, I think the traditional formulation implies the military character of the target, since it is the character of the target that specifies the military participant's intention. Accordingly, I am of the opinion that the difference between the traditional formulation and O'Brien's is largely one of interpreting what is or is not implicit in the traditional formulation.

and it is precisely when and because military personnel seek to destroy military or war-related targets that they can truly claim not to intend the collateral deaths of ordinary citizens.

Nonetheless, a military or war-related target may be of insufficient importance to justify the deaths of ordinary civilians collaterally resulting from an attack on the target, and the principle of proportionality, not the principle of discrimination, would be violated in such a case. And the more disproportional the number of collateral civilian deaths, the more suspect will be the sincerity of a belligerent's claim that the intended target is military or war-related.

Terrorism either principally or by definition signifies acts that are intentionally designed to kill (or hold hostage) undeniably innocent individuals in order to achieve political goals. Such acts violate the principle of discrimination as much as their moral equivalents in conventional war, countercity nuclear strategy, and revolutionary war. A broad consensus of Western public opinion condemns such terrorist acts[9]; even a revolutionary group like the I.R.A. claims to target only those it regards as guilty enemy, although the number of innocent persons killed in some I.R.A. attacks may cast doubt about the claim. Some non-Westerners, principally Arab terrorists, however, openly reject the principle of discrimination. Although it is beyond the scope of this study to assess strategies of deterring terrorists and terrorist acts, it is appropriate here to urge the universal validity of the principle of discrimination and the right of the world community to defend the inviolability of innocent human life in all forms of warfare.

One other point should be duly noted. The principle of discrimination requires military combatants to weigh carefully the effects of their actions on ordinary civilians. If military combatants either willfully do not consider the effects of their action on ordinary ci-

---

9. Western public opinion regarding the principle of discrimination is not always so strongly aroused or so broadly based. Although the West strongly and broadly condemns indiscriminate acts of terrorism, it does not so strongly or so broadly condemn other indiscriminate acts of killing (e.g., indiscriminate military retaliation). Indeed, abortion opponents claim that public tolerance of abortion reflects indifference to the inviolability of innocent human life.

vilians or act with reckless disregard of those effects, the combatants violate the principle of discrimination just as much as if they were deliberately to target innocent enemy civilians. The use of reason to discriminate between the guilty enemy and the innocent enemy as targets of military action is precisely what the principle of discrimination is about.

The Allied blockade of Germany during World War I and even after the armistice, as applied to foodstuffs, would seem to have been the functional equivalent of an indiscriminate military attack on ordinary citizens, and so unjust war conduct. Similarly, as elaborated in the next chapter, the United States in the middle years of the Cold War, to deter the Soviet Union from nuclear attacks against the United States and Western Europe, threatened nuclear retaliation against Soviet cities. This countercity strategy held ordinary Soviet citizens hostage and directly targeted them for destruction if deterrence were to fail.

The Principle of Proportionality

The principle of discrimination prohibits acts of war that target ordinary civilians: bombing civilian residential areas that include no military target, using nuclear weapons against cities and their civilian populations, and committing acts of terrorism or reprisal against ordinary civilians. But even acts of war that attempt to discriminate between enemy participants in war and war-related activities and enemy nonparticipants are likely to result in the death of ordinary civilians, and the principle of proportionality needs to be applied to such acts of war.

The principle of proportionality is itself subsumed under the so-called principle of double effect, of which proportionality is an integral part. When human agents consciously will to do something, they are morally responsible for the foreseeable consequences of their actions, and their actions can have several effects, for one of which they are morally permitted to strive, and for the other of which they are not.[10] The principle of double effect holds that human

---

10. Cf. St. Thomas Aquinas, *Summa theologiae*, II–II, Q. 64, A. 7.

agents are morally permitted to act in such cases if and only if certain conditions are satisfied.

First, the action itself, as defined in specific circumstances, should be at least morally neutral, that is, not morally bad. Thus, for example, the principle of double effect cannot be invoked to justify acts of murder or adultery. Second, the human agent should desire the morally good effect, that is, the effect that it is morally good to strive for, and not desire the morally bad effect, that is, the effect that it would be morally bad to strive for. Third, the morally bad effect must not be the means whereby the morally good effect is achieved, as, for example, would be the case if one were deliberately to kill an innocent human being in order to save one's own or another's life. Fourth, the morally good effect, one that it is morally permissible to desire, should equal or outweigh the morally bad effect, one that it is not morally permissible to desire. The fourth condition of the principle of double effect is the principle of proportionality.

Bombing military targets, at least doing so on a large scale, will, in addition to the destruction of the targets, almost inevitably result in the death of enemy civilians who are not participants in war or war-related activities. Such bombing would satisfy the first condition of the principle of double effect, since it is morally permissible to bomb military targets in a just war. The bombing would satisfy the second condition if the military personnel responsible for the bombing desire the destruction of the military targets without desiring the death of innocent civilians. The bombing would satisfy the third condition if the collateral death of ordinary civilians is not the means whereby the military targets are destroyed. But that is not the end of the moral matter; indeed, the fourth condition, that of proportionality, is the most difficult moral matter. The bombing will be morally permissible only if the importance of the military targets equals or outweighs the resulting deaths of ordinary civilians.

Technological developments in the instruments of war have made it a near-certainty that waging modern conventional war will result in incidental civilian deaths and so raise questions of proportionality. The Allied bombardment of the ancient Benedictine monastery of Monte Cassino, Italy, in 1944 is a classic example. German forces under Allied attack had entrenched themselves in the monastery, which occupied a lofty vantage point for the Germans against the Allied forces advancing up the Italian peninsula. Heavy Allied bombing almost totally destroyed the monastery. If the monastery was as militarily important a target as Allied commanders deemed it, then the foreseeable but indirectly intended damage to the monastery and its historical treasures would seem to fall within the limits of the principle of proportionality, especially considering the character and potential of the foe.

Critics of the Gulf War (1991) maintained that the month-long Allied air strikes before ground forces crossed into Iraq inflicted morally disproportional civilian casualties, destruction of utilities, and ecological damage to the region and its inhabitants. If the targets of the Allied bombings were legitimate and important military or other war-related targets, then destruction of the targets would have justified a relatively high level of collateral damage, assuming the justice of the Allies' cause to wage war. Since it is difficult to imagine how modern belligerents could wage war without inflicting considerable collateral damage, the critics of the proportionality of the air strikes may be implicitly, if tacitly, assuming that no modern war can satisfy the principle of proportionality. In any case, the critics gave no indication of what level of collateral damage they would have accepted as compatible with just warriors' observance of the principle of proportionality.

Unconventional warfare, that is, revolutionary guerrilla warfare, also poses problems of proportionality. Assuming the justice of a revolutionary cause and the legitimacy of certain military and political targets in a revolutionary war, attempts to destroy such targets will often involve the death of ordinary citizens unrelated to the military-political targets. For example, the remote-control detonation of explosives to destroy an enemy army post is very likely to cause some civilian deaths and property damage. In some cases, such a probability is an absolute certainty (e.g., tossing a bomb into a pub frequented by enemy soldiers). As in the case of conventional warfare, the importance of the military-political target will determine what level of civilian casualties and destruction is compatible with the principle of proportionality.

If the U.S. countercity nuclear strategy ran counter to the principle of discrimination, the counterforce strategy raised a serious problem of proportionality. The latter strategy threatened retaliatory nuclear destruction of Soviet weapons and forces. To have carried out such a strategy if deterrence were to have failed would have resulted in extensive collateral civilian deaths and destruction. We shall consider in the next chapter whether any effective counterforce strategy could satisfy the principle of proportionality. We shall also there consider whether any use of tactical nuclear weapons could satisfy the principle.

Estimating proportionality involves practical judgments about the likely outcomes of military actions. How many casualties is bombing a military target likely to inflict on enemy civilians unconnected with the enemy's war efforts? How important is the military target? Although morally responsible belligerents cannot reach absolutely (i.e., theoretically) certain judgments about hypothetical outcomes, they can and should strive to reach morally (i.e., practically) certain judgments about such outcomes and act accordingly.

Effect of Unjust War Conduct on Just Cause

Isolated acts of unjust war conduct, however morally reprehensible, will not render unjust a belligerent's otherwise just cause. But if unjust war conduct is systematic and pervasive, the very justice of the cause for which a belligerent is purportedly waging war will be tainted; a belligerent can hardly claim that it is fighting a just war if it wages war in a systematically unjust way. Critics leveled this charge against U.S. military action in Vietnam.

Observance of International Conventions

International conventions have established certain codes of war conduct. Some of these conventions specify how belligerents are to carry out general moral responsibilities. For example, belligerents have a general moral responsibility to treat prisoners of war humanely, since prisoners of war are no longer actual or potential war participants, and international conventions specify what constitutes humane treatment.[11]

11. See 1907 Hague Convention IV, Annex, Articles 4–19; 1949 Geneva Con-

Other international conventions do more than specify general moral responsibilities; such conventions outlaw behavior that might otherwise be morally permissible under certain conditions. The use of particular kinds of deadly weapons against important military targets might under certain conditions satisfy the principle of proportionality, but international conventions have categorically outlawed some such weapons (e.g., chemical and biological weapons).[12]

Belligerents have a self-interest in observing international conventions governing war conduct; their failure to do so would invite enemy retaliation in kind. But nations, in addition to their self-interest, have a moral responsibility to take reasonable means to lessen the casualties and hardships of war. Moreover, even if the enemy fails to observe international conventions, belligerents have moral responsibilities with respect to the subject matter of the conventions. For example, belligerents are morally obliged to treat prisoners of war humanely and not to use any weapon indiscriminately against ordinary civilians, irrespective of international conventions or an enemy's observance of the conventions.

---

vention on prisoners of war; 1977 Protocol I to the 1949 Geneva Convention, Articles 43–45.

12. See 1925 Geneva Protocol on the use of poisonous gas and biological weapons; 1972 Convention on Biological and Toxic Weapons.

7

NUCLEAR WEAPONS
AND JUST WAR CONDUCT

The age of nuclear weapons began at the end of World War II when the United States dropped atomic bombs on the Japanese cities of Hiroshima and Nagasaki in order to induce the Japanese government to surrender. In the subsequent Cold War, the United States and the Soviet Union embarked on a nuclear arms race to deter one another from a nuclear attack, and in the case of the United States, also to help deter a conventional Soviet attack on Western Europe. It was in this context that statesmen, theologians, philosophers, and political scientists debated the morality of nuclear weapons and warfare.[1] The debate served to clarify the issues and is still relevant despite the collapse of the Soviet Union and the end of the bipolar nuclear balance of terror. Although the U.S.-Russian détente and radical nuclear disarmament have undoubtedly reduced the risk of a nuclear holocaust, there remains a great risk of nuclear warfare and of blackmail by militant leaders of lesser nations with nuclear capability or by nationalist or terrorist groups supported by such leaders. Indeed, the collapse of the Soviet Union and the apparent

1. On various nuclear strategies and tactics, and the practical and moral issues they raise, see Richard J. Regan, *The Moral Dimensions of Politics* (New York: Oxford University Press, 1986), pp. 160–79; William V. O'Brien, "Just-War Conduct in a Nuclear Context," *Theological Studies* 44 (June 1983): 191–220.

disinclination of U.S. and Western European electorates to support longer-term, casualty-costly military operations against rogue nations may paradoxically increase the risk that minor powers or groups they support will use, or threaten to use, nuclear weapons.

The Bipolar Cold War Context

For a brief period after the end of World War II (1945–49), the United States (and Great Britain in a minor, allied capacity) had a monopoly of atomic weapons. In 1949, however, the Soviet Union became a nuclear power, and the two superpowers had developed the hydrogen bomb by the midfifties (the United States in 1952, the Soviet Union in 1955). By the end of the 1950s, both superpowers were well on the way to developing missile delivery systems for their nuclear arsenals. As a result, there existed a "balance of terror" between the superpowers, to use Winston Churchill's apt phrase: neither the United States nor the Soviet Union could inflict massive destruction on the other without itself suffering a similar fate. In this situation, each superpower sought to maintain enough nuclear capability to be able to inflict "unacceptable destruction" on the other after absorbing a nuclear first strike.

The projected strategic targets of U.S. nuclear weapons in the 1950s were Soviet cities, and the projected strategic targets of Soviet nuclear weapons were U.S. cities. The theory of deterrence underlying these strategies was that neither side would rationally initiate a nuclear strike against the other if it knew that the other would be capable of inflicting massive destruction on it after absorbing the strike. Each superpower effectively—and avowedly—held the other's civilian population hostage.

I have previously objected to this countercity strategy on the moral ground that carrying out the strategy if deterrence were to fail would violate the principle of discrimination: that is, executing the strategy would involve the direct killing of innocent enemy civilians.[2] Indeed, the strategy sought to maximize the number of potential enemy civilian deaths precisely in order to be more effective

---

2. Regan, *Moral Dimensions*, p. 165.

as a deterrent; the more enemy civilians the strategy threatened to kill, the greater its value for deterrence. From a purely practical point of view, one might also argue that the strategy was not credible and so not an effective deterrent, that it would be suicidal for the United States to carry out the strategy after a limited Soviet nuclear attack, and that the Soviets, knowing this, would discount the U.S. threat to retaliate massively.

In the late 1950s and early 1960s, the critics of the countercity strategy proposed an alternate, counterforce strategy: the strategic targets of U.S. nuclear weapons should be Soviet nuclear missile sites and air force installations.[3] This strategy seemed to satisfy the principle of discrimination, since its targets were avowedly military. But the counterforce strategy was criticized on both moral and political grounds. Moral critics argued that a counterforce strategy, to be effective, would need to target hundreds or even thousands of sites and installations, that many of these targets would lie close to populated areas, that statistically predictable error in delivery would inevitably lead to large-scale civilian casualties, and that these results would violate the principle of proportionality. Practical critics argued that a credible counterforce strategy would cause the Soviet leadership to fear that the United States was preparing to deliver a decisive first nuclear strike, and itself to strike preemptively in order to prevent the United States from doing so. Practical critics also argued that there were simply too many Soviet nuclear weapons for a U.S. second strike to be successful, not least because of the statistically predictable error in delivering missiles or bombs to intended targets.

In the early 1980s, a third strategy, a countercontrol strategy, was proposed.[4] According to this strategy, the target of a U.S. nuclear response to a Soviet nuclear attack should be the apparatus of Soviet military and political control, since means of military and political control are the assets that the Soviet leadership would value most highly. Proponents claimed that such a strategy would effectively

---

3. For a summary of the arguments for and against the counterforce strategy, see Regan, *Moral Dimensions*, pp. 167–71.

4. For a summary of the arguments for and against the countercontrol strategy, see Regan, *Moral Dimensions*, pp. 165–67.

deter the Soviet leadership from initiating a strategic nuclear strike on the United States because the Soviet leadership would most of all want to preserve its military and political control, and that the strategy would avoid directly targeting civilian populations. Moral critics counterclaimed that the strategy would still cause large-scale civilian casualties and thereby, in their view, violate the principle of proportionality. Practical critics pointed out that the strategy would be dangerously destabilizing and make all-out nuclear war more rather than less likely; the Soviet leadership, they argued, precisely because it valued its control apparatus so highly, would be strongly tempted to execute a preemptive nuclear attack against the United States in order to prevent the United States from striking first against the Soviet control apparatus.

The countercity, counterforce, and countercontrol nuclear strategies of deterrence were offensive strategies, that is, strategies that threatened retaliatory destruction of Soviet cities, forces, or control apparatus. In 1983, President Ronald W. Reagan proposed a supplementary defensive nuclear strategy, that is, one that threatened to destroy Soviet missiles between launch and arrival at their U.S. targets.[5] There was no moral objection, as indeed there could not be, to targeting activated hostile missiles for destruction. But there were a host of objections to the anti–ballistic missile strategy on other grounds. Critics said that the strategy would be doubly destabilizing. On the one hand, it might tempt an American president to presume (erroneously) that the United States was safe enough from nuclear destruction to launch a nuclear attack on the Soviet Union, with disastrous results for both nations. On the other, the strategy might cause the Soviet leadership to fear the imminence of such an attack so much that it would launch its own preemptive nuclear attack. Critics said that no space-based antiballistic defense system was possible, and that the system could be easily overwhelmed. And some thought that it would be a prodigal waste of resources that could be better spent to alleviate poverty at home and abroad.

The primary purpose of these nuclear strategies was to deter the

5. On the Reagan proposal, see *The New York Times*, March 24, 1983, p. A1. For a summary of the arguments for and against the anti–ballistic missile defense system, see Regan, *Moral Dimensions*, pp. 172–73.

Soviet Union from launching a nuclear attack against the United States or its Western allies. For any retaliatory strategy to deter a potential enemy, the threatened sanction needs to be both sufficiently repugnant to the would-be enemy and credible: that is, the potential attacker needs to regard the threatened sanction as worse than any advantage likely to accrue from initiating an attack and believe that the potential defender would, if attacked, actually carry out the threatened retaliation. Most commentators, therefore, assumed that the United States needed to be willing and prepared to carry out whatever offensive nuclear strategy it adopted if it were actually to deter the Soviet Union from initiating a nuclear attack against the United States or its Western allies. But if deterrence were to fail, then the consequences for both sides, and possibly other nations as well, would be disastrous.

Faced with such appalling consequences if deterrence were to fail, some commentators attempted to distinguish the possession of nuclear weapons, which the commentators were prepared to accept as morally tolerable for deterrence purposes until a general nuclear disarmament could be achieved, from the use of nuclear weapons, which the commentators deemed never to be morally acceptable, since any use would, in this view, inevitably violate the principle of proportionality, and a countercity strategy would violate the principle of discrimination.[6] In essence, these commentators would rest U.S. nuclear deterrence on a bluff: the United States would possess nuclear weapons and the capacity to use them, and the United States would threaten to use them in retaliation to a Soviet nuclear attack, but the United States would not in fact use them if deterrence failed. Although uncertainty about whether or not the United States intended to carry out its threatened nuclear retaliation might have caused the Soviet leadership to hesitate before launching a nuclear

6. Cf. National Conference of Catholic Bishops, *The Challenge of Peace: God's Promise and Our Response* (Washington, D.C.: U.S. Catholic Conference, 1983), ##157–61, 186, 188. See also Paul Ramsey, *The Just War* (New York: Scribner's, 1968), pp. 249–58. Ramsey subsequently abandoned this position; see "A Political Ethics Context for Strategic Thinking," in Morton A. Kaplan, ed., *Strategic Thinking and Its Moral Implications* (Chicago: University of Chicago Center for Policy Study, 1973), p. 142.

attack, there is good reason to doubt the long-term effectiveness of such a bluff, especially in a crisis. Moreover, nuclear pacifists doubted that U.S. leaders would be morally able in a crisis to resist the temptation to use the nuclear weapons they possessed.

To lessen Soviet civilian casualties of a U.S. retaliatory strike to a morally acceptable (proportional) level in the event that deterrence were to fail, other commentators suggested that the threatened retaliation should be severely limited. The commentators argued that it would be morally permissible to use a small number of nuclear weapons against a limited number of counterforce targets, and that the certainty of such a limited nuclear retaliation would be sufficient to deter the Soviet leadership from initiating a nuclear attack.[7] Both of the foregoing propositions were disputed. Nuclear pacifists argued that limits on nuclear warfare would not and could not be observed in times of crisis. Military experts and political scientists argued that a severely limited counterforce strategy would not be sufficient to deter the Soviet leadership from launching a nuclear attack. One difficulty about assessing either the moral acceptability or the deterrent value of a limited nuclear counterforce is that the strategy's proponents did not specify the number of weapons or the nature of the targets involved in the strategy. In any case, the central dilemma confronting a limited nuclear counterforce strategy was this: How could the strategy include a large enough number of nuclear warheads against important enough targets to deter the Soviet leadership from initiating a nuclear attack, and at the same time result in small enough collateral death and destruction to satisfy the moral principle of proportionality if deterrence were to fail?

The North Atlantic Treaty Organization (N.A.T.O.) did not rely on a threat to use strategic weapons to deter the Soviet leadership from attacking Western Europe with conventional forces. Rather, N.A.T.O. relied on its conventional forces with an unspecified combination of conventional weapons and tactical nuclear weapons to defend Western Europe from a conventional Soviet and Warsaw Pact attack. Since it was then commonly thought that the Soviet Union

7. Cf. Regan, *Moral Dimensions*, pp. 170–71, 176.

and the Warsaw Pact nations had overwhelming superiority in conventional forces, N.A.T.O. declined to disavow a possible first use of tactical nuclear weapons. According to pre-1990 N.A.T.O. planning, the Soviet leadership could and would be deterred from initiating a conventional attack against Western Europe by the implied threat that N.A.T.O. might use tactical nuclear weapons against Soviet and Warsaw Pact attack forces if N.A.T.O.'s own conventional forces relying on conventional weapons were being overwhelmed, and Western Europe about to be overrun.

Critics contended that the use of tactical nuclear weapons in Europe would involve disproportional collateral civilian casualties and destruction of the very societies in whose defense the weapons were avowedly being used; that N.A.T.O.'s unleashing of tactical nuclear weapons against the armed forces of the Soviet Union and its Warsaw Pact allies would inevitably lead the Soviets to retaliate in kind; and that the United States might well then exacerbate the war to domesday proportions by launching strategic nuclear weapons.[8] Moreover, N.A.T.O. nations had more than enough military and economic potential to match the Warsaw nations in conventional forces, and technically advanced, precision nonnuclear missiles and other weapons could destroy most military targets as well as tactical nuclear weapons could, with vastly lower numbers of collateral casualties and destruction.

The New Nuclear Superpower Context

During the Cold War, the Soviet Union professed the Communist ideology of world revolution and committed itself to the forcible overthrow of democratic capitalism and non-Communist regimes everywhere. But the Soviet Union collapsed in 1991, and the successor Russian regime has repudiated that ideology. The friendly intentions of the present Russian leadership could change, or a new, hostile Russian leadership could come to power, but Russia itself will remain economically impoverished and dependent on the West for

8. For a summary of arguments for and against tactical nuclear weapons, see Regan, *Moral Dimensions*, pp. 171–72.

the foreseeable future, and a nuclear arms race will accordingly be both prohibitively expensive and contrary to Russia's paramount interest in reviving its domestic economy.

The new Russia, no longer hostile and cognizant of its relative impoverishment, reached a sweeping nuclear arms control agreement with the United States in 1992.[9] That agreement called for the destruction over the next eleven years of two thirds of the nuclear arsenals of the two nuclear superpowers. As a result, even in the unlikely eventuality that relations between the two superpowers were to become hostile, neither would be capable after the next decade of launching a knock-out nuclear strike against the other, and yet each would retain the capability of inflicting serious damage on the other after absorbing a nuclear first strike. The agreement vindicates the view that the two nuclear superpowers would have as much or more security with less nuclear weaponry if they could trust one another, and/or if they had sufficiently reliable means of verification to disarm radically. Moreover, they might be able to disarm even more radically without risk to their mutual security. How much nuclear weaponry the nuclear superpowers would need to deter other actual or potential nuclear powers, however, is another question.

Both Russia and the United States will retain enough nuclear capability after execution of the agreement to threaten severe retaliatory damage on the other, and the same questions and roughly the same parameters remain concerning the moral acceptability of different strategies of deterrence, that is, what targets of nuclear weapons are morally acceptable if deterrence were to fail.

9. *The New York Times*, June 17, 1992, p. A1. The agreement was incorporated in a treaty signed on January 3, 1993; *The New York Times*, January 4, 1993, p. A1. Domestic political instability poses a credible risk that a new, militant regime might come to power in Russia and repudiate the agreement. Moreover, the agreement presupposes the cooperation of the three other successor republics of the Soviet Union possessing nuclear weapons (Belarus, Ukraine, and Kazakhstan). Belarus and Ukraine have indicated that they will cooperate and divest themselves of their nuclear weapons, but the Ukrainian parliament is insisting on financial compensation and security guarantees. Kazakhstan, like Russia, is politically unstable, and so its cooperation is particularly problematic.

By the year 2003, of course, a countercity strategy would threaten less destruction than it currently would, but it would still target civilian populations as such and so still violate the moral principle of discrimination. A countercontrol strategy by the year 2003 might be less threatening to Russia because the United States would be incapable of delivering a knock-out first strike, but it might well still be sufficiently threatening for a hostile Russia to conclude that it would be better off using its nuclear weapons first. A severely limited counterforce strategy might satisfy the principle of proportionality, but there would remain the problem of how such a strategy could involve a large enough number of targets to be an effective deterrent. (A postreduction counterforce strategy, however, would need only to threaten large enough retaliation to deter a nonmassive first strike.) And having eliminated the possibility of a knock-out nuclear first strike, the nuclear superpowers might be more disposed to cooperate in developing an antiballistic missile defense system, not least because of its potential for limiting the effectiveness of blackmail threats by minor nuclear powers.

The China Context

China is today the only strategic nuclear power openly committed to the Communist ideology of world revolution and the forcible overthrow of democratic capitalism and non-Communist regimes everywhere.[10] Although there may be reason to hope that events similar to those in the last years of the Soviet Union, or a popular revolt, will transform China into a democratic nation, the free world would be foolish to bank on it, certainly foolish to assume that it will transpire in the near future. This means that the free world needs very much to keep in mind the potential threat posed by China's nuclear capability.

Fortunately for the free world, the ratio of China's nuclear ca-

---

10. Great Britain and France also have strategic nuclear capabilities but no hostile designs on other nations. Nor, given the stability of their democratic regimes, is there more than a mathematical possibility that they ever would have such designs. On China's nuclear capability and strategy, see Chong-Pin Lin, *China's Nuclear Weapons Strategy* (Lexington, Mass.: Lexington Books, 1988).

pability to that of the United States is incomparably inferior to the equal or nearly equal ratio of the former Soviet Union's, now Russia's, nuclear capability to that of the United States. In the latter case, the strategic nuclear force of the two nuclear superpowers was, is, and will remain symmetrical or nearly symmetrical; in the former case, the strategic nuclear forces of China, on the one hand, and of the United States and Russia, on the other, are vastly asymmetrical in favor of each of the superpowers. Because of this asymmetry, the United States and Russia could agree to disarm two thirds of their nuclear arsenals without affecting the capacity of each to deter China from initiating a nuclear first strike. China, although incapable at present or in the foreseeable future of posing a credible nuclear threat to the security of the United States or Russia, might be capable of attempting nuclear blackmail against a nonnuclear neighbor (e.g., Japan), and it is for this reason that the nuclear superpowers cannot completely divest themselves of strategic nuclear capability vis-à-vis China. In this asymmetrical context, we need to consider the efficacy and morality of various strategies by the United States, whether alone or in collaboration with Russia, to deter China from engaging in nuclear blackmail against third parties.

The vastly superior nuclear capability of the United States makes it almost certain that the threat of massive countercity nuclear retaliation would deter China from using, or threatening to use, nuclear weapons against a third nation, despite the fact that the present Chinese leadership evidently values the lives of its citizens so much less than the West does. From the moral perspective, however, carrying out a countercity strategy against China if deterrence fails would violate the principle of discrimination as much as carrying out the countercity strategy against the Soviet Union during the Cold War would have.

A counterforce strategy would face the previously indicated problem of how to make such a threat substantial enough to be an effective deterrent and simultaneously small enough to satisfy the moral principle of proportionality with respect to the indirectly resulting but inevitable civilian casualties. The limited nuclear capability of China, however, might make even a severely limited U.S.

counterforce threat against China more credible than a similar threat against the former Soviet Union would have, or a similar threat against Russia would.

A countercontrol strategy against China would certainly be credible. It would, moreover, not significantly add to any existing fear of a preemptive U.S. nuclear strike, since the United States already has the nuclear capability of such a strike. There would remain, however, the moral question whether or not the collateral civilian casualties in carrying out the strategy if deterrence were to fail would be duly proportional.

The fact that the United States and Russia have such overwhelming asymmetrical nuclear capability vis-à-vis China should also serve to render China amenable to a strategic nuclear arms reduction agreement with the nuclear superpowers. China would, of course, expect the superpowers to make asymmetrically greater reductions, and the nuclear superpowers, given their overwhelming superiority, could reasonably do so. But the nuclear superpowers and China distrust one another, and China might be especially unwilling to agree to accept on-site verification.

Even a limited antiballistic missile defense system would further disadvantage China in the ratio of its nuclear capability to that of the United States and Russia. Again, such a system would not significantly add to China's fear of a preemptive nuclear first strike by the United States or Russia, which capability already exists, and it might further induce her to agree to a mutually verifiable strategic nuclear arms reduction.

With the collapse of the Soviet satellites of Eastern Europe, the breaking up of the Soviet Union, and the disintegration of the armed forces of the former Soviet Union, Western Europe no longer needs to fear a conventional attack from that quarter. But China remains capable of a conventional attack on its neighbors, and such an attack, if promising success, would be consistent with its professed Communist ideology. In this context, the question arises whether or not the United States and its Western allies should threaten to use tactical or intermediate nuclear weapons to deter such an attack, and be accordingly prepared to use the weapons if deterrence failed.

A combination of geographical advantages and U.S. air support strongly suggests that the most likely targets of Chinese aggression (Taiwan, Japan, India, Pakistan) would be capable of defending themselves against a conventional attack with U.S. air and naval (in the case of Taiwan and Japan) support and without the use of tactical nuclear weapons. Moreover, from a moral perspective, the objections to the use of such weapons in Asia are just as strong as the objections to their use against Soviet aggression in Europe were.

Nonetheless, although it seems both practically possible and morally necessary to wage defensive war without tactical nuclear weapons in the case of a Chinese conventional attack against one of her neighbors, and so practically prudent and morally correct for the United States (and Russia) to disavow any first use of the weapons, it would be practically prudent for the United States (and Russia) not to disavow any *second* use; ambiguity about U.S. (or Russian) intentions with respect to retaliating in kind if the Chinese used the weapons helps to deter the Chinese from doing so, whereas disavowal of any retaliation in kind might encourage the Chinese to think that they could use the weapons with impunity. Whether or not any U.S. retaliatory use of tactical nuclear weapons is morally tolerable is a hard question; the high civilian casualties and destruction that would be very likely to result from extensive use of tactical nuclear weapons argue that only a very limited tactical nuclear response might be able to satisfy the moral principle of proportionality.

The Context of Other Nations' Nuclear Capability and the Problem of Proliferation

A dozen or so other nations reputedly possess or are in the process of developing nuclear-weapons capability. But those nations' actual or potential nuclear weapons are relatively short-range and designed either to guarantee defense against hostile neighbors or to further regional aspirations. Although those nations' tactical and intermediate nuclear-weapons capabilities do not and will not pose any direct threat to the United States or the West, such capabilities could dangerously destabilize particular regions, and proliferation of nuclear-weapons capabilities necessarily increases the risk that one or more of the nations with such capabilities will use them.

Most students of military affairs and international relations believe that Israel already possesses tactical and intermediate nuclear-weapons capability. It is not hard to understand why Israel feels it necessary to develop and possess such capability. Israel is surrounded by hostile Islamic nations, whose populations outnumber Israel's by fifty to one. (If one includes more remote Islamic nations like Pakistan, the margin is one hundred to one.) Moreover, Israel is too small geographically to suffer much penetration of its defense perimeter without being overwhelmed.[11] Israel's nuclear capability serves two purposes: (1) it deters potential enemy neighbors without nuclear weapons from attacking Israel, and (2) it deters potential enemy neighbors with nuclear weapons from using the weapons in conjunction with a conventional attack against Israel. It is also especially in Israel's security interest to ensure that neighboring nations do not develop nuclear-weapons capability, since Israel would then have less ability to deter a conventional attack or defend against a conventional attack if deterrence failed.

It is public knowledge since the Gulf War that Iraq was developing nuclear-weapons capability before the war and within several years of achieving it. Other Islamic Middle Eastern nations (e.g., Iran, Syria) would like to have nuclear weapons in their arsenals, and the oil revenues of the Middle East would be able to finance development of nuclear-weapons capability. The collapse of the Soviet Union has made a large number of its nuclear scientists and technicians unemployed or underpaid, and so Islamic nations aspiring to develop nuclear-weapons capability might be able to procure the services of those scientists and technicians. Moreover, the predominantly Islamic republics of the former Soviet Union might sell nuclear materials to Iran. In short, there is grave danger—and Israel is well aware of it—that Iran or some other Islamic nation will acquire nuclear-weapons capability in the not-too-distant future.

---

11. It should be noted, however, that the collapse of the Soviet Union has in one important respect improved Israel's security: neighboring Islamic nations no longer have a major nuclear power on whom to rely either for deterrence or for defense. China is now the only nuclear power that might conceivably support Israel's hostile neighbors, and China is both too remote geographically and too inferior in nuclear weaponry to counterbalance Western support for Israel.

The problem of nuclear weapons proliferation in the Middle East, however, is only the tip of that region's conflictual iceberg. Underlying the nuclear problem is the political problem posed by Israel's existence. With the exception of Egypt, Arab and Islamic nations do not accept Israel's legitimacy, and no firm peace is possible in the region until they do. Resolution of the Palestinian question is a prerequisite for Arab and Islamic recognition of Israel and stability in the region. Until recently, Israel had not been prepared to make substantial concessions to the Palestinians (e.g., local but demilitarized autonomy for the West Bank,[12] compensation for confiscated Arab land), and Palestinian spokesmen (Yasir Arafat and the P.L.O.) had not been disposed to accept anything less than an independent militarized Palestinian state. The United States and the United Nations were able to do little to break this impasse beyond offering their good offices. Recently, however, Israel and the P.L.O. reached breakthrough accords on limited Palestinian self-rule in the Gaza strip and the Jericho area (May 4, 1994) and autonomy for 30 percent of the West Bank (September 28, 1995).

The United States, the European Community, and the pertinent successor states of the Soviet Union, however, can do something about Islamic nations' access to nuclear materials and technology by imposing and vigorously enforcing export controls. The West could and should collaborate with the pertinent successor states of the Soviet Union to develop financially attractive civilian employment opportunities for former Soviet scientists and technicians either in the new republics or in the West. And the West and Russia can collaborate more broadly with the United Nations to control the proliferation of nuclear weapons.

Israel's nuclear capability is designed to deter its hostile neighbors from attacking it, not to acquire or regain disputed territory. The same cannot be said about the purpose of other nations' actual or potential nuclear-weapons capabilities, and nuclear-weapons capabilities that are designed to help nations acquire or regain disputed territories are far more destabilizing than nuclear-weapons

12. Cf. Security Council Resolution 242 (November 22, 1967).

capabilities for deterrence or defense. If, for example, Pakistan or North Korea or Iran were to acquire nuclear-weapons capability, those nations might readily use their capability to gain possession of disputed territory (Pakistan to gain Indian Kashmir) or hegemony over neighbors (North Korea over South Korea, Iran over the Middle East). And if the target nation also possessed nuclear weapons (e.g., India in the case of Kashmir), or if a nuclear power were to intervene on behalf of the target nation (e.g., Israel to prevent Iranian hegemony in the Middle East), the end product might be a regional nuclear disaster. Major nuclear powers might need to intervene in order to deter such minor-power nuclear confrontations.

Proliferation of nuclear weapons capability seriously destabilizes the security, and threatens holocausts in, regions where such weapons are introduced. Western nuclear powers (the United States, Great Britain, and France) and most of the successor republics of the Soviet Union with nuclear weapons or materials[13] have a common interest in nonproliferation. They need to maintain the strictest controls on the export of materials, technology, and delivery systems that could be used to develop nuclear weapons capability. Developed nations in possession of nuclear materials convertible to military use, and of nuclear technology, have a similar interest and a similar need to maintain strict export controls. If nuclear materials or technology is exported for professedly peaceful uses, the exporting nations should insist on the right of on-site inspection of the importing nations' facilities. Unless all nations with access to nuclear materials and technology cooperate closely and act vigorously, irresponsible entrepreneurs will attempt to circumvent the export controls of one country by shipment to another, whence the materials and technology can be transshipped to the nation of ultimate destination.

13. Of the four successor republics of the Soviet Union that possess nuclear weapons (Russia, Belarus, Ukraine, and Kazakhstan), only Kazakhstan, with its largely Islamic population, might be tempted to sell or transfer its nuclear weapons to a would-be nuclear power (presumably an Islamic nation). Four successor republics of the Soviet Union (Russia, Ukraine, Kazakhstan, and Uzbekistan) produce uranium. All four might be tempted to sell uranium to other nations for profit, but only in the case of Kazakhstan is there any credible fear that uranium would be sold or transferred to would-be nuclear powers for political reasons.

The United Nations plays a key role, and could play a stronger role, in preventing the proliferation of nuclear weapons. The Nuclear Nonproliferation Treaty recognizes the right of U.N. officials to inspect the facilities of signatory nations. And the Security Council by reason of Chapter VII of the United Nations Charter could prohibit nuclear-weapons proliferation, mandate inspection of facilities whether or not nations were signatories of the Nuclear Nonproliferation Treaty, and enforce compliance by sanctions or military action.

The U.S. Central Intelligence Agency (C.I.A.) by late spring 1993 concluded that North Korea had diverted plutonium from peaceful uses in 1989 and produced one or two atomic bombs. Moreover, the government of North Korea was stalling on allowing officials of the International Atomic Energy Agency (I.A.E.A.) to inspect that government's nuclear facilities. Military options against the North Korean facilities were deemed unacceptable, in part because of the nuclear risk to the region, and China and Japan were unwilling to participate in economic sanctions against North Korea. Despite the weakness of its bargaining position, the United States reached an agreement with North Korea on October 21, 1994: North Korea agreed to freeze its nuclear program, and the United States and a consortium of nations promised economic and other aid to North Korea. The agreement did not mention, much less consider, the problem that would be posed by any atomic bombs that North Korea already possessed.

China is the most important nuclear power that might regard the export of nuclear weapons and technology to certain nations—and resulting regional instability—as beneficial to its national and ideological interests. China might regard the introduction of nuclear weapons and the promotion of instability in regions remote from China as harmful to its capitalist adversaries. For example, China might decide to help Islamic nations of the Middle East to acquire nuclear-weapons capability in order to enable those nations to destabilize the oil supplies of the West and Japan. On the other hand, it would clearly be in China's interest to prevent Pakistan and India from acquiring nuclear-weapons capability. China might, therefore, be persuaded to join efforts by the major nuclear powers and

the United Nations to prevent nuclear-weapons proliferation everywhere. Although China would thereby lose the opportunity to destabilize oil-producing regions vital to the economies of the West
and Japan, China would gain security on her own frontiers.

Some nations other than the Big Five (e.g., Israel) very probably
already possess tactical and intermediate nuclear-weapons capability. Since these nations cannot be reasonably expected to give up
their nuclear-weapons capability without ironclad guarantees, the
world community and some or all of the Big Five nuclear powers
would need to be prepared to go to the brink of war—or beyond—
to force such powers to agree to disarm themselves of the nuclear
weapons they already possess. Public opinion in the West, especially
concerning Israel, would not support such a confrontation, which
would in any case be foolhardy, unnecessary, and prima facie unfair
in the absence of alternate security guarantees. It would be far less
dangerous and more practical to try to induce minor nuclear powers
to relinquish their nuclear-weapons capability voluntarily in return
for adequate security guarantees that would make possession of
those weapons unnecessary. Effective U.N. enforcement of nuclear
nonproliferation and defense treaties between nations relinquishing
nuclear-weapons capability and major powers, especially the United
States, might provide adequate security to the former.

Some nations (e.g., Pakistan, India, North Korea) seem to be actively attempting to attain nuclear-weapons capabilities but may not
yet have achieved their objective. As previously indicated, nations
with nuclear-weapons capabilities or vital components thereof need
to maintain and enforce strict controls on the export of materials,
weapons, technology, and delivery systems that could be used by
aspiring nations to develop or improve nuclear-weapons capabilities.
As also previously noted, the United Nations currently oversees observance of the Nuclear Nonproliferation Treaty, and the Security
Council could mandate and enforce nonproliferation with or without reference to that treaty.

The creation of a U.N. nuclear force under the special agreements
provided for by Article 43 of the charter would not only help to enforce compliance to the Nuclear Nonproliferation Treaty and poten-

tial Security Council nonproliferation resolutions but also offer a shield to provide security against hostile neighbors for nations without nuclear weapons. As such, this nuclear force would offer some security to nonnuclear nations and might even help to persuade minor powers with nuclear weapons to relinquish the weapons.

The creation of a nuclear force at the disposal of the Security Council would not affect the Big Five, since each of them would retain a veto power over use of the force. The Big Five, therefore, would remain as secure (or insecure) against the first use of nuclear weapons as they are at present, and they will not relinquish all or part of their own nuclear arsenals unless they mutually agree or unilaterally decide to do so. The United States and Russia have already gone far to disarm themselves of nuclear weapons, and the two nuclear superpowers might be able to go further, especially if China were to agree to disarm on an asymmetrically lesser scale. The creation of a U.N. nuclear force would also enhance the prospects for the Big Five to disarm more of their nuclear arsenals because the U.N. nuclear force would help to deter rogue minor powers from nuclear blackmail.

Nuclear Proliferation and Terrorism

In addition to the problem of mutual deterrence, the two superpowers have long recognized an internal control problem, namely, how those higher in each superpower's chain of command ought to communicate authoritative commands to subordinates and assure compliance. Thanks to the highly ordered structures of the U.S. and Soviet military, the customary obedience of their personnel to political authorities, and the extensive steps the two superpowers took to ensure communications between different levels of command, no breakdown of the three C's (command, control, communication) occurred during the Cold War.

The main problem of control now is to prevent the proliferation of nuclear weapons, materials, and technology to other nations. Five successor republics of the Soviet Union (Russia, Belarus, Ukraine, Uzbekistan, and Kazakhstan) possess the nuclear weapons that previously belonged to the Soviet Union and/or produce uranium, and one of those republics (Kazakhstan) is very unstable politically.[14] Second, many former Soviet nuclear scientists and technologists are now unemployed or underpaid, and nations with nuclear aspirations may seek to hire them. Third, China may for its own reasons export nuclear weapons or materials to other nations. Fourth, Western businesses may cooperate with agents of aspiring nations to deliver components of nuclear-weapons systems to those nations. Lastly, if rogue nations acquire nuclear weapons, those nations may make nuclear devices available to terrorist groups.

The latter scenario is particularly frightening because terrorists cannot be deterred by threats of retaliation, and many of them do not fear even self-immolation, which their religious beliefs regard as a form of martyrdom meriting heavenly bliss. In short, unlike the powerholders of nation-states or even organized crime, terrorists will not be deterred by any rational calculus of potential gains and losses.

The most effective way to prevent nuclear terrorism is to prevent aspiring nations from acquiring nuclear-weapons capability. This involves keeping the sources of nuclear-weapons capability out of the hands of nations without them. Nuclear-weapon materials in the hands of Belarus, Ukraine, and Kazakhstan should be destroyed, neutralized, or transferred to Russia, with Western subsidies and security guarantees; former Soviet scientists and technologists should be guaranteed civilian employment with adequate pay either in their own country or in the West; China needs to be induced to support nonproliferation; Western nations need to impose and vigorously enforce export controls on the components of nuclear weapons.

If, in spite of precautions, rogue nations do manage to achieve nuclear-weapons capability, the West and Russia will need a strategy to deter such nations from providing terrorists with nuclear devices. Such a deterrence strategy would probably need to threaten military retaliation against nations that supply terrorist groups with the nuclear devices that the groups detonate anywhere. The threatened retaliation would not need to involve nuclear weapons, nor should it

14. Cf. nn. 9 and 13.

target rogue-nation civilians; the targets could be the nuclear facilities and political control apparatus of the rogue nation. The U.N. Security Council should ideally legitimate such a deterrence policy and authorize any enforcement action under Article 42 if deterrence fails.

If terrorists succeed in acquiring nuclear devices, the United States and Europe would have only conventional means of counterterrorism at their disposal (e.g., border controls, domestic surveillance, maximum security at rail and air terminals, espionage, infiltration). But even the most vigorous and efficient counterterrorist operations are not likely to be leak-proof. And so the prospects of preventing nuclear terrorist acts once terrorists have access to nuclear devices are not very comforting.

PART 2

CASES AND QUESTIONS

WORLD WAR I (1914-18)

Austria-Hungary formally annexed Bosnia-Herzegovina (part of postwar Yugoslavia), a former Turkish province of Muslim and Christian population, in 1908. With two accomplices, Gavrilo Princip, a Serbian nationalist, crossed the frontier of Serbia into Bosnia and assassinated the heir to the Austro-Hungarian throne, Archduke Franz Ferdinand, and his wife in Sarajevo (the capital of Bosnia-Herzegovina) on June 28, 1914. The head of the Serbian Intelligence, Colonel Dragutin Dimitrijevic, was generally believed to have inspired the plot, but the evidence of this involvement is inconclusive. There is no certainty about how much, if anything, the Serbian government knew about the plot, or about what steps, if any, the Serbian government took to prevent its execution. The Austrian official in Sarajevo in charge of investigating the assassination reported to Vienna that he could not establish Serbian responsibility for the assassination.

Nonetheless, the Austrian government was determined to crush Serbia, which it regarded as the breeding ground of nationalist agitation in its Slavic dependencies. The Emperor Franz Joseph of Austria-Hungary wrote to Emperor Wilhelm II of Germany that Austria-Hungary must aim at "the isolation and diminution of Serbia," which he wanted "eliminated as a factor in the Balkans." The Austro-Hungarian foreign minister, Count Leopold von Berchtold, sent a memorandum to Berlin urging that Bulgaria be admitted into the Triple Alliance (the alliance of Germany, Austria-Hungary, and Italy), and that it was "imperative" to take strong action against

Serbia. Austria also sent a special emissary, Count Alexander von Hoyos, to Berlin. Von Hoyos communicated orally to the German government that Austria-Hungary proposed "to march into Serbia" without warning and to partition that country among Austria-Hungary, Albania, and Bulgaria.

The German emperor and his government received the plan cordially and urged Austria-Hungary to take immediate action. Wilhelm believed that, because a fellow prince had been murdered, Czar Nicholas II of Russia would not come to the aid of Serbia. But Wilhelm promised to support Austria-Hungary and to fight on her side against Russia and France, Russia's ally, if the czar did decide to support Serbia.

Wilhelm held no consultations with his chancellor Theobald von Bethmann-Hollweg, or his military advisers, before he gave his blanket promise to the Austro-Hungarian government. The German government did not raise any objections, nor did it ask its ambassador in St. Petersburg whether or not the emperor's belief about the czar's intentions was correct. Moreover, the emperor assumed that Great Britain would remain neutral in the event of a general war, but the German ambassador in London had been reporting to Berlin for eighteen months that Britain would join Russia and France if such a war broke out.

With the German emperor's assurance of support, Austria-Hungary considered itself free to act against Serbia. Count István Tisza, the Hungarian prime minister, however, opposed immediate action, and so the Austrian prime minister abandoned plans to march immediately into Serbia. The Joint Austro-Hungarian Council of Ministers decided on July 7 to issue a forty-eight-hour ultimatum to Serbia, and the council was sure that Serbia would find the demands unacceptable. The ultimatum would demand that Serbia make "rectifications" of its frontier with Austria-Hungary in favor of the latter, cede other territories to Bulgaria and Albania, and tie itself to Austria-Hungary by a military convention signed by a new monarch.

On July 23, Austria-Hungary served an ultimatum of ten demands on Serbia, with forty-eight hours to reply. The ultimatum made no mention of territory but required Serbia to allow Austro-

Hungarian officials to operate in Serbia to suppress agitation against Austria-Hungary and to take action against putative instigators of the assassination. French President Raymond Poincaré and Prime Minister René Viviani, then completing a state visit to Russia, promised the czar and his ministers that France would support Russia against Austria-Hungary and Germany if Russian support for Serbia led to war with those countries.

On July 25, the Serbian government replied to the Austro-Hungarian ultimatum in a conciliatory tone, agreed to most of the Austro-Hungarian demands, and expressed its willingness to submit the rest to international arbitration. The Austro-Hungarian minister in Belgrade, after a cursory reading of the reply, deemed it unsatisfactory and left Belgrade. The Austro-Hungarian government broke diplomatic relations with Serbia and ordered partial mobilization of its army.

On July 26, the British government proposed a peace conference of the major powers in London to find a solution to the dispute between Austria-Hungary and Serbia. The German government rejected the proposal on July 27.

On July 28, encouraged by the German Foreign Office, Austria-Hungary declared war on Serbia and bombarded Belgrade. The German emperor, returning from a two-week cruise, now decided that the Serbian reply to the Austrian ultimatum had removed "every reason for war," and proposed that Austria-Hungary should halt its attack on Serbia with the occupation of Belgrade and offer to negotiate.

On July 29, Great Britain made an almost identical proposal, and the German government advised the Austrian government that evening to accept it. Sir Edward Grey, the British foreign secretary, also advised the German ambassador in London that, if a general war broke out in Europe, Britain would be drawn in against Germany.

On the same day, Russia ordered partial mobilization of its army, but the army had no plan for such mobilization. Accordingly, the czar had to choose between total mobilization or none. After giving and revoking his consent on the twenty-ninth, the czar definitively authorized general mobilization on the thirtieth, and the order was published on the thirty-first. The czar promised that Russian armies would not attack as long as negotiations continued.

When rumors of Russian mobilization reached Berlin on July 30, General Helmut von Moltke, chief of the German General Staff, pressed for war. By evening, he had persuaded the German chancellor to relax pressure on Austria-Hungary to accept the British proposal. Von Moltke also telegraphed General Franz von Hötzendorf, the Austro-Hungarian chief of staff, urging rejection of the British proposal and promising German support.

Austria-Hungary, following von Moltke's advice, ordered general mobilization of its army on July 31, before news of Russia's general mobilization reached Vienna. On the same day, the German chancellor, at the insistence of von Moltke and the emperor (who had again changed his mind), issued a war-danger proclamation as the groundwork for a general mobilization order.

The German government regarded Russian general mobilization as equivalent to an act of war, since that would enable Russia and France to mount an attack on Germany on two fronts, and so informed the Russian government on July 31. Germany demanded that Russia halt its mobilization within twenty-four hours. Germany also demanded that France declare within eighteen hours its intention to remain neutral.

On August 1, Germany ordered general mobilization of its army and declared war against Russia when the latter failed to halt its mobilization. On the same day, France declined to promise neutrality, saying only that it would consult its own interests. France also ordered general mobilization of its army.

On August 2, Germany invaded Luxembourg and demanded that Belgium permit German troops free passage through that country.

On August 3, Germany declared war on France, and when Belgium refused to permit German troops free passage, Germany invaded it that evening.

As a guarantor of Belgian neutrality, Great Britain on August 4 issued an ultimatum to Germany to withdraw its troops from Belgium by midnight (German time). When Germany failed to do so by the deadline (11:00 P.M., British time), Great Britain declared itself at war with Germany. Britain had already promised France on August 2 to help the latter defend its northern coast if Germany attacked.

Many other nations subsequently entered the war. On August 7, 1914, Montenegro (part of postwar Yugoslavia) declared war against Austria-Hungary. On August 23, 1914, Japan declared war against Germany. On October 29, 1914, Turkey attacked Russia. On May 23, 1915, Italy declared war against Austria-Hungary. On September 6, 1915, Bulgaria joined the Central Powers (Austria-Hungary and Germany). On August 27, 1916, Romania joined the Allies (Britain, France, and Russia). Japan sought to acquire Germany's Pacific possessions, Turkey part of the Caucasus, Italy Austrian territories bordering its northeastern border, Bulgaria part of Serbia, and Romania Transylvania.

British Naval Blockade and German Submarine Warfare

On November 2, 1914, Great Britain declared the North Sea a war zone and warned all neutrals that their merchant ships traveled there at risk unless they used prescribed routes. The British initially indicated that they would adhere to the Declaration of London (1909), which attempted to limit the list of contraband goods to war material and items that could be used for war purposes, but they soon expanded the list to include as contraband goods not traditionally so regarded. They included food in the contraband list in February 1915, and cotton on August 21, 1915. On July 7, 1916, they altogether abandoned adherence to the declaration. The blockade brought German sea trade to a halt from the outset of the war.

In March 1915, the British instituted an undeclared blockade of the ports of neutral nations bordering on Germany (Holland and Denmark). By various devices, the British successfully "rationed" neutral nations' imports to goods for local consumption and thereby prevented their transshipment to Germany. The British blockade was so effective that the German civilian population experienced considerable hardship when the domestic crop failed in 1916.

On January 30, 1915, German submarines without warning sank the British liners *Tokemaru* and *Ikaria*. On February 4, Germany declared a war zone around the British Isles and warned that, on and after February 18, all enemy ships in the zone would be destroyed, and that neutral merchant ships would travel at their own risk. On May 7, a German submarine sank the British liner *Lusitania* off the southwestern coast of Ireland without warning and without provision for the safety of passengers or crew. The ship was carrying 173 tons of ammunition. The death toll from the sinking was 1,198 persons, including 128 U.S. citizens. On August 17, a German submarine without warning sank the British liner *Arabic*, with the loss of U.S. and neutral passengers aboard. On October 5, the German government disavowed the action, offered indemnity, and promised to order its submarine commanders to observe the traditional rules of warfare with respect to passenger and neutral merchant ships, but not before a German submarine sank another British liner, the *Hespernia* (September 18).

In March 1916, the German naval high command authorized submarines to sink without warning all but exclusively passenger vessels traveling in the war zone. On March 24, a German submarine without warning sank the British liner *Sussex*, causing the loss of several American lives. On April 18, the U.S. government demanded assurances from Germany that the latter's submarines would give warning to passenger and neutral merchant ships before attack and provide for the safety of the ships' passengers and crew. On May 4, the German government yielded and again suspended its unrestricted submarine warfare.

On January 31, 1917, Germany announced that it would resume unrestricted submarine warfare on the next day. The United States broke diplomatic relations on February 3. After German submarines attacked several U.S. merchant ships and without warning sank the British liner *Laconia*, with the loss of several American lives (February 25), President Woodrow Wilson on April 2 asked Congress to declare war against Germany, and Congress did so on April 6.

Peace Attempts

In early 1916, President Wilson sent his aide, Colonel Edward M. House, to London and Paris to sound out Great Britain and France about the possibility of United States mediation of the conflict. On February 22, Colonel House and British Foreign Secretary Grey signed a secret memo in which the United States indicated that it would probably join the Allies if Germany rejected the offer of U.S. mediation, and Secretary Grey reserved the right to initiate the call for U.S. mediation. After the sinking of the *Sussex*, which seemed likely to draw the United States into the war on the side of the Allies, efforts to press Grey to initiate the call for mediation were in vain.

On December 12, the German chancellor publicly called for peace talks under terms militarily favorable to the Central Powers, but the Allies rejected the offer, insisting on reparations and the principle of nationalities (self-determination).

By the end of 1916, President Wilson gave up waiting for the British to initiate a call for U.S. mediation. On December 18, Wilson invited the belligerents to communicate their war objectives to him. The Allies did so in sweeping terms, but the Central Powers did not elaborate their terms beyond the German chancellor's statement of December 12.

On January 22, 1917, President Wilson publicly called for "peace without victory." A confidential British reply expressed readiness to accept Wilson's mediation. The German chancellor, in his reply of January 31, repeated his support for peace talks and urged Wilson to continue his efforts. On the same day, however, the German government announced its resumption of unrestricted submarine warfare, upon which it had decided on January 9, and so this Wilson initiative failed.

In February, the new Austro-Hungarian emperor Karl, with his brother-in-law Prince Sixtus of Bourbon-Parma as intermediary, initiated discussions with the Allies for a separate peace. The British and French prime ministers reacted favorably to Karl's first letter (March 24), which Sixtus took to Paris, but the Italian government demanded more territory from Austria than Karl was willing to grant. Although Karl wrote a second letter (May 9), and Sixtus visited London in June, the talks ended without any result.

On July 19, the German Reichstag (parliament) passed the "Peace Resolution," which renounced German annexation of any territory as a result of the war.

On August 1, Pope Benedict XV proposed a far-reaching peace plan: Germany was to withdraw from Belgium and France; the Allies were to restore German colonies; Serbia, Montenegro, and Romania were to be restored; an independent Poland was to be created; the principles of arbitration, disarmament, and freedom of the seas were to be accepted. Britain and France declined to reply until Germany agreed to the restoration and indemnification of Belgium. The German reply avoided committing itself to do so. The U.S. reply expressed moral objections to negotiating with Germany's current political and military leaders, thus implying that the German army's destruction and the German emperor's abdication were necessary conditions for peace. The Pope's plan accordingly failed.

The Armistices and Peace Treaties

The new Bolshevik government of Russia reached an armistice with the Central Powers on February 15, 1918. On March 3, Russia signed the Treaty of Brest-Litovsk with the Central Powers and gave up claim to Finland; the Baltic areas of Estonia, Latvia, and Lithuania; prewar Russian Poland; and the Ukraine.

By September, however, the Central Powers were collapsing on all fronts. Bulgaria signed an armistice with the Allies on September 29, Turkey on October 30, Austria-Hungary on November 4, and Germany on November 11. The Allies maintained the blockade on Germany (food included) until the Treaty of Versailles was signed.

Germany signed the Treaty of Versailles on June 28, 1919. The treaty ceded eastern territory to Poland and Alsace-Lorraine to France; gave the coal mines of the Saar basin to France and put the administration of the Saar in the hands of the League of Nations for fifteen years; abrogated the Treaty of Brest-Litovsk and required German troops to withdraw from the Baltic areas of Estonia, Latvia, and Lithuania at the behest of the Allies; and stripped Germany of its African and Asian colonies. The Rhineland was permanently demilitarized, and the Allies were permitted to occupy different parts of it for five to fifteen years. Germany acknowledged its responsibility for the war and liability for reparations and agreed to the trial of accused war criminals and the deposed emperor. The treaty limited the size and arms of the future German army and navy, forbade an air force, and renounced compulsory military service.

Austria signed the Treaty of St. Germain-en-Laye on September 10, 1919. The treaty ceded territory to Italy, Czechoslovakia, Poland, and Yugoslavia. The territory ceded to Czechoslovakia included 3.5 million ethnic Germans, mostly on the northwest borders of that country, and the territory to Italy included 250,000 ethnic Germans in the South Tyrol. Austria recognized the Allies' right to try Austrians accused of war crimes, and its liability for reparations. The treaty limited the size of Austria's army and renounced compulsory military service.

Bulgaria signed the Treaty of Neuilly on November 27, 1919. The treaty ceded territory on Bulgaria's western border to Yugoslavia, and western Thrace, which included access to the Mediterranean, to Greece. Bulgaria recognized the Allies' right to try Bulgarians accused of war crimes, and its liability for reparations. The treaty limited the size of Bulgaria's army.

Hungary, now a separate nation, signed the Treaty of Trianon on June 4, 1920. The treaty ceded territory to Czechoslovakia, Romania, Austria, and Yugoslavia and reduced Hungary to one third of its prewar size. The territory ceded to Romania included 2.5 million ethnic Hungarians, and that to Czechoslovakia, 1 million ethnic Hungarians. Hungary agreed to Allied trials of Hungarians accused of war crimes, reparations, and renunciation of compulsory military service. The treaty limited the size of Hungary's army.

Turkey signed the Treaty of Sèvres on August 10, 1920. The treaty ceded eastern Thrace to Greece and reduced Turkey to the environs of Constantinople and the Anatolian peninsula of Asia Minor. Turkey agreed to the independence of Kurdistan and Armenia and to Greek administration of Ionia (western Anatolia). The Dardanelles were to be demilitarized and internationalized. (The Treaty of Lausanne, signed on July 24, 1923, modified the Treaty of Sèvres.)

The Casualties and Economic Cost of the War

The casualties of the war included 8.5 million military dead, 28 million civilian dead, 7.75 million missing persons, and 21 million wounded. The war was estimated to have cost $186 billion.

In addition to its physical casualties and economic costs, World War I had significant, longer-term, adverse political consequences. The war led to the collapse of the czarist regime in Russia, the subsequent rise of the Communist party to power there, and the threat of worldwide exportation of Communist revolutions. The severity of the Treaty of Versailles led to revanchist German sentiments that contributed to the rise of Hitler and generated support for his pan-German aspirations. And the more than literal decimation of a generation of young men, including prime leadership potential, engendered strong antiwar sentiments in the United States and Western European democracies, sentiments that operated to constrain leaders of those countries from directly confronting Hitler before the latter's invasion of Poland in 1939.

SUGGESTED READINGS

Joll, James, *The Origins of the First World War.* London; New York: Longman, 1984.
Stokesbury, James J. *A Short History of World War I.* New York: Morrow, 1981.

QUESTIONS

1. Do you think that the Slavic peoples living under Austro-Hungarian rule in 1914 regarded it as legitimate? If not, do you think that Croatians, Slovenes, and Muslims preferred independence under Serbian hegemony to Austrian or Hungarian rule?

2. Assuming the legitimacy of Austro-Hungarian rule in those dependencies, was Austria-Hungary, after the assassination, justified in demanding virtual control of the Serbian police in the absence of proof of Serbian complicity? Was the Austrian cause, even if otherwise just, proportional to the risk of world war? How reasonable was it to expect that Russia would not intervene? What probability of a larger war would have rendered the Austro-Hungarian cause proportionally unjust? As-

suming a 50 percent probability, would the potential casualties of a larger war have rendered the Austro-Hungarian cause proportionally unjust? What if the probability of a larger war were only 10 percent?

3. Assuming the general justice of Austria-Hungary's cause, was Germany proportionally justified in giving Austria carte blanche to attack Serbia and promising support for Austria if Russia came to the support of Serbia? How reasonable was the German emperor's expectation that Russia would not intervene? That Great Britain would stay neutral? Even if those expectations were more likely than not, if the event proved otherwise, would the potential casualties have rendered the German promise of support proportionally unjustified?

4. After the Serbian reply to the Austro-Hungarian ultimatum, did Austria-Hungary have any just cause to declare war? To reject the British proposal for a ceasefire?

5. Given Germany's warning that it would regard full Russian mobilization as a prelude to war, was Russia proportionally justified in doing so, assuming the justice of Serbia's cause?

6. Was Germany justified in regarding the Russian mobilization as a casus belli? Should Germany have been satisfied with the czar's promise not to attack Austria-Hungary while negotiations were in progress, and have pressured Austria-Hungary to negotiate?

7. Assuming that Germany was justified in declaring war against Russia, was Germany justified in demanding that France declare its intention to remain neutral? In declaring war against France when the latter failed to do so and mobilized its forces?

8. Assuming that Germany was justified in declaring war against France, was Germany justified in invading Belgium to attack France? Even if Germany's survival depended on doing so? Did Germany's treaty obligation to respect Belgian neutrality ipso facto render Germany's invasion of Belgium unjust?

9. Would an early unequivocal British declaration of support for the Allies have been likely to deter Austria-Hungary and Germany from initiating hostilities? If so, and assuming the justice of the Allied cause, should Britain have made such a declaration? Even if there was an equal likelihood that Britain would not deter Austria and Germany from initiating hostilities? Would Britain have been justified in declaring war on Germany if the latter had not violated Belgian neutrality?

10. Japan, Turkey, Italy, Bulgaria, and Romania entered the war, at least in part, in order to gain territory. Assuming that they had some

historical claim to, and/or kindred ethnics living in, the territory, did such a reason justify those nations' waging war?

11. Both the British and German blockades violated traditionally accepted rules of war. Why did the American government find the German violations so much more objectionable? Was it because human lives were involved, or because the American government was more sympathetic to the Allies?

12. Were the Germans justified in attacking passenger ships because those ships could be, and sometimes were, used to carry war material (e.g., the *Lusitania*) and/or to transport war-connected personnel? Were the Germans justified in attacking neutral merchant ships irrespective of the ships' content because the British were preventing such ships from transporting goods traditionally regarded as noncontraband to Germany or to neutral nations for transshipment to Germany? Did the vulnerability of the submarine justify the Germans' not giving passenger and neutral merchant ships warning of attack, and not rescuing the ships' crews and passengers?

13. Assuming that Germany was not justified in waging unrestricted submarine warfare, did the United States have a proportional just cause to declare war against Germany? Did not American passengers and merchant ships have adequate warning about the risk of traveling in the German war zone, and had they not assumed that risk by doing so? Apart from the cause of Germany's unrestricted submarine warfare, did the Allied cause or the cause of democracy justify American intervention? If so, should not the United States have declared war against Germany earlier or even indicated its intention to side with the Allies before the outbreak of hostilities?

14. Was it morally justifiable for Britain to refuse to initiate a call for U.S. mediation in the spring of 1916, when, after the sinking of the *Sussex*, it appeared likely that the United States would enter the war and provide the Allies with the margin for a decisive military victory?

15. Were the Allies morally justified in refusing the German chancellor's call for peace talks (December 12, 1916) without prior German agreement to reparations and the principle of self-determination?

16. Were the Allies morally justified in demanding indemnification of Belgium before giving a reply to Pope Benedict XV's peace plan? Was the German government morally justified in refusing to commit itself to do so? Was the United States morally justified in virtually demanding the German army's destruction and the German emperor's abdication

as necessary conditions for peace? Was any single issue more important than ending the war?

17. Was the Italian government morally justified in demanding more territory than Austro-Hungarian emperor Karl was prepared to grant when he proposed a separate peace in the spring of 1917? Should the British and French, despite their secret promises of territory to Italy, have accepted Karl's proposal anyway? Should Karl have yielded to the Italian demands in order to secure peace?

18. Was there any moral justification of the Allies' maintaining the blockade of foodstuffs to Germany after the armistice?

19. Given the complexity of the war's origin, were the Allies justified in holding Germany solely responsible for the war? Were the Allies justified in exacting German reparations for Belgium? For France? Even if the people of Germany were thereby impoverished? Even if the reparations sowed the seeds of World War II?

20. Were the Allies justified in stripping Germany of her colonies? In taking over the colonies?

21. Were the Allies justified in transferring territories with ethnic German and Hungarian populations to Czechoslovakia, territory with ethnic German population to Italy, and territory with ethnic Hungarian population to Romania? If so, what about the principle of self-determination?

22. Were the Allies justified in requiring Turkey to grant independence to Kurdistan and Armenia? In giving Greece administration of Ionia?

23. Was any participant's cause proportional to the war's casualties, costs, and political consequences?

THE VIETNAM WARS (1946–75)

The Colonial Period

France gained control over Vietnam in the second half of the nineteenth century and established direct French rule there at all levels by the end of the century, effectively replacing the native emperor and his court. The French instituted a network of public works to facilitate exploitation of Vietnam's wealth for the benefit of France. The chief Vietnamese resources exploited by the French were rice, coal, minerals, and later, rubber. The French were not interested in promoting local industry except to provide goods for immediate local consumption.

Although the construction of irrigation projects between 1880 and 1930, chiefly in the Mekong delta (southern Vietnam), quadrupled the surface land available for growing rice, the rice produced by individual peasants for local consumption declined during the same period without an increase in the production of other foods. The new lands were distributed by sale to the highest bidders and by virtual gifts to native favorites. The new landlords (six to seven thousand) exacted up to 60 percent of the crop from their tenants, and the product was exported.

Individual peasants lost their land to large landowners when they were unable to repay loans provided at exorbitantly high interest rates. As a result, large landowners in the Mekong delta (2.5 percent of the landowners) owned 45 percent of the land in 1939, whereas small peasants (71 percent of the landowners) owned no more than 15 percent of the land, and 50 percent of the population was landless.

The peasants' share of the crop was further reduced by direct and indirect taxes imposed to finance the public works, and Vietnamese natives were forced to contribute their labor to produce the public works.

No more than 15 percent of school-age children received any kind of schooling in 1939, and 80 percent of the population was illiterate, although a majority of the population had been literate before the French arrived.

There were in that year only two doctors for every 100,000 Vietnamese, compared with seventy-six in Japan and twenty-five in the Philippines.

There were no civil liberties for the native population, and the Vietnamese were excluded from nontraditional industry and trade.

Opposition to French rule in the nineteenth century was mainly traditionalist, but a new nationalist movement favorable to Western modernization arose in the twentieth century. The failure of moderate reformist efforts led to the formation of revolutionary groups during and after World War I. The unified and disciplined Communist party, formed by Ho Chi Minh in 1930, was at the outbreak of World War II the most effective organization in the national liberation movement.

After the fall of France (June 1940), the defeated French appointed a new governor general of Indochina. The latter concluded an agreement with Japan that allowed Japan to station thirty thousand troops in Indochina and to use the major Vietnamese airports. Indochina thus became for all practical purposes a French-administered possession of Japan.

Nationalist Vietnamese exiles in southern China organized opposition to the Japanese occupation. In May 1941, Ho Chi Minh founded the Viet Minh, an umbrella organization of nationalist groups under Communist direction. The anti-Communist Nationalist Chinese government orchestrated the formation of a Vietnamese non-Communist counterfront, the Dong Minh Hoi, and imprisoned Ho in 1942. The Dong Minh Hoi, however, proved incompetent, and the Chinese and the Americans relied principally on the Viet Minh for intelligence about Japanese activities in Vietnam. Ho himself reentered Vietnam in October 1944.

In March 1945, the Japanese, fearful that the French forces in Indochina would turn against them, disarmed the French and allowed Bao Dai, the last French-appointed emperor of Vietnam, to proclaim the country's independence and set up a national government in Hue (central Vietnam) under Japanese control.

The War for Independence

After the Japanese government sued for peace on August 15, 1945, Viet Minh cadres revolted and took possession of the city of Hanoi (northern Vietnam). The Bao Dai government resigned on August 22, and the emperor abdicated in favor of the Viet Minh. A provisional revolutionary committee in Saigon (southern Vietnam), dominated by the Viet Minh, put itself under the authority of the Hanoi government on August 25. On September 2, Ho proclaimed the independence of Vietnam.

The leaders of the victorious Allies at the Potsdam Conference in July 1945 confirmed French rule in Indochina. The Chinese, who occupied northern Vietnam in September, refused to interfere with the Viet Minh government there. (The Chinese government was opposed to restoration of French rule.) British forces, who occupied southern Vietnam the same month, disarmed the Japanese, freed interned French troops, and armed and assisted the latter to oust the Viet Minh–dominated Revolutionary Committee of South Vietnam. The French reconquest of southern Vietnam began on September 23 and broke resistance there in several weeks. The French gained control of the southern cities, but armed guerrillas, supplied by the Viet Minh government of Hanoi, continued to operate over the countryside of southern and central Vietnam.

The Chinese reached an agreement with the French on February 28, 1946, to withdraw from northern Vietnam by March 15. Ho Chi Minh permitted the French to station fifteen thousand French and ten thousand allied Vietnamese troops in northern Vietnamese cities, and the French promised to recognize the Viet Minh government as a free state in the French Union. The French also agreed to withdraw their troops from Vietnam over a five-year period and to allow southern Vietnam to be integrated with northern Vietnam if the merger were approved in a referendum.

To placate the Chinese, the Viet Minh included anti-Communist nationalists in the government but retained firm control. The anti-Communist nationalists did not receive enough votes in the National Assembly elections of January 6 to win the 70 of 380 seats allotted them, and they denounced the Viet Minh–French agreement of March 6 as a sell-out. The French entered Hanoi on March 18 and cooperated with the Viet Minh in suppressing the anti-Communist nationalists; the Viet Minh and French eliminated those nationalists from every position and region they held during the Chinese occupation.

The French high commissioner of Indochina, Admiral d'Argenlieu, proclaimed South Vietnam an autonomous republic on June 1, 1946, and the French navy bombarded the area of Haiphong (the chief port in northern Vietnam) on November 23 and caused the death of six thousand civilians. The Viet Minh attacked French troops on December 19.

The French gained control of the cities and highways of northern and central Vietnam within a few weeks, and the Viet Minh retreated to the mountains north and west of Hanoi. Viet Minh forces controlled the countryside and waged guerrilla warfare. The supply of weapons from China after the Communist victory there in 1949 enabled the Viet Minh to assume the offensive and to force the French out of positions along the Chinese border in September and October 1950.

Despite the French attempt to gain native political support by reestablishing Bao Dai as the nominal emperor of Vietnam in June 1949, French military victories under the able General Jean de Lattre de Tassigny in 1951, and large-scale U.S. military and financial aid to the French, the Viet Minh retained control over most of northern and central Vietnam exclusive of the Red River delta, and wide areas in the southern Mekong River delta. Finally, on May 7, 1954, the Viet Minh inflicted a crushing defeat on the French when the former overran the latter's strong garrison at Dien Bien Phu. The French government then sued for peace.

At an international conference in Geneva, the French and Viet Minh agreed on July 21, 1954, to a ceasefire and a temporary partition of Vietnam at the seventeenth parallel. All Viet Minh forces were to withdraw north of the parallel, and all French forces and the Vietnamese forces allied with them were to withdraw south of the parallel. For a limited time, refugees were to be permitted to move from one zone to the other. An international commission, composed of Canadian, Indian, and Polish representatives, was to supervise execution of the agreement. The participants in the conference—the United States, the United Kingdom, the Soviet Union, Red China, France, and the Viet Minh—issued a Final Declaration providing for all-Vietnam elections in July 1956 to establish a united government. No one seriously doubted that the Viet Minh would win those elections.

Two Vietnams

On June 16, 1954, Bao Dai chose Ngo Dinh Diem, a Catholic leader, to head the provisional government in the south. Over the next year, with large-scale financial aid from the United States, Diem eliminated francophile native army officers, established control over regions dominated by the Cao Dai and Hoa Hao religious sects, and resettled some 700,000 refugees from the north (mainly Catholics). A government-controlled referendum in 1955 abolished the monarchy, and Diem became president of South Vietnam.

Diem attempted to institute a modest land-reform program in 1956, but the landlord class entrenched in the administration sabotaged the plan. Diem used army and police terror against the Viet Minh and suspected collaborators. The regime openly favored Catholics. Critics were harshly punished. Loyalty to the president and his family became the criterion for advancement, and punishment the reward of personal disloyalty to them. Government appointees replaced traditionally elected village councils, and the government manipulated elections when they took place.

In North Vietnam, the Hanoi government took over most industrial and trade enterprises. Farmland was organized into cooperatives, in three quarters of which the state by 1968 owned the land, the animals, and the tools. The role of women was vastly expanded. Almost every segment of human activity was tightly controlled by the Communist party. Foreign Catholic priests were expelled in

1959, "patriotic" Catholic and Buddhist associations established under party control, and "scientific materialism" promoted. Party elites became the equivalent of the traditionally privileged mandarins, enjoying access to special shops and medical care at special hospitals. The party enjoyed a monopoly of political and economic power.

South Vietnam had a population of nearly 19,000,000 in 1971. This included 5,000,000 active Buddhists, more than 1,500,000 Catholics, 1,500,000 adherents of the Cao Dai sect, and 750,000 to 3,000,000 members of the Hoa Hao sect.

North Vietnam in the early 1970s had a population of 21,500,000, most of whom identified themselves as Buddhists. The Catholics who remained after the flight of 1954–55 numbered around 800,000.

The Revolutionary War in South Vietnam

In 1957, one year after Diem refused to participate in the all-Vietnam elections set by the Geneva Accord, the Communists inaugurated a guerrilla war against the Diem regime. In December 1960, various groups warring against the Diem regime formed the National Liberation Front (N.L.F.) under Communist direction. The N.L.F. platform called for South Vietnam to be neutralized, foreign troops to be withdrawn, and South Vietnam to be united with North Vietnam. The Hanoi government supplied the N.L.F. forces (the Viet Cong) with weapons and personnel, and the U.S. government supplied the Diem regime with money, military equipment, and advisers to the South Vietnamese army. The number of U.S. military advisers had increased from seven hundred in 1960 to seventeen thousand by the end of 1963, but they were instructed not to participate in combat with South Vietnamese army units.

A series of Buddhist riots and demonstrations against the Diem regime, including several self-immolations, erupted in the cities of South Vietnam in 1963. Apparently with the passive or active support of U.S. officials, South Vietnamese army officers overthrew the Diem regime on November 1, assassinating Diem and his brother Nhu, the head of the secret police.

On August 2 and 4, 1964, North Vietnamese torpedo boats fired on two U.S. destroyers in the Bay of Tonkin, and U.S. planes bombed North Vietnamese torpedo-boat bases and oil-storage facilities in retaliation. At the request of President Lyndon B. Johnson, the U.S. Congress overwhelmingly passed the so-called Tonkin Bay Resolution, which authorized him to take "all necessary means to repel attacks . . . and prevent further aggression." (Congress repealed the resolution in 1970.)

There were nine changes of government between November 1, 1963, and June 1965, when Air Marshal Nguyen Cao Ky assumed control of South Vietnam. Militant Buddhists opposed the Ky regime as much as they had the Diem regime, but Ky was able to break their resistance, which was centered in Hue and Da Nang. Like Diem, Ky suppressed civil liberties and imprisoned political opponents.

The Americanization of the War

By early 1965, American military experts had reached the opinion that the South Vietnamese regime could not survive without direct U.S. involvement in the war, as the Viet Cong continued to gain ground despite the assistance provided by U.S. military advisers and helicopter pilots. When the Viet Cong attacked a U.S. military base on February 7 and killed eight soldiers, President Johnson ordered U.S. planes to bomb North Vietnam to stop North Vietnamese infiltration of weapons and personnel into South Vietnam. Four weeks of bombing failed to halt the infiltration, and North Vietnam sent more regular battalions into the south in March. (Regular North Vietnamese battalions were already entering South Vietnam by the fall of 1964.)

The United States sent its first combat troops to South Vietnam on March 7, when 3,500 marines landed at Da Nang. U.S. troops numbered 75,000 by July, 188,000 by December 31, 389,000 by 1967, and 510,000 early in 1968. Regular South Vietnamese forces numbered 600,000. Those forces were augmented by several hundred thousand members of regional and local defense forces.

On September 3, 1967, General Nguyen Van Thieu and Ky were elected president and vice president of South Vietnam, respectively.

They received 35 percent of the vote, and ten civilian candidates received the other 65 percent. Opponents charged that the election results were obtained by fraud, and the civilian candidate who had received the largest number of votes after Thieu and Ky was jailed after the election because he favored negotiations with the N.L.F.

U.S. and South Vietnamese forces removed civilians in the countryside to fortified hamlets, defoliated areas of heavy vegetation, established free-fire zones, engaged in search-and-destroy missions, and attacked Viet Cong sanctuaries in Cambodia. (An important by-product of the accelerated tempo of the war was the displacement of South Vietnamese civilians from the countryside to the cities; whereas only 15 percent of the South Vietnamese lived in cities in 1955, 45 to 55 percent did so in the 1970s.) Neither the aforementioned American–South Vietnamese tactics nor the superiority of American equipment nor the continuous American bombing of North Vietnam undermined the will or fighting capacity of the Viet Cong and North Vietnamese forces. This became evident when, on January 30, 1968, Viet Cong forces launched the so-called Tet offensive against more than 36 of the 43 provincial capitals, 5 of the 6 autonomous cities, 34 of the 242 district capitals, and 50 hamlets. Moreover, they were able to hold some of these for three to four weeks.

Although the Tet offensive was a military failure, and the Viet Cong suffered heavy losses, the intensity and scope of the offensive shocked U.S. military and political leaders. Moreover, the offensive, mounting casualties in Vietnam, and higher draft call-ups induced widespread public demonstrations in the United States against the war, especially on college campuses.

President Johnson denied the request of General William C. Westmoreland, the American commander in Vietnam, for an additional 206,000 troops. On March 31, 1968, the president announced that he would not be a candidate for reelection, and that the United States would halt its bombing of North Vietnam above the twentieth parallel.

The United States opened negotiations with the Hanoi government in Paris on May 13. The talks were expanded in the fall to include representatives of the N.L.F. and South Vietnamese government. The United States halted all bombing of North Vietnam after October 31.

The Vietnamization of the War

On June 8, 1969, President Richard M. Nixon announced the first withdrawal of U.S. combat troops from Vietnam. By April 1970, 115,000 troops had been withdrawn, and another 150,000 were scheduled to be withdrawn in the next twelve months. Although U.S. ground forces joined with the South Vietnamese army in a major assault on Viet Cong sanctuaries in Cambodia in May 1970, and U.S. planes simultaneously bombed the whole of Indochina on an unprecedented scale, the withdrawals continued. By the end of 1971, U.S. ground forces no longer engaged in military actions.

When the peace talks in Paris broke down in March 1972, and the North Vietnamese some days later launched a major offensive against South Vietnam across the demilitarized zone (the seventeenth parallel), Nixon ordered the mining of Haiphong (and six other ports) and renewed bombing of North Vietnam. After the failure of the North Vietnamese spring offensive, peace talks resumed in July and made some progress in the summer and early fall of 1972. But the talks stalled in the late fall, and this induced President Nixon to order U.S. planes to bomb North Vietnam for eleven days in mid-December.

The N.L.F. and the governments of the United States, North Vietnam, and South Vietnam finally reached a cease-fire agreement on January 27, 1973. According to the agreement, the United States would withdraw all its forces in sixty days, all prisoners of war would be released, the South Vietnamese would determine their own future, and an International Commission, composed of representatives of Indonesia, Iran, Hungary, and Poland, would oversee observance of the agreement with a peacekeeping force of 1,160 troops. North Vietnam was to send no replacements of its troops in South Vietnam, and a National Council for Reconciliation and Concord, composed of N.L.F., Saigon government, and neutralist representatives, was established to facilitate the formation of a unified

Vietnam. (Irreconcilable differences, however, doomed the council to failure.)

The last U.S. troops were withdrawn in March, North Vietnamese and Viet Cong forces in South Vietnam remained active, and fifty thousand Vietnamese were reported killed in battle in the year after the truce. The International Commission failed to reach the unanimous agreement required for it to act and would probably have been unable to prevent violations of the ceasefire in any case.

In the spring of 1974, the South Vietnamese government began defensive withdrawals from areas dominated by North Vietnamese and Viet Cong forces. In July, the North Vietnamese and Viet Cong forces launched disruptive attacks against South Vietnamese forces, and, supplied with Soviet tanks, penetrated to within sixteen miles of Saigon. By the end of the year, 1,313 South Vietnamese troops were being killed, and 20,000 deserting, each month.

The South Vietnamese government continued to receive substantial U.S. support but on a drastically reduced scale. In 1974, the United States gave South Vietnam $700 million in military aid and $400 million in economic aid. Congress refused a presidential request for supplementary aid.

Political opponents in 1974 charged that there was widespread corruption in the South Vietnamese government, and that Thieu and his family were personally involved. Demonstrators took to the streets of major cities in the fall of 1974, some immolating themselves, and the government responded with repressive measures. Inflation that year ran at the rate of 60–70 percent, and 20 percent of the work force (50 percent in some areas) was unemployed.

The Fall of South Vietnam

North Vietnamese and Viet Cong forces, mainly North Vietnamese, probing weak spots, attacked isolated South Vietnamese army outposts north and south of Saigon at the close of 1974. In January 1975, they attacked a province seventy-five miles north of Saigon, and South Vietnamese troops surrendered the province's capital on January 7. On March 13, North Vietnamese and Viet Cong forces, in a surprise attack, captured a central highlands provincial capital.

Thieu then ordered the evacuation of two other major provincial capitals, and the civilian population there fled in a stampede. On March 20, large-scale North Vietnamese forces crossed the demilitarized zone into South Vietnam. Hue fell on March 25, 500,000 Vietnamese fled south, and the South Vietnamese army in the area disintegrated. On March 30, Da Nang fell. By April 18, three quarters of South Vietnam was in the hands of North Vietnamese and Viet Cong forces. In Saigon, the government cracked down on dissidents and thwarted two attempted coups.

On April 21, Thieu resigned in a radio broadcast in which he castigated the United States for its failure to live up to an alleged promise to defend South Vietnam from the North Vietnamese attack. Saigon surrendered to North Vietnamese and Viet Cong forces on April 30, but not before U.S. ships offshore rescued 100,000 refugees. In all, 145,000 Vietnamese refugees were resettled in the United States.

The North Vietnamese dominated the new Provisional Revolutionary Government of South Vietnam and moved to integrate the two Vietnams. All-Vietnam elections were held on April 25, 1976, with no candidates opposed to unification permitted to participate. The unification of North and South Vietnam was announced on July 2.

The victory of the Viet Cong and North Vietnam brought the oppression of Communist rule to the people of South Vietnam. The new regime punished leaders and elites of the former regime, and repressed the freedom of ordinary citizens not fortunate enough to have escaped. The severity of the new regime induced thousands of South Vietnamese to flee the country at great risk of death at sea and under arduous conditions, and the exiles did not usually find themselves welcome in the countries where they sought refuge. Although the Communist regime in the newly united Vietnam did assist fellow Communist revolutionaries in Laos and Cambodia, the regime did not export or support Communist revolutionaries in other countries of southeast Asia.

Casualties and Other Costs of the War

The South Vietnamese army suffered casualties of 220,357 killed and 499,000 wounded, and the U.S. Department of Defense estimated that there were 100,000 civilian casualties in South Vietnam in 1968 alone. North Vietnamese and Viet Cong forces' casualties have been estimated at 440,000 dead. U.S. casualties included 57,605 killed and 303,700 wounded. The direct cost of U.S. participation in the war was $165 billion.

At the war's end, half of the population of South Vietnam had become refugees from their homes, and the economies of both Vietnams were devastated. Prices in South Vietnam rose 800 percent between 1963 and 1975. A fifth of the forested areas of South Vietnam had been sprayed with herbicides, and a substantial portion of these had been destroyed.

SUGGESTED READINGS

Arnett, Peter, and Maclear, Michael. *The 10,000 Day War: Vietnam, 1945–1975.* New York: St. Martin's Press, 1981.

Duiker, William J. *Vietnam: Nation in Revolution.* Boulder, Colo.: Westview Press, 1983.

Herring, George C. *America's Longest War: The United States and Vietnam.* 2nd ed. Philadelphia: Temple University Press, 1986.

QUESTIONS

1. Were the victorious World War II Allies at the Potsdam Conference justified in confirming French rule in Indochina? If not, what should they have done?

2. Assuming that most Vietnamese in 1946 wished to be governed by the Viet Minh, or at least that more Vietnamese so wished than wished to be governed by the French, were the French justified in resisting a Vietnamese government under Viet Minh control because the latter were Communists or Communist-dominated? Because the Viet Minh would export Communist revolutions to Laos, Cambodia, and other parts of southeast Asia? In resisting independence under broader democratic auspices? Were the French justified in reneging on their agreement (March 6, 1946) with Ho Chi Minh to recognize the Viet Minh government in the north, to withdraw their troops

within five years, and to allow the south to be integrated with the north?

3. After the 1954 Geneva Accord, was the United States justified in providing economic aid to the Diem government? Military aid? If so, was the United States justified in continuing either aid after Diem refused to participate in the all-Vietnam elections that the Geneva Conference set for 1956?

4. Did the U.S. Constitution require that Congress authorize the president to send military advisers to assist the South Vietnamese army?

5. Did the Diem regime have acceptable reasons for its authoritarian and repressive policies after guerrilla warfare broke out in 1957? If not, was U.S. aid to the Diem regime nonetheless justified because a Communist regime would be equally or more repressive, as Viet Minh rule in North Vietnam demonstrated? What about the fact that the Diem and successor governments effected no significant land reform in South Vietnam?

6. Assuming that U.S. officials of the C.I.A. instigated or antecedently approved the coup against Diem, should it have done so? If the coup was justified, who was legally permitted or required to authorize U.S. involvement? The chief C.I.A. official in South Vietnam? The director of the C.I.A.? The president? Congress? Who should have been responsible?

7. Can any of the governments of South Vietnam from the fall of Diem (November 1963) to the election of Thieu (September 1967) be regarded as legitimate? If not, was it just for the United States to aid them?

8. Did the killing of eight soldiers at a U.S. base in South Vietnam on February 7, 1965, justify retaliatory U.S. bombing of Hanoi? As punishment and/or deterrence?

9. Aside from the Tonkin Bay Resolution, did the president have authority as commander in chief of U.S. armed forces to dispatch marines in March 1965 to combat duty in South Vietnam? To dispatch 50,000 troops? 188,000 troops? 389,000 troops? 500,000 troops? A million troops?

10. Did the U.S. government have just cause to commit armed forces to the defense of South Vietnam? For the security of the United States? For the security of other southeastern Asian nations? For the good of the South Vietnamese people? If the war was "unwinnable," or at least unwinnable without massive U.S. involvement? If the war would cost

the Vietnamese people, south and north, hundreds of thousands of lives, economic devastation, and social disintegration, and would cost the American people tens of thousands of lives, large-scale domestic unrest, and $165 billion?

11. If South Vietnamese forces could not defeat the insurgent North Vietnamese and Viet Cong forces with the active support of 500,000 U.S. troops and air power, was it plausible to expect that the South Vietnamese forces alone could do so? If not, assuming the justice of the South Vietnamese government's cause, was it just for the United States to withdraw its forces? Conversely, assuming that the South Vietnamese government's cause was unjust, was it just for the United States *not* to withdraw its forces with all deliberate speed, at the cost of additional American casualties?

12. Assuming the justice of the South Vietnamese government's cause, was the United States justified in invading neighboring Cambodia in the spring of 1970 to search for Viet Cong sanctuaries?

13. Did the North Vietnamese invasion of South Vietnam across the demilitarized zone in March 1972 justify the retaliatory U.S. actions of mining North Vietnamese harbors and bombing Hanoi? If so, was the United States morally obligated to do more, namely, to recommit forces to defend South Vietnam?

14. Assuming the justice of the South Vietnamese government's cause and at least a tacit U.S. promise, was the United States morally obligated to undertake military action when large-scale North Vietnamese forces crossed the demilitarized zone on March 20, 1975? If so, what action? To bomb North Vietnam? To provide air support for South Vietnamese forces? To recommit U.S. troops? Had the United States at least implicitly committed itself to defend South Vietnam against a conventional North Vietnamese attack?

15. Should the United States have done more to help refugees escape from South Vietnam before the fall of Saigon on April 30, 1975? After the fall? What more could the United States have done?

16. Did the repression in South Vietnam after the Viet Cong and North Vietnam came into power there in 1975 demonstrate that the United States correctly evaluated such a prospect as a proportionate justifying cause of its intervention in Vietnam? On the other hand, did the absence of any effort by the Communist regime in the newly united Vietnam to export or support Communist revolutions in Southeast Asia beyond Laos and Cambodia demonstrate that the United States incor-

rectly evaluated such a prospect as a proportionate justifying cause of its intervention in Vietnam?

17. Do the casualties and other costs of U.S. participation in the war prove that the United States lacked a proportionally just cause of its intervention in Vietnam, however otherwise just that cause might have been?

THE FALKLANDS WAR (1982)

The Falkland Islands lie 250 miles east of Argentina and 8,000 miles from Great Britain. An English navigator, John Davis, reported sighting the Falklands in 1592, and another Englishman, John Strong, reported landing there in 1690. A French navigator founded the first recorded settlement on East Falkland in 1764, and the British the first recorded settlement on West Falkland in 1765. The Spanish bought the East Falkland settlement from the French and drove the British off West Falkland in 1770. The Spanish returned West Falkland to the British in 1771. The British, for reasons of economy, abandoned their settlement in 1774 but left a plaque claiming sovereignty.

Spain maintained its Falklands settlement until 1811. In that year, when news of the revolution in Argentina against Spanish rule reached the settlers, the latter abandoned the islands. Argentina declared its independence from Spain in 1816 and its sovereignty over the Falklands in 1820. Argentine colonists settled there in 1829. In 1831, a U.S. corvette destroyed the Argentine fort on the islands, and most of the settlers left. In 1833, the British ejected the handful of remaining Argentine colonists and resettled the islands.

The British held unchallenged possession of the islands from 1833 to 1982. The British administered the islands as a crown colony, and residents in 1982 shared in its governance. There were in that year eighteen hundred to two thousand residents on the islands, mainly of British stock. The London-based Falklands Company owned most of the land.

In 1964, the U.N. Special Committee on Colonization debated the rival claims of Britain and Argentina to the Falklands. In 1965, the U.N. General Assembly approved Resolution 2065, which called on the British and Argentines to enter discussions for a peaceful solution to the Falklands dispute that would respect the interests of the residents. Britain and Argentina held such U.N.-sponsored talks intermittently over the next seventeen years.

In December 1980, British Prime Minister Margaret Thatcher suggested a leaseback arrangement in which the British would recognize Argentina's sovereignty over the islands, and Argentina would grant the British the right to administer the region for a period of years. This suggestion foundered because of the islanders' opposition. The British on another occasion proposed that the sovereignty question be frozen for twenty-five years, but the Argentines rejected the proposal.

On February 26 and 27, 1982, Great Britain and Argentina held the last of the U.N.-sponsored talks. At the unsuccessful conclusion of those otherwise cordial talks, Nicanor Costa Méndez, the Argentine foreign minister, declared that Argentina would take alternate measures to resolve the sovereignty question if negotiations did not quickly arrive at a solution.

Argentine Occupation of the Falklands

On March 19, 1982, a group of Argentine scrap-metal merchants raised the flag of Argentina on South Georgia, a barren, independently administered island dependency eight hundred miles east of the Falklands. A British and an Argentine naval vessel converged on the scene, but military action was averted, and the Argentine merchants left the island peacefully.

On March 31, the British Foreign Office informed Prime Minister Thatcher that an Argentine invasion of the Falklands was imminent. On April 2, an Argentine force of two thousand men, subsequently increased to eighteen thousand to twenty thousand, occupied the Falklands, and Britain broke diplomatic relations with Argentina. On April 3, an Argentine force of around 150 men occupied South Georgia. On the same day, at the conclusion of an emergency session of Parliament, the British government announced that it would send a naval task force to recover the Falklands. Mrs. Thatcher gave two reasons for the prospective military action: (1) to show that aggression does not pay; (2) to vindicate the islanders' right of self-determination. The main task force set sail for the Falklands from Portsmouth, England, on April 5. On April 7, Britain declared a two-hundred-nautical mile exclusion zone around the Falklands, that is, a zone in which Argentine naval vessels would be attacked if they entered its waters.

The British government reported to the U.N. Security Council on April 1 that Argentina was preparing an invasion. On the following day, when the Argentine force occupied the Falklands, Britain requested an emergency session of the Security Council. The Security Council met on April 3 and passed Resolution 502, which called for Argentine forces to withdraw from the Falklands and for an end of hostilities. Ten members of the council voted for the resolution, none voted against it, and four members abstained.

Diplomatic Efforts and International Reactions

U.S. Secretary of State Alexander Haig shuttled between Washington, London, and Buenos Aires from April 8 to 19 in an attempt to find a peaceful solution to the Falklands crisis. Argentina, however, declined to accept Haig's proposals for an interim solution because the proposals involved withdrawal of Argentine forces from the Falklands. The proposals also fell short of the British objective of allowing the islands' residents to determine their sovereignty.

On April 12, Argentina declared that it would comply with the U.N. Security Council Resolution 502 if the British would also. Britain refused to do so, asserting that Argentina had already disregarded the resolution by occupying South Georgia and by increasing its forces on the Falklands. Since winter weather in the South Atlantic would severely hamper naval and amphibious operations after mid-June, the British were unwilling to forgo military action unless Argentina immediately and unconditionally withdrew its forces from the Falklands and South Georgia.

President Fernando Belaunde Terry of Peru and U.N. Secretary

General Javier Pérez de Cuéllar also sponsored peace talks. But the Peruvian-sponsored talks broke off on May 6, and the U.N.-sponsored talks, despite promising signs during the week of May 10, broke off on May 20. The British would not agree to forgo military action and to enter negotiations about the future status of the Falklands unless Argentina immediately withdrew its occupying forces, and Argentina would not negotiate the future of the Falklands unless the British antecedently recognized Argentine sovereignty there.

The forty-six-member Commonwealth of Nations unanimously supported the British military action to recover possession of the islands and joined Britain in imposing trade sanctions against Argentina. (Neighboring nations were claiming sovereignty over all or part of the territory of several of the formerly British nations; Guatemala, for example, claimed the whole of Belize, and Venezuela claimed part of Guyana.)

On April 17, the European Community condemned the Argentine invasion of the Falklands and imposed trade sanctions for thirty days. Ireland and Italy, however, withdrew their support of the sanctions after the military action in the Falklands commenced on May 1, and the *Belgrano* was sunk on May 2 at the cost of 321 lives. Spain, not yet a member of the European Community, declared its support of Argentina. Most members of the European Community renewed the trade sanctions at the end of the thirty days.

The Organization of American States in late April approved a resolution supporting Argentina's claim to the Falklands but calling for a truce. Seventeen American nations voted in favor of the resolution, none voted against it, and five nations (including the United States) abstained. Peru and Bolivia offered Argentina limited military assistance, but Argentina did not take up the offer. Brazil pledged to transship Argentine exports abroad and to provide military supplies. Chile, which was currently involved in a dispute with Argentina over sovereignty of the islands of Picton, Lennox, and Nueva in the Beagle Channel at the southern tip of Latin America, maintained strict neutrality.

On April 30, the United States concluded that Argentina did not want to negotiate the sovereignty question and declared its unequivocal support of Great Britain. More importantly, the United States suspended military exports and aid to Argentina and provided the British with military supplies and intelligence.

British Reoccupation of the Falklands

The British naval task force arrived in the South Atlantic at the end of April. The British reoccupied South Georgia on April 25 and 26. On May 2, a British submarine sank the Argentine cruiser *Belgrano*. (The British claimed that the *Belgrano* was inside the exclusion zone when sunk, but the Argentines claimed that the ship was outside the zone.)

From May 1 to 21, a heavy air battle took place. Although the British suffered air and naval losses, the Argentines suffered heavier—and crippling—air losses.

The British forces landed on the Falklands on May 21, and the Argentine forces there surrendered on June 14.

Casualties and Aftermath

About 700 Argentines, including the 321 on the *Belgrano*, and 255 British were killed in the war. The Argentine forces captured in the Falklands were repatriated by June 19. Although the actual battle losses in the war were light, the destruction of the British destroyer *Sheffield*, costing $145 million, by an Exocet missile, costing $45,000, demonstrated the destructive potential of modern electronically directed weapons.

On June 18, Argentina reported to the U.N. Security Council that its forces on the Falklands had surrendered to the British, and called for the British to negotiate the sovereignty question. On June 23, Britain indicated that it would not negotiate, and that its troops would remain on the Falklands to defend possession of the islands.

The British government reported in September 1982 that it proposed to spend £75 million from 1984 to 1988 to reconstruct and enlarge the airfield at Port Stanley, the capital of the Falklands; to improve defenses on the islands; and to develop potential offshore fisheries. Another £35 million was to be spent to aid tourism, agriculture, and fisheries on the islands.

On November 4, Latin nations sponsored, and the U.N. General Assembly approved, a resolution calling on Great Britain and Argentina to renew negotiations on the sovereignty question. Ninety nations (including the United States) supported the resolution, twelve nations (including Great Britain) opposed the resolution, and fifty-two abstained. Britain opposed the resolution because it thought the moment too soon after the war for meaningful negotiations, and because the islanders in any case should decide the question.

SUGGESTED READINGS

Freedman, Lawrence, and Gamba-Stonehouse, Virginia. *Signals of War: The Falklands Conflict of 1982*. Princeton: Princeton University Press, 1991.
Hastings, Max, and Jenkins, Simon. *The Battle for the Falklands*. New York: Norton, 1984.

QUESTIONS

1. At the time of the Argentine invasion of the Falklands, did Argentina or Britain have the better claim to the islands? Assuming that Argentina had a superior claim, did that give it a proportionally just cause to use military force to gain possession of the islands? How should this and other territorial disputes be resolved?

2. Do the residents of the Falklands have a right of self-determination? If so, and assuming that the Falklanders wish to remain British, would it be just for Britain to negotiate a leaseback arrangement or local autonomy for the islands under the sovereignty of Argentina? For Britain to have acquiesced in the Argentine occupation of the Falklands against the wishes of the residents?

3. The U.S. government, when informed by the British Foreign Office on April 1 that an Argentine invasion of the Falklands was imminent, instructed the American ambassador in Buenos Aires to communicate personally to the president of Argentina the U.S. government's view that Argentina should undertake no military action against the Falklands. The president of Argentina would not receive the American ambassador. Should the United States have broken diplomatic relations with Argentina when the president would not receive the ambassador? Should the U.S. government have delivered its message to the Argentine ambassador in Washington? Should the U.S. government have made its view public? Would a stronger message, namely, one that explicitly indicated

U.S. support for the British in the event of hostilities, have probably persuaded Argentina to call off its projected invasion of the Falklands? If so, and assuming the justice of Britain's cause, did the United States have a moral obligation to make such a declaration? Would fear of alienating Latin Americans justify the United States' not doing so?

4. Did Secretary of State Haig's efforts at mediation give Argentina good reason to hope that the United States would remain strictly neutral in the event of hostilities? If so, and if the U.S. government had moral certainty that the British were determined to fight to recover the Falklands unless Argentina withdrew its forces, did Haig's peace efforts make war more rather than less likely? If so, and if the United States intended to support and aid Britain in the event of hostilities, as the United States did on and after April 30, were Haig's peace efforts not only counterproductive but also dishonest?

5. Assuming that Britain had a claim to the Falklands superior to Argentina's, did that give Britain a proportionally just cause to use military force to regain possession of the islands? Should the Argentine invasion of the Falklands be considered essentially the same as an invasion of Britain? Would acceptance of the Argentine occupation of the Falklands have encouraged similar attacks on other British dependencies (e.g., by Spain on Gibraltar, by China on Hong Kong) or former British colonies (e.g., by Guatemala on Belize)? Does the relatively small number of residents affect the proportion? Was there due proportion between the British cause, if otherwise just, and the likely casualties and costs of waging the war?

6. Should the British have called off their projected military action to recover the Falklands when Argentina offered on April 12 to comply with Security Council Resolution 502 if the British would? Was there any assurance that Argentina would withdraw its forces from the Falklands before the onset of winter in the South Atlantic? If Argentina's offer was not a ruse to gain time, could a U.N. peacekeeping force have played a role in providing such assurance?

7. Was it just war conduct for the British submarine to have sunk the *Belgrano* if the latter had not yet entered the exclusion zone? Given that the *Belgrano* was at least near, and presumably about to enter, the exclusion zone, and that Argentina and Britain were in a state of undeclared war, should it make any difference whether or not the *Belgrano* was actually inside the zone? Assuming that the British decision to wage war was just, but that its sinking of the *Belgrano* was unjust war conduct, did

the latter act vitiate the justice of Britain's cause? If not, should Ireland and Italy have withdrawn their previous support for trade sanctions against Argentina after the sinking?

8. In view of the casualties and outcome of the war, did Argentina have a proportionally just cause to occupy the Falklands, however just the cause may have been in the abstract? In view of the casualties and strong antecedent possibility of failure and far heavier casualties, economic war costs of possibly a billion dollars, and postwar expense of millions of pounds to shore up the islands' defenses, did Britain have a proportionally just cause to wage war to recover the Falklands, however just the cause may have been in the abstract? Assuming the justice of Britain's cause, would Britain have had a proportionally just cause to use nuclear weapons against mainland Argentine bases if its task force had been destroyed or severely damaged?

9. The Argentines thought that the British would not attempt to recover the Falklands, and the logistics were very much against the British doing so. The Argentines guessed wrong. What does this indicate about the hazards of predicting a potential enemy's actions and estimating its capabilities?

10. After its reconquest of the Falklands, should Britain have cooperated with the U.N. General Assembly Resolution of November 4, 1982, and entered discussions with Argentina about the future status of the islands? Should Britain do so now?

REVOLUTION AND CIVIL WAR
IN NICARAGUA (1978–90)

The Central American Republic of Nicaragua covers an area of some fifty thousand square miles and had a 1993 population of 4.1 million people, with a per capita income of some five hundred dollars.

After more than a year of riots, general strikes, and open warfare against the regime of Anastasio Somoza, the Nicaraguan dictator, the latter resigned on July 17, 1979. The Sandinista National Liberation Front seized control of Managua on July 19, and the civil war ended. The war had resulted in 10,000 dead and 500,000 homeless.

Despite the promulgation of a bill of rights on August 21, 1979, doubts arose about the democratic intentions of the new regime. Several Sandinista cabinet ministers, including the minister of the interior (the minister of charge of the police), were avowed Marxists. The government reached an economic and military agreement with the Soviet Union in March 1980. The Cuban Marxist president, Fidel Castro, visited Nicaragua in July 1980. Thousands of Marxist teachers arrived from Cuba. The junta established neighborhood "Defense Committees." The junta also repudiated $600 million of foreign debt.

In January 1981, the U.S. government (the Carter administration) suspended American aid, $75 million that the U.S. Congress had voted in 1980, because the U.S. government claimed that the Sandinista regime was shipping arms to rebels, allegedly Marxist, in

El Salvador. The Nicaraguan government nationalized private companies on September 9.

On the third anniversary of the Sandinistas' coming to power, July 19, 1982, President Daniel Ortega boasted that the regime had organized the workers and reduced illiteracy from 50.3 percent to 12.9 percent. According to Ortega, spending on health had quadrupled, six thousand homes had been built, and $90 million worth of food distributed. On the other hand, critics noted that the state-controlled economy had failed to produce enough consumer goods, and that the freedoms of press and religion had been restricted. Also, with the aid of Cuban advisers, the Sandinistas maintained the largest army in Central America and part-time neighborhood militias.

By 1983, Nicaraguan counterrevolutionaries (the Contras), operating from bases near the Honduran and Costa Rican borders, were an active force. In April 1984, U.S. citizens hired by the C.I.A. were said to be directly involved in the mining of Nicaraguan harbors. In October, the U.S. government disavowed a manual attributed to the C.I.A. that advised Contras how to kill Sandinista officials.

On November 4, 1984, Ortega won 63 percent of the votes in the presidential election. Although the main opposition candidate did not participate in the election, 75 percent of those eligible voted.

In May 1985, the U.S. government embargoed trade with Nicaragua and banned Nicaraguan ships and aircraft from the United States. In June, Congress authorized $27 million of nonmilitary aid for the Contras. On October 12, the Nicaraguan government imposed curbs on civil liberties (speech, press, travel, strikes) and suspended the writ of habeas corpus.

On October 21, 1985, Ortega told the United Nations that the Contra insurgency had since 1981 resulted in 11,000 dead, 5,000 wounded, and 5,000 kidnaped. Moreover, Ortega said that 250,000 people had had to be relocated.

By 1986, the Nicaraguan armed forces numbered sixty-three thousand, many of whom had been trained in Cuba, the Soviet Union, and Eastern Europe. A quarter of the Nicaraguan budget was allocated to military expenses. In October, the U.S. Congress for the first (and last) time voted $70 million of military aid to the Contras.

On November 25, 1986, the Iran-Contra scandal broke. To circumvent the pre-fiscal-1987 ban on U.S. employees' rendering military assistance to the Contras, key members of the U.S. National Security Council had conspired to divert to the Contras through third-party arrangements funds accruing from the sale of arms to Iran.

In September 1987, the Nicaraguan government loosened restrictions on the press and lifted the ban on the opposition newspaper *La Prensa* and the Roman Catholic radio station. The government also agreed to indirect negotiations with the Contras for a ceasefire. The U.S. Congress that year voted only nonmilitary aid to the Contras.

On March 23, 1988, the government and the Contras agreed to a ceasefire to begin on April 1. (Some twenty-five thousand lives had been lost in the war since 1981.) The Contras agreed to stop fighting and to enter a ceasefire zone in Nicaragua but not to surrender their weapons; the government agreed to grant amnesty to thirty-three hundred Contra prisoners and to guarantee complete freedom of expression. On July 11, Nicaragua expelled the U.S. ambassador for interfering in Nicaraguan affairs, and the speaker of the U.S. House of Representatives, James Wright, revealed that the C.I.A., with presidential approval, was secretly supporting political opponents of the Sandinistas. The U.S. Congress that year voted $27 million of nonmilitary aid to the Contras.

On September 2, 1989, Violeta Barrios de Chamorro became the united opposition's candidate for president. The Soviet Union discontinued its annual $600 million of aid to the Nicaraguan government, a sum that constituted one third of the government's total income. The U.S. Congress approved $4.5 million of nonmilitary aid to the Contras until the elections.

After ten years of Sandinista rule, the Nicaraguan economy was in shambles. Per capita income had fallen 25 percent, the standard of living had declined 60 percent, and production was below that of 1979.

On February 25, 1990, Violeta Chamorro was elected president and inaugurated on April 25. Chamorro retained General Humberto Ortega (brother of Daniel) as commander of the armed forces.

Strikes by Sandinista workers forced the new government to grant 100 percent pay raises. The Contras disbanded.

Three years after Chamorro's inauguration, the government's promises to privatize the economy, to return confiscated private property, and to secure land for disbanded Contras remained largely unfulfilled, and the political situation unstable. Most conservative supporters of Chamorro in the 1990 election now opposed her; former Contras, renaming themselves Recontras, organized along the Honduran border; Sandinistas, in addition to their control of the armed forces and the public unions, exercised de facto control of particular areas. In July 1993, Sandinista rebels seized the town of Estelí, which revolt the government suppressed at the cost of 150 dead. In August, Recontras took dozens of legislators hostage, and Sandinistas retaliated by seizing dozens of conservative leaders. Although all of the hostages were released in a few weeks, the Recontra hostage takers were granted a security zone, and the Sandinista hostage takers were flown to their stronghold in Quilalí. Moreover, U.S. authorities accused Sandinistas of making Nicaragua a center of international terrorism, and twenty-four caches of Sandinista arms were discovered in Nicaragua during the spring and summer of 1993.

Chamorro promised on September 2 that she would dismiss General Humberto Ortega from his post as commander of the armed forces. A three-way dialogue on national reconciliation among the left, right, and center began later the same month.

SUGGESTED READINGS

Christian, Shirley. *Nicaragua: Revolution in the Family.* New York: Random House, 1985.

Cockburn, Leslie. *Out of Control.* New York: Atlantic Monthly Press, 1987.

Kinzer, Stephen. *Blood of Brothers: Life and War in Nicaragua.* New York: Putnam, 1991.

QUESTIONS

1. Would a Marxist regime in Nicaragua alone have posed a threat to U.S. security? Would a Marxist regime in Nicaragua allied with the Soviet Union? What if such a regime were to possess nuclear capability?

2. Would a Marxist regime in Nicaragua have been able to foment Marxist revolutions in neighboring nations if the governments of those nations enjoyed broad popular support, as, for example, was the case in Costa Rica?

3. Would a Marxist regime in Nicaragua have posed a realistic threat to the Panama Canal? Was it likely that such a regime would risk its own destruction if it attacked the canal, presupposing that it had the capability to do so?

4. Did the cause of Nicaraguan freedom justify U.S. aid to the Contras? Even though Nicaraguans seem to have voted freely and overwhelmingly for the Sandinistas in 1984? Even if the Contras were dominated by former officials of the Somoza regime?

5. If nonmilitary aid to the Contras was justified for whatever reason, wasn't military aid also justified? Conversely, if military aid to the Contras was not justified, wasn't nonmilitary aid also unjustified?

6. Did the presence of non-Marxists in the Sandinista regime indicate that the regime was not under the control of the Marxists? Did the presence of self-styled Marxists in the Sandinista regime indicate that those officials were Marxist-Leninists? Are there not other kinds of Marxists? Does the fact that the Sandinistas relinquished power to Violeta Chamorro cast doubt on the assumption that the Sandinista regime was Marxist in the Leninist sense or dominated by such Marxists? Or does it only indicate that Marxist-Leninists in the Sandinista regime, if they dominated the Sandinistas, guessed wrong about the election result and could no longer rely on Soviet support if they repudiated the result? Or are the Marxist-Leninists biding their time, holding on to their power in the armed forces and public employee unions?

7. Could a U.S. policy of cooperation with the Sandinista regime, along with aid, have weaned it away from its alliance with Moscow? Would such a policy have strengthened the hand of the non-Marxists in the regime? Or did U.S. support for the Contras force the regime to hold the 1990 elections and accept the results?

8. In any case, were the human and material costs of the Contra war proportional to the cause?

9. What authority did the C.I.A. have for aiding the Contras before fiscal 1987? If it had authority from the president, was that enough?

10. Suppose the United States sold arms to a third party, and the third party sold the arms to the Iranians at a profit. Suppose further that the third party violated no U.S. law and donated the profits to the Con-

tras. Would that have been illegal? What then was the crime if U.S. officials participated in the Iran-Contra deal? Even if they had the approval of the president?

11. What can or should the United States, the Organization of American States, and/or the United Nations do currently to facilitate the democratic process and the rule of law in Nicaragua? What can or should they do if there is a Sandinista (or Recontra) revolution there?

THE CIVIL WAR IN EL SALVADOR

(1979–92)

El Salvador is a country in Central America, with Guatemala to the north and northwest, Honduras to the north and east, a tip of Nicaragua across the Gulf of Fonseca to the southeast, and the Pacific Ocean to the south. El Salvador is densely populated (five million people in eighty-two hundred square miles).

A military junta ruled El Salvador in 1979. Leftist rebels, many of whose leaders were self-declared Marxists, waged guerrilla war against the junta. Rightist militias terrorized peasants and workers.

In January 1980, violence in the capital, San Salvador, left twenty dead. In February, the junta approved a plan to break up farms larger than 125 acres and to distribute land to peasants working on the large farms. On March 29, Archbishop Oscar Romero, an outspoken critic of the regime and the rightist death squads, was assassinated in the capital. Some twenty-five thousand people turned out for his funeral. By October, six thousand people had been killed by acts of terrorism and left-right confrontations in the countryside. On December 2, three American nuns and a social worker were murdered by a right-wing death squad. The United States suspended its $25 million program of military and economic aid. On December 10, the junta stepped aside to allow José Duarte, a Christian Democrat, to become president. Elections were scheduled to choose members of a Constituent Assembly that would draft a new Constitution.

In January 1981, the rebels launched a "final" offensive. The offensive failed. On January 3, two U.S. advisers on peasant cooperatives were assassinated. The United States sent fifty-four military advisers to assist the government and appropriated $161 million in military and economic aid. The armed forces and extremists of the left and right committed various atrocities. The government failed to put the land reform plan into effect. The toll of civilian dead mounted to thirty thousand.

The election of a Constituent Assembly was held on March 28, 1982. A record number of voters participated, although the leftists boycotted the elections. The rightists won a majority of the assembly seats, and the extreme rightist National Republican Alliance of Roberto D'Aubuisson won 29 percent of the vote. The Constituent Assembly voted in May to suspend the land redistribution program but backed off when the United States threatened to cut off aid. U.S. military advisers now numbered one hundred.

On December 13, 1983, the assembly reduced by 80 percent the amount of land to be redistributed to peasant workers. The United States had increased aid to $300 million a year. The rebels were inflicting heavy damage on the Salvadoran infrastructure (roads, bridges, electric power, communications) and agricultural production.

On May 6, 1984, Duarte was elected president. On May 24, five members of the National Guard were convicted of the nuns' murder. In October, Duarte agreed to negotiate with rebel representatives. Both sides, however, launched military offensives. The rightist-dominated assembly declined to extend phase three of the land reform plan, which would have allotted up to 17.5 acres apiece to landless peasants.

In 1985, the rebels were on the defensive in the countryside, but they launched a new wave of urban terrorism. On June 19, thirteen patrons of a San Salvadoran restaurant were killed, including four U.S. marines and two U.S. businessmen. On September 10, rebels kidnaped Duarte's daughter and killed her bodyguard. On October 10, guerrillas killed forty government soldiers and wounded sixty-eight in a raid on a training base.

In 1986, U.S. aid increased to $365 million, and the government appeared to be winning the war.

On March 31, 1987, rebels destroyed a government base, killing seventy soldiers. On October 4, Duarte met with negotiators representing the rebels. On November 23, he accused D'Aubuisson of masterminding the assassination of Romero.

At the beginning of 1988, right-wing death-squad activity intensified to protest the assembly election of March 20. The National Republican Alliance defeated the Christian Democrats in the election.

In the presidential election held on March 19, 1989, the Christian Democratic party split, and the National Republican Union candidate, Alfredo Christiani, was elected. There was an abstention rate of 50 percent, and the leftists boycotted the election. Following the election, there was an upsurge of violence, including the assassination of the attorney general. The new president was inaugurated on June 1 and declared a state of siege. The assembly curtailed civil liberties.

The government held peace negotiations with rebel representatives in Costa Rica on October 16–18, but the negotiations were broken off after the bombing of a leftist labor federation office on October 31. On November 11, the rebels launched one of their largest offensives, including an assault on the capital. They were routed; thirteen hundred persons were killed and thirteen hundred wounded, including many civilians in neighborhoods bombed and strafed by government forces. On November 16, uniformed soldiers murdered six Jesuit priests, their housekeeper, and her daughter. (The priests had been critical of the right-wing death squads, claiming that the latter were responsible for seventy thousand deaths.) On November 26, the government broke diplomatic relations with Nicaragua after shooting down an airplane, allegedly Nicaraguan, carrying surface-to-air missiles.

On January 13, 1990, Christiani announced the arrest of three officers and five enlisted men for the murder of the Jesuits. Because of that murder, the U.S. Congress cut fiscal-1991 military aid to El Salvador in half, to $42.5 million.

From May 1989 to May 1990, 3,219 civilians were killed. In May 1990, U.N.-monitored peace talks began but failed to establish a permanent ceasefire.

On March 10, 1991, a new assembly was elected, and leftist parties participated in the election. In September, the U.N.-sponsored peace talks moved to New York City, the headquarters of the United Nations. On September 25, the government and the rebels signed accords there calling for the creation of a new civilian police force with rebel participation, the reduction and purging of the Salvadoran armed forces, and land redistribution. On September 28, a Salvadoran court convicted two military officers and acquitted seven others of the murder of the Jesuit priests. In mid-November, the rebels agreed to an indefinite ceasefire. (The military position of the rebels had weakened in part because of the collapse of the Soviet Union and the Sandinista electoral defeat in Nicaragua.)

On January 1, 1992, the government and the rebels, under intense international pressure, signed an accord to end the civil war. Beginning February 1, a formal ceasefire was to go into effect, and the warring forces were to begin to enter "isolation zones." The process was to be concluded by October 31, with the complete dismantling of the rebels' military apparatus (six thousand to seven thousand men). The government forces were to be cut to half their then-existing size (fifty-three thousand men). Corrupt government officers and government officers guilty of human rights violations were to be purged. Government military education and training were to be restructured. Government mobile infantry battalions, the National Intelligence Directorate, the Treasury Police, the National Guard, and the National Police were to be disbanded. A new national police force under civilian control was to be created, and former rebels and former members of the old National Police were to be eligible to serve in the new national police force. The government pledged to recognize the right of peasants to land they currently occupied in rebel-held areas. The government also pledged to redistribute landholdings in excess of around six hundred acres to landless peasants and to create social programs to alleviate the effects of economic austerity policies.

Although it was clear by the end of October 1992 that the demobilization deadline would not be met, and each side accused the other of dragging its feet regarding full implementation of the accord, the ceasefire held.

The U.N.-sponsored Commission on Truth established under terms of the peace accords to investigate human-rights abuses during the civil war issued its report on March 15, 1993. The commission found that there had been widespread violence against civilians, most and worst by the Salvadoran military and right-wing "death squads" but some by the rebels. The commission recommended punishment of at least the chief offenders (after reform of the judicial system), extensive changes in the military and judicial systems, dismissal of fifteen senior military officers, exclusion of implicated government and rebel officials from leadership positions in the government and political parties for at least ten years, and further investigation of the activities of right-wing "death squads." The report also criticized U.S. officials who had denied or attempted to justify the Salvadoran military's worst violence. The commission interviewed two thousand Salvadorans but did not identify the witnesses on whose testimony the report relied.

The National Assembly reacted to the report by approving a general amnesty of all those accused of human-rights abuses during the civil war, over the opposition of the center and the left. On July 1, however, Christiani retired Defense Minister René Emilio Ponce and three other generals. (The Commission on Truth had named Ponce and two of the generals as persons responsible for the murder of the Jesuit priests.)

On August 18, U.N. officials reported that the rebels had now surrendered the bulk of their weapons, including more than 120 stashes, since the December 15, 1992, deadline.

SUGGESTED READINGS

Berryman, Philip. *Inside Central America.* New York: Pantheon, 1985.
White, Richard A. *The Morass: United States Intervention in Central America.* New York: Harper, 1984.

QUESTIONS

1. Assume, as seems probable, that the military junta ruling El Salvador in 1979 lacked legitimacy, that is, that most Salvadorans did not regard the junta as rightfully entitled to make authoritative decisions for Salvadoran society, and that the junta perpetrated or tolerated pervasive human-rights violations. Assume further that the rebels lacked

legitimacy and aimed to impose a repressive Marxist-Leninist regime. From the humanitarian perspective, was there justification for the United States' providing the relatively small military and economic aid to the junta?

2. Did the junta's transfer of power to Duarte in December 1980 and the promise of elections to draft a new constitution legitimate Duarte's presidency? Affect the justice of the regime? Justify U.S. military and/ or economic aid to the regime?

3. Was the election of the Constituent Assembly in 1982 legitimate? Did the leftist boycott of the election taint its legitimacy? Did the plurality vote in favor of the wealthy landowners' party make suspect the freedom of the voters and the honesty of the count? Is it likely that a democratically elected assembly would effectively scuttle the agrarian reform that favored the vastly larger number of landless peasants over the vastly smaller number of wealthy landowners?

4. Was Duarte's election in 1984 legitimate? The election of the rightist-dominated assembly? Did the conviction of those accused of murdering the nuns indicate that the regime was moving to rectify injustice? Did the Duarte administration's agreement to negotiate with the rebels do so? Did the regime's failure to implement phase three of the agrarian reform plan indicate the contrary? Was the United States on balance justified in continuing aid?

5. The Duarte and Christiani administrations were apparently unable to prevent the armed forces from working in consort with rightist death squads. Does this indicate that the armed forces were the de facto government of El Salvador? If so, does this mean that the civilian administrations were illegitimate? Or does the prosecution of the military personnel for the murder of the Jesuit priests indicate a turning point?

6. Given the armed forces' complicity with rightist death squads and involvement in the murder of the Jesuit priests, was continued U.S. aid justified? If so, why cut the military aid in half? If not, why provide any military aid?

7. In the 1980s, the Reagan administration claimed that many leaders of the revolution in El Salvador were Marxist-Leninists tied to Moscow, and that Communists controlled the revolutionary movement. The Reagan administration relied on C.I.A. reports and conclusions. If you were a member of Congress asked to approve large-scale military and economic aid to the Duarte government, would you defer to the C.I.A. conclusions if the Reagan administration did not make available the evi-

dence on which the C.I.A. based its conclusions, or would you want to examine the evidence? Is such evidence necessary for you to reach an informed decision about the aid? How would you vote if the Reagan administration on the grounds of national security and executive privilege declined to make the evidence available?

8. Would a Marxist regime in El Salvador, even a Marxist-Leninist regime, pose a threat to U.S. security? A threat to neighboring nations?

9. Did the civil war in El Salvador vindicate the critical importance of outside military assistance for successful suppression of social revolutionaries? Or did it indicate the opposite? Did it vindicate the critical importance of outside military assistance for the success of social revolutionaries? Or did it vindicate the opposite?

10. What were the most important factors contributing to the accord to end the civil war? Salvadoran public opinion? World public opinion? Mediation by the United Nations? U.S. pressure on the government? Pressure by neighboring Central and South American nations on the rebels? The willingness of government and rebel leaders to compromise and/or to take risks? The military weakness of the rebels? The rebels' loss of Soviet and Sandinista support?

11. The U.N.-sponsored Commission on Truth criticized Reagan administration officials as cynical or very misinformed about the Salvadoran military's complicity in many abuses. How likely is it that the officials did not have a pretty good idea of what was taking place? If they did, were they justified in trying to hide the truth? To mislead Congress and the public? To lie? What would have been the likely result for U.S. aid to the Salvadoran government if the U.S. officials had publicly acknowledged the abuses, and what would have been the likely result if the United States discontinued aid to the Salvadoran government?

12. The Commission on Truth recommended that at least the worst human-rights offenders should be punished, but the Salvadoran National Assembly, in the alleged interest of national reconciliation, approved a general pardon of all those accused of human-rights abuses. Do you agree with the commission or the National Assembly?

THE GULF WAR (1991)

The Persian Gulf Emirate of Kuwait became a British protectorate at the end of the nineteenth century, although it remained under the nominal suzerainty of Turkey until the latter's defeat in 1918. Iraq, a nation to the north and west of Kuwait, became an independent nation after the defeat of Turkey in World War I, and a member of the United Nations after World War II. Kuwait became an independent nation in 1961 and was admitted into the United Nations. Although Iraq had previously claimed that Kuwait was part of Iraq because the Turks had administered both as one unit, Iraq recognized Kuwait as an independent nation. In 1990, Kuwait was ruled autocratically by its emir, and Iraq autocratically by its president, Saddam Hussein, and a socialist party apparatus.

In July 1990, Iraq accused Kuwait of flooding the world oil market in consort with the other Gulf emirates, of encroaching on Iraqi territory, of exceeding its allotment of oil from the jointly owned Rumalian fields, and of failing to cancel its loans to Iraq during the latter's war with Iran (1980–88). Kuwait and the other emirates agreed henceforth to abide by the quotas of the Organization of Petroleum Exporting Countries (O.P.E.C.).

Iraq invaded Kuwait on August 2, 1990. The U.N. Security Council condemned the invasion on August 3; on August 6, the council imposed an economic embargo against Iraqi oil exports and against Iraqi imports other than humanitarian aid. Iraq formally annexed Kuwait on August 8 and ordered diplomats accredited to Kuwait to leave. The Security Council imposed a naval blockade on Iraq on August 18 and on October 27 declared Iraq liable for war damages.

On November 29, the council authorized the use of military force to eject Iraq from Kuwait if Iraqi forces were not withdrawn by January 15, 1991 (S.C. Resolution 678). On January 12, the U.S. Congress authorized the commitment of U.S. forces to military action if Iraq failed to observe the U.N. deadline for withdrawal (Senate: 52–47; House: 250–183).

Immediately after the Iraqi invasion of Kuwait, President George H.W. Bush dispatched warships and aircraft carriers to the area, and ground and air forces to Saudi Arabia. The declared purpose of the disposition of these forces was to deter an Iraqi attack against Saudi Arabia and/or the Gulf emirates. By early November, the U.S. forces in Saudi Arabia numbered 230,000. After the 1990 congressional elections, the Pentagon announced plans to increase the U.S. forces there to 430,000 by January 1, 1991. Great Britain, France, Egypt, Saudi Arabia, and Syria also contributed forces to "Operation Desert Shield."

There were various attempts at mediation. All failed. The last was by President Mikhail Gorbachev of the Soviet Union. The United States and Great Britain rejected the Soviet proposal, which called for Iraq to withdraw from Kuwait without specifying a timetable.

Iraq had not withdrawn from Kuwait by the U.N. deadline of January 15, 1991. The Allies commenced air strikes against Iraqi military targets on January 17. A month later, President Bush delivered an ultimatum to Iraq to commence withdrawal from Kuwait by noon, February 23, and to complete the withdrawal within forty-eight hours. Iraq failed to comply with the ultimatum, and the Allied armies crossed the Saudi Arabian border into Iraq on February 24. The Allied armies outflanked and routed the Iraqi army and entered Kuwait City on February 27. Iraq and the Allies concluded a ceasefire, permitting Iraqi forces to return home without their equipment.

The war cost several hundred Allied casualties. The number of Iraqi military casualties was much higher. In addition, Allied bombing inflicted heavy damage on the Iraqi infrastructure and resulted in large-scale civilian casualties. Kuwait was a shambles, six hundred of its oil wells ablaze, the air over and around it polluted with carbon dioxide and sulfur, and the Persian Gulf awash in oil.

The ceasefire left the Iraqi leader, Saddam Hussein, in power.

Shiites in southern Iraq and Kurds in northern Iraq rebelled, but Saddam crushed the revolts. To halt alleged atrocities against the Kurds and their mass migration into neighboring Turkey, U.S. forces were sent into the Kurdish area of northern Iraq as a peacekeeping force, and Kurdish and Iraqi leaders entered into negotiations. Four months later, the U.S. forces withdrew. (After the withdrawal, there was sporadic fighting between the Kurds and the Iraqis, but the United States did not intervene.)

The ceasefire accords provided that Iraq would destroy its offensive weapons, including nuclear, chemical, and biological weapons and materials. Security Council Resolution 687 permitted the Allies to enforce the ceasefire accords. Security Council Resolution 688 demanded that Iraq end "repression" of its civilian population and allow humanitarian aid to be delivered to the Kurds and Shiites. The ceasefire accords also left intact the economic sanctions against Iraq until Iraq complied fully with the accords and the U.N. resolutions. The accords forbade Iraqi military flights in zones south of the thirty-second parallel and north of the thirty-sixth parallel; the accords also recognized the right of Allied aircraft to fly in the zones.

In January 1993, Iraq flew jet fighters in the southern no-flight zone, deployed surface-to-air missiles in both no-flight zones, sent small contingents of troops across a newly established border with Kuwait to recover weapons, and refused to allow U.N. weapons inspectors to fly into Baghdad, the capital of Iraq, in U.N. planes. The Allies responded with three air strikes and a missile attack on Iraqi military facilities. Iraq relented on the U.N. inspectors flying into Baghdad in U.N. planes, and the inspectors did so on January 21. Iraq also ended its jet-fighter flights in the southern no-flight zone.

Conspirators planned to assassinate former president Bush during his visit to Kuwait in mid-April to receive a decoration. On June 26, after U.S. authorities concluded that the plot was the work of the Iraqi government, President William J. Clinton ordered a missile attack on Iraq's intelligence center. The target was destroyed, but three missiles went off course and killed eight civilians in Baghdad suburbs. Also, in several incidents over the summer, U.S. airplanes in

the southern no-flight zone fired on Iraqi antiaircraft missile bat-
teries after the latter allegedly targeted or fired on the planes.

Iraq's challenge to U.N. monitoring of weapon production reached
a climax in early July when Iraq refused to allow U.N. inspectors to
install cameras or seal operating switches at missile sites. (Security
Council Resolution 687 had imposed a ceasefire condition limiting
the Iraqi missile program to the development of missiles with a range
of 150 kilometers [93 miles], and Security Council Resolution 715
authorized ongoing inspection of Iraqi missile activity or material
"at any time . . . at any site or facility.") On July 19, however, Rolf
Ekeus, chairman of the U.N. Special Commission on Iraq, reached
an agreement with the Iraqi government. Under terms of that agreement, Iraq for the first time accepted long-term monitoring of its
missile weapons programs, as Resolution 715 required, and agreed
to the installation of cameras at the sites. Ekeus in turn agreed that
the United Nations would not activate the cameras until later negotiations resolved technical issues. The agreement also stipulated
that Iraq would be permitted to resume oil sales after full compliance
with the monitoring. On September 23, Iraq reported that the monitoring cameras at the two sites had been activated.

As of 1995, four years after the war, there were conflicting statements about the current status of Iraq's weapons of mass destruction. On August 3, the U.S. ambassador to the United Nations,
Madeleine K. Albright, claimed that Iraq had failed to dismantle the
weapons. On August 23, Ekeus declared that Iraq had substantially
complied with U.N. mandates regarding them. (Ekeus nonetheless
said on October 12 that Iraq had not yet fully disclosed information
about the weapons.)

SUGGESTED READINGS

Freedman, Lawrence, and Karsh, Efraim. *The Gulf Conflict (1990–1991): Diplomacy
and War in the New World Order.* Princeton: Princeton University Press, 1993.
Johnson, James T., and Weigel, George, eds. *Just War and Gulf War.* Washington:
Ethics and Public Policy Center, 1991.
Moore, John Norton. *Crisis in the Gulf: Enforcing the Rule of Law.* Dobbs Ferry, N.Y:
Oceana, 1992.
Schacter, Oscar. "United Nations Law in the Gulf Crisis." *American Journal of In-
ternational Law* 85 (July 1991): 452–73.

QUESTIONS

1. Assuming the validity of Iraq's claims to all or part of Kuwait, did Iraq have legitimate authority in terms of the U.N. Charter to invade Kuwait? Proportionate just cause?

2. Did the Emir's authoritarian rule in Kuwait give Iraq just cause to invade Kuwait? If the Kuwaiti people had rebelled against the emir and invited Iraq to intervene?

3. Immediately after Iraq's invasion of Kuwait, President Bush dispatched U.S. forces to Saudi Arabia and the Gulf for the avowed purpose of deterring Iraqi attacks against Saudi Arabia and other Gulf nations. Did the War Powers Resolution require the president to consult with Congress before his deployment of U.S. forces, to notify Congress after their deployment, and to obtain congressional approval of the deployment within sixty days?

4. In view of Saudi Arabia's authoritarian regime, did the United States have just cause to commit its forces to defend Saudi Arabia against an Iraqi attack?

5. If the War Powers Resolution did not apply to the initial deployment of U.S. forces in Saudi Arabia and the Gulf, did it apply when the United States increased the number of its troops in Saudi Arabia to nearly a half million?

6. Did the U.S. Congress need to authorize the commitment of U.S. forces to military action before the U.N. Security Council adopted Resolution 678 (November 29, 1991)? After the Security Council did so?

7. Why were the negotiations to prevent the Gulf War unsuccessful? Is it reasonable to conclude that negotiations to avoid war without a credible threat to use force are unlikely to succeed when one of the parties to the negotiations is an aggressor-in-possession?

8. What is the likelihood that economic sanctions alone would have induced Iraq to withdraw from Kuwait within a reasonable period? Is the survival of the Saddam regime after its overwhelming military defeat and despite the existence of economic sanctions for more than five years relevant evidence? Is it reasonable to conclude that economic sanctions alone are unlikely to succeed when the target nation is ruled autocratically, or at least that economic sanctions alone will take a protracted period to persuade an autocratic aggressor to alter his international behavior—or to induce a successful internal revolution?

9. If Iraq had not invaded Kuwait, would the United Nations have

had just cause to authorize military action against Iraq to force elimination of the latter's nuclear, chemical, and biological weapons?

10. Would the fact that Iraq, with the acquisition of Kuwait, would control 25 percent of the world's export oil supply have in itself provided proportionate just cause for the United Nations to authorize military action to restore Kuwait's independence? What if there was tangible evidence that Iraq intended to cut off oil exports to oil-importing nations or to set such high prices on oil exports that the economies of oil-importing nations would be severely depressed? What if there was tangible evidence that Iraq would intimidate other Middle Eastern oil-exporting nations to follow her lead?

11. Were the actual Allied casualties of the war duly proportional to its cause? Were the actual Iraqi casualties and economic destruction? Was it reasonable to have anticipated higher casualties and losses? If so, were the potential, reasonably anticipated casualties and losses duly proportional to the justice of the war's cause?

12. After the defeat of the Iraqi forces and Iraq's willingness to withdraw from Kuwait, did the Allies have just cause to continue the war to force the ouster of Saddam Hussein? To secure the destruction of nuclear, chemical, and biological weapons? Did the Allies have legitimate authority to do so?

13. Was it just to continue the economic embargo on Iraqi exports after the ceasefire? The embargo on Iraqi imports (except food and medicine)?

14. After the ceasefire, did the Allies have just cause to dispatch troops into northern Iraq to prevent Iraqi forces from killing Kurds or driving them out of their homes into exile? Did the Allies have legitimate authority to do so apart from Security Council Resolutions 687 and 688? On what legal basis in the charter did Security Council Resolution 688 have the authority to demand that Iraq end repression of its own citizens (the Kurds and Shiites)?

15. Did Iraq's refusal to allow U.N. weapons inspectors to fly into Baghdad in U.N. planes proportionately justify the subsequent Allied air strikes and missile attack? Did the Allies have legitimate authority to do so without a new Security Council resolution? Did the U.S. forces have legitimate authority to participate in the Allied actions without new authorization from Congress? Did the Iraqi provocations of January 1993 proportionately justify the Allies' renewing hostilities to force Saddam's overthrow? Would new authorization by the U.N.

Security Council and the U.S. Congress be necessary for U.S. participation?

16. Did the plot to assassinate former president Bush, assuming Iraqi government involvement, give the United States proportionate just cause for the June 26 missile attack on Iraq's intelligence center? As retaliation? As deterrence of future assassination plots? In conjunction with other Iraqi provocative actions? Did President Clinton have the legal authority to do so? On what basis?

17. In view of the series of provocative and recalcitrant actions by Iraq since January 1, 1993, would the Security Council have had or still have proportionate just cause the give Iraq an ultimatum that any future provocation or recalcitrant action would result in a massive attack on Iraqi antiaircraft missile sites?

THE INTERVENTION IN SOMALIA
(1992–94)

The territory of greater Somaliland is situated on the Horn of Africa, the easternmost territory of Africa, south of the Gulf of Aden, east of the Indian Ocean, and west of Ethiopia and Kenya. The territory is inhabited by a relatively homogeneous ethnic group, the Somalis, and has been since ancient Egyptian times. The Somalis became Muslim in the second half of the first millennium of the Christian era.

France, Great Britain, and Italy competed to colonize Somaliland in the second half of the nineteenth century, and they agreed to a partition of the territory toward the end of the century. France acquired the northern section, Great Britain the central section, and Italy the southern section. In 1960, British and Italian Somaliland became independent and promptly merged to form the Republic of Somalia.

The Republic of Somalia covers 246,199 square miles. Most of the country is a hot, desertlike, low plateau, although there is some mountainous territory in the north and northeast. At the beginning of 1991, Somalia had an estimated population of nearly eight million, not including three quarters of a million Somali refugees from the adjacent Ogaden area of Ethiopia. The Somalis are divided into clans and subclans. The population is 99.8 percent Muslim.

Somalia is economically undeveloped. Three quarters of the economy derives from livestock (sheep, goats, camels) raised by nomadic herdsmen. There is some agriculture, primarily sugarcane and bananas grown on low-productivity lands. The per capita annual income is one of the lowest in the world ($170).

Somalia was under parliamentary rule from 1960 to 1969. The Somalian Youth League dominated the government and maintained a loose alliance with, and received arms from, the Soviet Union (some $210 million worth in 1961–74). Elections in 1967 resulted in a shift of power to groups favorable to the West, but a military coup returned Somalia to the Soviet orbit. The leader of the coup, Major General Mohammed Siad Barre, established a military government dominated by him and his party, the Somali Revolutionary Socialist party (S.R.S.P.).

From its establishment in 1960, Somalia disputed the claim of Ethiopia to the Ogaden territory, an Ethiopian province largely inhabited by Somali nomads. A rebel group, the West Somalian Liberation Army (W.S.L.A.), operated in the territory with the support of Somalia. The conflict between the W.S.L.A., with Somalian support, and Ethiopia erupted into full-scale war in June 1977. A revolution in Ethiopia in September 1974 had brought a Marxist regime to power there, and the Soviet Union supplied and supported Ethiopia in the Ogaden war. Ethiopia decisively defeated the W.S.L.A. and Somalian forces, and one to one and a half million Somali refugees from the region poured into Somalia.

Somalia, embittered by the Soviet support of Ethiopia, broke relations with the Soviet Union on November 13, 1977; expelled Soviet advisers; and renounced the Soviet-Somalia treaty of friendship. Somalia also broke diplomatic relations with Cuba and expelled all Cubans from the country. Somalia then turned to the United States for economic and military aid. From 1981 to 1989, the United States provided some $40 million of defensive arms to Somalia.

The military government under Barre ruled Somalia throughout the 1980s, although there were several attempts to give the regime a facade of civilian government and popular legitimacy. Northern Somali entrepreneurs and members of the Issaq clan became disgruntled with the Barre regime and lent support to the guerrilla Somali National Movement (S.N.M.), which in the 1980s commenced operations in the north from across the Ethiopian border. By 1988, the rebellion there became a full-scale civil war. Another rebel group, the Somali Patriotic Movement (S.P.M.), created unrest in southern cities in 1989, and yet another rebel group, the United Somali Congress (U.S.C.), did likewise in the central capital city, Mogadishu. The U.S. government ended military aid to Barre, who then turned to Libya, and cut off economic aid in early 1990. By the end of 1990, most of the country was in the hands of the rebels. The S.N.M. and the powerful Issaq clan controlled northern urban centers, the S.P.M. the south, and the U.S.C. the center. The capital, under siege by the U.S.C., was controlled by armed rebels drawn from military deserters.

On January 26, 1991, Barre fled the capital. The U.S.C. proclaimed an interim government under Mohammed Ali Mahdi, but Mahdi failed to restore order in the capital. General Mohammed Farah Aidid, the U.S.C. chairman, and other rebel groups declined to recognize Mahdi's self-declared interim government. In the north, the S.N.M. on May 18 declared the territory of the former British Somaliland independent. (No foreign government recognized the newly declared Somaliland Republic.) In the south, the civil war between clans and subclans continued, and particularly sharp violence between the forces of Mahdi and Aidid broke out in the capital on November 17.

On January 23, 1992, the U.N. Security Council voted to impose an embargo on the shipment of weapons and equipment to Somalia (S.C. Resolution 733). On April 24, the council voted to set up a U.N. operation in Somalia (UNISOM). The purposes of the operation were to facilitate and maintain an immediate ceasefire, to promote a political settlement, and to carry out a ninety-day plan of action for humanitarian assistance (S.C. Resolution 751). The plan provided for fifty U.N. observers and a five-hundred-member security force to escort the delivery of relief supplies to distribution centers in and around the capital.

The U.N. relief efforts were unequal to the need and frustrated by armed clansmen and irregulars. A severe famine was putting one and a half million Somalis at risk of starvation, and three and a half million lacked adequate nourishment. Relief airlifts landing at Somali airports were either attacked or subjected to extortion. Stored relief supplies were looted, and overland transportation of relief supplies was subjected to both looting and extortion. At the end of July, the United States concluded that the U.N. airlifts were failing to reach needy Somalis, and the United States in mid-August, in cooperation with the United Nations, undertook a military airlift of relief supplies to Somalia. On August 28, the U.N. Security Council authorized the deployment of thirty-five hundred peacekeeping forces in Somalia to protect the distribution of relief supplies (S.C. Resolution 775).

When, in mid-September, U.S. aircraft and U.N. relief convoys came under attack from the warring clans and irregular gangs, the United States dispatched twenty-four hundred marines to ships in the Indian Ocean. At the same time, five hundred Pakistani soldiers of the U.N. peacekeeping force arrived in Mogadishu but were not deployed; the rival clans would not agree to their deployment at the city's airport and seaport.

On October 13, the forces of the Somali National Front (S.N.F.), fellow clansmen of former President Barre under the leadership of Barre's son-in-law, Mohammed Siad Hersi Morgan, occupied the southern town of Bardera after the forces of General Aidid abandoned it. U.N. and other relief agencies evacuated the town, and the death rate there soared to two hundred deaths a day.

By mid-October, armed gangs had forced the closing of the southern seaport of Kismayu, Somalia's second largest. At the end of October, the U.N. secretary general, Boutros Boutros-Ghali, forced the resignation of Mohammed Sahnoun, the U.N. special representative in Somalia, because of his outspoken criticism of the slow response of U.N. agencies to the plight of starving Somalis.

By the end of October and early November, warring gangs had virtually forced the seaport of Mogadishu, Somalia's largest, to close, and the city was blockaded. The port closed completely on November 7. By that date, only 20 percent of all relief shipments were reaching starving Somalis; the rest were being looted. During the week of November 8, some of the U.N. peacekeeping forces were for the first time deployed at the Mogadishu airport.

By the end of November, observers estimated that 300,000 Somalis had died in the violence and famine since the fall of Barre in January 1991 and 100,000 since March 1992. From the fall of Barre to the end of 1992, one million Somalis fled the country. Most became refugees in Ethiopia and Kenya, but a few fled by boat to Yemen. The only good news for Somalis in the fall of 1992 was the end of the drought.

The northern section of Mogadishu was in the control of the forces of Mahdi, who controlled little else, and the southern section in the control of the forces of Aidid. (Mahdi and Aidid belonged to the same clan but different subclans.) In addition, there were irregular gangs there under the control of neither Mahdi nor Aidid. In the south, Bardera was in the hands of forces under the command of Morgan (although under siege by the forces of Aidid), and Kismayu was under the control of Colonel Omar Jess, a local clan leader. In the north, the S.N.M. controlled a self-declared but internationally unrecognized independent state, which was relatively stable.

On November 24, a U.N. relief ship carrying ten thousand tons of supplies was hit by artillery fire as it attempted to dock at the seaport of Mogadishu. President George H.W. Bush decided on November 25 to make U.S. forces under U.S. command available to the United Nations for deployment in Somalia to guarantee the delivery of relief supplies to starving Somalis.

On December 3, the U.N. Security Council unanimously voted to approve deployment of U.S.-led forces in Somalia to "establish as soon as possible a secure environment for humanitarian relief" (S.C. Resolution 794). The resolution authorized the secretary general to establish a liaison staff in the headquarters of the U.S. commander, a special commission to monitor the resolution, and regular reports from nations sending forces to Somalia. The secretary general was also authorized to continue deployment of the thirty-five hundred peacekeepers approved by Resolution 775.

Resolution 794 noted the unique character of the situation, the need for an immediate and exceptional response, the threat to international peace and security constituted by the magnitude of the human tragedy, the deterioration of the situation and need for prompt humanitarian assistance, conditions that continued to impede the delivery of such aid (in particular, looting of supplies and armed attacks on aircraft, ships, and the U.N. peacekeeping forces in Mogadishu), and the inadequacy of UNISOM alone to respond to the tragedy.

The resolution also sought to facilitate the process of a political settlement under U.N. auspices and recognized the ultimate responsibility of the Somali people for national reconciliation and reconstruction of the country. The resolution reaffirmed the council's demand that all factions in the civil war cease hostilities (cf. S.C. Resolution 751) and cooperate with the U.N. special representative in Somalia and the military forces to be deployed there. The resolution condemned violations of international humanitarian law, particularly deliberate obstruction of the delivery of food and medical supplies to the civilian population, and declared that those guilty of such violations would be individually held responsible.

Once the U.S.-led armed forces had accomplished their mission to secure humanitarian relief operations, all or most of them were to be withdrawn, and U.N. peacekeeping forces were to take over supervision of relief efforts. It was to be up to the secretary general to propose, and the Security Council to approve, a plan to that effect in cooperation with the Somalis, a plan that might call for additional peacekeeping forces.

After obtaining broad support for intervention from leaders of Congress and the governments of other nations, and the cooperation of the two chief Somali warlords, Mahdi and Aidid, President Bush on December 4 ordered U.S. forces into Somalia to "save thousands of innocents from death." He assured the American public that the intervention had only the limited humanitarian objective of assuring the delivery of food and medicine to starving Somalis, that the U.S. forces had no intention of remaining in Somalia once they had accomplished that mission, that the United States would not dictate a political settlement to the Somali people, and that some dozen other nations were expected to contribute armed forces to the operation. He also told House and Senate leaders that the Defense Department did not anticipate any serious resistance to the intervention, that

U.S. commanders would have broad leeway with regard to defense of their forces, and that the costs of the military operation would be offset by contributions from affluent nations like Germany and Japan.

On December 9, the first U.S. forces landed in Mogadishu and quickly secured the airport and seaport without incident. The U.S. forces were joined by the forces of other nations. Fighting and looting continued in the interior for some days until the U.S.-led forces secured the areas.

On December 11, the two chief warlords in Mogadishu, Mahdi and Aidid, agreed to a ceasefire. On December 21, the warring clans in Mogadishu placed their armed vehicles in depots outside the city administered by the U.S.-led forces, but the vehicles were subject to the clans' control. U.S. forces then proceeded to prevent the operation of rogue armed vehicles in the city.

On January 4, 1993, a conference of the leaders of fourteen warring Somali clans met in Addis Ababa, Ethiopia. On January 8, they agreed to a ceasefire, convocation of a national reconciliation conference in Addis Ababa on March 15, and cooperation with international relief organizations. On January 15, they signed an accord declaring an immediate ceasefire and pledging complete disarmament of their militias by early March. On March 28, leaders of the fifteen principal Somali clan leaders agreed in Addis Ababa to complete substantial disarmament within ninety days, to establish an interim national council to govern the country, and to create within two years a permanent national government under a new constitution. The agreements to disarm and form an interim national council were not implemented.

On March 26, the U.N. Security Council voted to establish a peacekeeping force in Somalia to replace the U.S.-led forces (S.C. Resolution 814). The peacekeepers, ultimately to number twenty-eight thousand military personnel and two thousand civilians, were to help deliver relief supplies, to disarm the warring factions, to promote national reconciliation, and to rebuild the nation. Some five thousand U.S. military personnel were to be part of the forces, with two thousand U.S. combat troops in reserve on ships offshore.

On May 4, the U.N. peacekeepers took control of the relief and rehabilitation operations. Eight U.S. servicemen and ten from the forces of other countries lost their lives in Somalia between December 9, 1992, and May 4, 1993, and the U.S. Department of Defense estimated the financial cost of the first four months' deployment of U.S. forces there at more than $500 million. Despite initial looting and attacks on the personnel of relief organizations, the U.S.-led forces had largely succeeded in safeguarding the delivery of relief supplies to the countryside. The capital city of Mogadishu, however, remained in a state of near-anarchy, although the U.S.-led forces seized some caches of weapons in the hands of irregulars and checked vehicles for possession of guns. The U.S.-led forces also made no attempt to disarm the warring clans in the countryside or the militias in Mogadishu.

On June 5, in what was assumed to be a reaction to U.N. peacekeepers' attempts to inspect Aidid's stockpiles and rumors that the peacekeepers would seize his radio station, Aidid's militiamen attacked and killed twenty-four Pakistani peacekeepers on patrol. On June 6, the Security Council authorized the arrest of those responsible for the attack on the Pakistanis and demanded that all Somali parties implement disarmament (S.C. Resolution 837). On June 11, the U.N. command in Somalia ordered the arrest of Aidid and offered a twenty-five-thousand-dollar reward for his capture on July 10. From June 11 to June 17, U.S. gunships conducted air strikes on Aidid's suspected headquarters and weapon compounds.

On September 22, the Security Council voted to set March 1995 as the cut-off date for terminating U.N. peacekeeping operations in Somalia and handing over responsibility to an elected Somali government (S.C. Resolution 865). The resolution committed the United Nations to the disarmament of Aidid's forces in Mogadishu and the capture of Aidid himself. The main goal of the peacekeepers was to promote national reconciliation in, and reconstruction of, Somalia. Specifically, the peacekeepers were to create a national police force and a functioning judicial system.

On October 3, a raid on an Aidid compound in Mogadishu resulted in the death of eighteen U.S. soldiers and the wounding of more than seventy-five others. (The Red Cross estimated that some three hundred Somalis were killed, and some eight hundred others wounded, in the raid and its aftermath.) Four days later, on October 7, President William J. Clinton announced that all U.S. forces would be withdrawn from Somalia by March 31, 1994. U.S. forces thereafter assumed a purely defensive position in and around the American embassy in Mogadishu, and otherwise functioned only as a backup for U.N. peacekeepers. Within a week of the announcement of the U.S. decision to withdraw its forces from Somalia, Western European nations with forces there followed the lead of the United States. Belgium, France, and Sweden scheduled withdrawal of their forces by January 15, and Italy by March 31.

The imminent withdrawal of U.S. and Western European forces from Somalia induced the Security Council to jettison the anti-Aidid provisions of Resolution 865. On November 16, the Security Council formally called off the manhunt for Aidid and cancelled the authorization of his arrest, although the council took steps to set up a special commission to determine responsibility for attacks on U.N. peacekeepers (S.C. Resolution 885). On January 18, 1994, the U.N. command in Somalia released eight Aidid lieutenants whom it had been holding in custody.

From May 4, 1993, when the United Nations took control of police operations in Somalia, to the end of that year, 83 peacekeepers were killed, and 302 wounded. This total includes 26 U.S. military personnel killed and 170 wounded. Somali sources estimated 6,000 to 10,000 Somali casualties killed or wounded.

Twelve Somali factions attended a U.N.-sponsored peace conference in Addis Ababa on November 29, 1993. The conference quickly ended on December 1 because of Aidid's opposition to the U.N. sponsorship. A successor conference under Ethiopian auspices assembled the following day, with fifteen Somali factions attending. (The United States Air Force flew Aidid to Addis Ababa to attend the conference.) The successor conference ended on December 12 with no significant results. Mahdi and Aidid, however, reached a peace accord on January 16, 1994.

As the countdown to the exodus of U.S. and Western European

forces tolled, banditry and looting increased, especially in the south and the countryside, and clan warfare intensified in Kismayu. The last eleven hundred U.S. troops left Somalia on March 25, 1994. (Fifty marines, however, continued to guard the U.S. embassy in Mogadishu and its personnel; the diplomats and marines were withdrawn in September.)

Some nineteen thousand U.N. peacekeepers, consisting mainly of reinforced contingents from Egypt, India, and Pakistan, remained in Somalia after the departure of U.S. and Western European forces. On October 4, the Security Council voted to end the peacekeeping mission in Somalia by March 31, 1995, and the evacuation of the peacekeepers was completed by March 3.

SUGGESTED READING

Metz, Helen C. *Somalia: A Country Study.* Washington, D.C.: Federal Research Division, Library of Congress, 1993.

QUESTIONS

1. Should the U.N. Security Council have authorized military action in the spring or summer of 1992 to ensure the delivery of relief supplies to starving Somalis? Should the United States have pushed at that time for U.N. action and offered to provide most of the armed forces? Since 1992 was a presidential election year, did the president have any grounds for fearing potentially negative political consequences if he did so? Should a statesman allow such domestic political considerations to be decisive?

2. Should the United Nations have been so slow to reinforce and deploy its peacekeeping force in Mogadishu in October and early November 1992? Should the United States have offered at that time to provide back-up military forces? Should the president allow the potentially negative political consequences of doing so only weeks or days before the presidential election to be decisive?

3. U.N. Security Resolution 794 (December 3, 1992) "determined" that the "magnitude of the human tragedy caused by the conflict [in Somalia] . . . constitutes a threat to international peace and security." Were the civil war and anarchy in Somalia any threat to *international* peace and security? Were the warring clans and irregular gangs intending or likely to export the war and violence to neighboring countries (Ethiopia, Kenya)? If, as reported, Kenya was providing arms to General

Morgan's forces in southern Somalia, did such a threat to international peace and security justify U.N. action to intervene in the civil strife in Somalia, or only to stop arms traffic by Kenya? Did the flow of refugees to neighboring countries pose a threat to international peace and security? Should the power of the Security Council under Article 39 to determine whether or when a threat to international peace and security exists mean that its "determination" is legally conclusive even when there is no plausible evidence or argument to support that finding?

4. If neither the warfare and violence in Somalia nor the exodus of refugees from Somalia constituted a threat to international peace and security, and if the determination of the Security Council to the contrary was not legally conclusive, on what basis could the Security Council authorize military intervention in Somalia? Can the Security Council be argued to have implied power to do so in order to deliver humanitarian aid to the civilian population? To enforce unwritten international law relating to human rights? To enforce the Declaration on Human Rights (assuming Somalia to be a signatory)? To undertake a quasi trusteeship over a nation in a state of anarchy? If so, can such powers be derived from provisions of the U.N. Charter? Can such powers become legitimated by the international community's de facto acceptance of them? Were they?

5. Did the consent of the warring clans in Somalia to the U.N.-authorized military intervention legitimate the operation? What if one or more of the warring parties opposed the intervention? Can the consent of the Somali people to the intervention be assumed? If so, would that presumed consent legitimate the intervention in spite of the opposition of one or more of the warring parties?

6. Is the War Powers Resolution inapplicable to the deployment of U.S. forces in Somalia in response to Security Council Resolution 794 because Resolution 794 "called on" member states to intervene? Because the U.S. forces committed were not likely to become engaged in conflict? How likely was it that the U.S. forces would not become engaged in some combat situations and suffer casualties? If the War Powers Resolution was applicable, Section 2 facially precluded the president from maintaining forces in Somalia without formal congressional approval. Notwithstanding, did the president as commander in chief of the armed forces have independent constitutional authority to do so? Why should he if there was no military necessity to defend U.S. interests or citizens, or the territorial integrity of Somalia, from external attack?

7. Assuming that humanitarian aid to starving peoples is a theoret-

ically just cause for outside military intervention, does this mean that the United Nations, relying on the armed forces of the United States and other nations, should do so in every such case, for example, in Bosnia and Sudan? What of the cumulative potential casualties? What of the cumulative economic costs? If the cumulative costs of military intervention in every case of humanitarian need would be prohibitive, how should the United Nations and the nations that would have to bear the bulk of the costs distinguish humanitarian causes that warrant intervention from humanitarian causes that do not? Should the gravity of the humanitarian need be a critical factor? The military difficulty of carrying out the humanitarian mission? The likelihood of limiting the military involvement? The likelihood of quick success? The likelihood of sufficiently high and sustainable levels of popular support by the electorates of the nations furnishing armed forces for the intervention? Does any or all of these factors affect the proportionality of just cause?

8. The United States took the lead and provided most of the armed forces for the initial intervention in Somalia. Should African nations have done so? What about the allocation of costs? Should the affluent nations of Western Europe, the Middle East, and the Far East pay more? To deal with future situations, should the United Nations and member nations set clear goals, time limits, and global priorities in interventions of this type? Should the United Nations and member states establish standby armed forces under Article 43 of the charter and adopt a fixed formula of allocating the costs of peacekeeping and peacemaking operations? Should regional organizations like N.A.T.O. be the operative agents to carry out the operations?

9. The U.N. peacekeepers' attempts to inspect Aidid's stockpiles in June 1993 are assumed to have provoked the subsequent attacks on the peacekeepers, and Security Council Resolution 814 and especially Resolution 865 committed the United Nations to the disarmament of Aidid's forces as well as the capture of Aidid himself. Were these goals possible? At what cost in casualties? At what financial cost? Did the United Nations thereby commit itself to long-term intervention in Somalia? Assuming the legality and abstract justice of the U.N. goal of disarming Aidid's and possibly other forces, was the cause proportionately just in terms of its costs?

10. Security Council Resolution 865 also and principally committed the United Nations to the political reconstruction of Somalia. How could the United Nations do more than broker an agreement by the clans to

accept the legitimacy of a national political unit without establishing an interim protectorate? How could the United Nations create a national police force and a judicial system without direct rule if the warring clans failed to reach a political solution? How would such a protectorate differ from nineteenth-century colonialism? Would such a protectorate be just?

11. President Clinton announced on October 7, 1993, that U.S. forces would be withdrawn from Somalia by March 31, 1994, and they were by March 25. Was the U.S. withdrawal effectively capitulation to Aidid and other warlords? If so, did the withdrawal shirk a moral responsibility to the Somali people? Did the Security Council effectively shirk such a moral responsibility when it called off its manhunt for Aidid?

12. After the United States and Western European nations decided to withdraw their forces from Somalia, and after the Security Council abandoned its efforts to disarm Aidid (and presumably other factions at a later date), could the United Nations play any role in the political reconstruction of Somalia? If the United Nations could do more than broker a confederation of armed factions, what was the point of continuing the peacekeeping operation in Somalia, nineteen thousand strong, until March 1995? What about the cost of doing so? (Each ordinary peacekeeper receives a monthly salary of almost one thousand dollars.)

THE BOSNIAN WAR (1992–95)

In the second half of the fifteenth century, Bosnia (1463 A.D.) and Herzegovina (1482 A.D.) were conquered by the Turks and became outposts of the Turkish Empire's ongoing war against Austria, Hungary, and Venice. Turkish power had waned by the middle of the nineteenth century, and Austria-Hungary was granted administrative charge of Bosnia-Herzegovina in 1877, although the latter continued to be recognized as a Turkish province. Austria-Hungary formally annexed Bosnia-Herzegovina in 1908.

At the conclusion of World War I, Bosnia-Herzegovina, in union with Serbia, Croatia, Slovenia, Montenegro, and Macedonia, became part of the new nation of Yugoslavia. The Serbs dominated the union. At the conclusion of World War II, Yugoslavia was restored under Communist rule. Although technically a federation of the six republics, Yugoslavia was actually ruled by one man, Marshal Josip Tito, until his death in 1980. The political and military apparatus of the federation was Serbian-dominated. Tito split with the Soviet Union in June 1948.

Bosnia-Herzegovina is a triangularly shaped territory comprising nearly twenty thousand square miles. It is bounded on the north and west by Croatia, on the east by Serbia, and on the southeast by Montenegro. Bosnia-Herzegovina has only thirteen miles of coastline on the Adriatic, but this coastland has no natural harbor. The terrain is principally mountainous, and only one half of the land is arable. The bulk of the economy is based on agriculture and livestock. Before the dissolution of Yugoslavia in 1991, the per capita income of Bosnians was only two thirds that of the Yugoslav federation as a whole, and only one half that of citizens of Slovenia, the most prosperous republic.

At the beginning of 1992, Bosnia had a population of 4.4 million (43.7 percent Muslim, 31.3 percent Serb, 17.3 percent Croat, and 7.7 percent other). The ethnic groups lived in a checkerboard pattern of close proximity, although there were a considerable number of pockets dominated by a single ethnic group.

Yugoslavia Disintegrates; Bosnia Declares Independence

In 1990, the central government of Yugoslavia began to relax its autocratic rule. Democratization led to independence movements in several of the federal republics. Voters in Slovenia and Croatia on December 23, 1990, and May 19, 1991, respectively, overwhelmingly approved resolutions calling for independence, and the two republics formally declared their independence on June 25, 1991. After brief border skirmishes, the Yugoslav army withdrew from Slovenia in the summer of 1991. But in parts of Croatia where ethnic Serbs (12 percent of the population) were concentrated, the Yugoslav army (now mainly Serb) and local Serbs resisted. By early October 1991, one quarter to one third of the territory of Croatia was in the control of Serbs.

Against a backdrop of on-again, off-again ceasefires and rising numbers of casualties, the U.N. Security Council on September 25, 1991, imposed a general and complete embargo on the delivery of weapons and military equipment to the area of former Yugoslavia (S.C. Resolution 713). On February 21, 1992, the Security Council established the United Nations Protection Force (UNPROFOR) to create conditions of peace and security in troubled areas of the former Yugoslav state in preparation for negotiating an overall settlement (S.C. Resolution 743). Beginning in March 1992, troops and officials of UNPROFOR arrived in Croatia, and the open warfare between Serbs and Croats there ground to a virtual halt during the spring.

As open warfare in Croatia subsided, the desire of Croats and

Muslims in Bosnia to end Bosnia's ties to Serb-dominated Yugoslavia was precipitating a new and more devastating war.

On February 23, 1992, Bosnian Croat, Muslim, and Serb leaders agreed to form a confederation of three distinct ethnic states. The agreement of the Muslim leader, Alija Izetbegovic, to the partition plan shocked many Bosnian Muslims, and the United States opposed the plan; most Bosnian Muslims and the United States desired that Bosnia become an independent, unified nation. After Warren Zimmerman, the U.S. ambassador to Yugoslavia, personally communicated his government's objections to the partition plan, Izetbegovic renounced the agreement. (Izetbegovic agreed to another partition plan on March 16 but again several days later recanted.)

On March 1, Bosnian voters approved a resolution calling for the creation of an independent nation. Croats and Muslims voted almost uniformly for the resolution, and Serbs almost uniformly abstained or voted against it. The United States pressured the European Community to recognize the newly declared Bosnian government, and the community did so on April 6. The United States followed suit on April 7.

The War

Shortly after the Bosnian declaration of independence, Bosnian Serbs, supported by irregulars from Serbia and with the complicity of the Yugoslav/Serb army, began systematically to expel non-Serbs, mainly Muslims, from areas close to Serbia and beyond, a process euphemistically called "ethnic cleansing." On April 14, the Bosnian government reported mass massacres by the Serbs. Estimates of casualties ran in the thousands, and hundreds of thousands were forcibly made refugees. By midspring, there were reports, later confirmed by journalists, that Bosnian Serbs were setting up detention camps in which Muslims were being tortured, raped, and killed. And the Serbs laid siege to Sarajevo, the capital of Bosnia, with their artillery deliberately targeting the city's civilian population. Croats also carried out lesser-scale expulsions of non-Croats. The warfare and expulsions intensified in April and May.

The Yugoslav/Serb army formally withdrew from Bosnia on May

19, according to Yugoslavia's report to the United Nations on June 5 (S/24074). Most irregulars from Serbia had also probably withdrawn by mid-May. But Bosnian-Serb Yugoslav army personnel remained to form the bulk of the rebel Serb forces, now styled the Bosnian-Serb army. The Yugoslav army left behind vast amounts of equipment for the Bosnian-Serb army, which, according to the U.N. Secretary General Boutros Boutros-Ghali's report of June 15 (S/24100), continued to receive at least logistical and economic support from Serbia. Besides the Bosnian-Serb army, local Serb warlords maintained defense forces, and a few thousand local freebooters were active.

On the Bosnian-Croat side, there were the regulars, most of whom were veterans of the Yugoslav army who defected to Croatia after the latter country declared independence in 1991, and a smaller group of combatants, the Croatian Defense Force, which was composed of Bosnian Croats and some Bosnian Muslims. The regulars were part of the Croatian army, and the secretary general's report of June 15 stated that they were receiving logistical and economic support from Croatia, just as the Bosnian-Serb army was from Serbia.

Bosnian-government forces, mainly under Muslim leadership and mainly composed of Muslim combatants, were much smaller than the Serb and Croat forces, equipped only with light arms and concentrated in the Sarajevo area and a number of other pockets.

During the summer and early fall of 1992, the Yugoslav air force conducted hundreds of bombing and strafing raids on Bosnian-government towns.

By the end of October, Serb forces controlled more than 60 percent of the territory of Bosnia, and Croat forces nearly 20 percent. Bosnian-government forces controlled only most of Sarajevo and its environs, and a number of other pockets. Up to 150,000 Bosnians, mostly Muslim, had died in the first nine months of fighting, and up to one and a half million Bosnians, also mostly Muslim, had become refugees. Sarajevo (population: 380,000) and its environs were under siege, the city in ruins, and residents living in dire conditions. Already deprived of food, water, and electricity, the residents of Sarajevo faced the onslaught of winter without adequate heating supplies.

In the spring of 1993, the Bosnian government's military position deteriorated further. Bosnian-Serb forces conquered towns and villages in eastern Bosnia; refugees flooded into Srebrenica and then into Tuzla, swelling the latter's population to 700,000 by April 21. In addition to Sarajevo, Bosnian-government forces were besieged in four towns of eastern Bosnia (Gorazde, Srebrenica, Tuzla, and Zepa) and one town in northwestern Bosnia (Bihac). The six enclaves held 1.2 million Bosnians, two thirds of the remaining Muslims. Bosnian-Serb forces prevented most relief supplies from reaching the besieged enclaves.

In response to a N.A.T.O. ultimatum provoked by the shelling of a marketplace in Sarajevo on February 5, Bosnian-Serb forces either withdrew their heavy weapons from striking distance of the city or turned the weapons over to U.N. peacekeepers by the deadline date of February 21. In response to another N.A.T.O. ultimatum, Bosnian-Serb forces withdrew their heavy weapons from striking distance of Gorazde by the deadline date of April 26, and almost all of their footsoldiers three kilometers from the center of the town by the deadline date of April 23.

The tenuous alliance of Bosnian Croats and Bosnian Muslims collapsed in the spring of 1993. After almost a year of fighting in central Bosnia, Bosnian Croats and the Bosnian government agreed to a ceasefire (February 23, 1994) and a political federation (March 1, 1994).

In the third year of the war (from the spring of 1994 to the spring of 1995), Bosnian-Serb and Bosnian-government forces engaged in heavy fighting in the Bihac area. To deter N.A.T.O. air strikes at one point, the end of November, the Bosnian Serbs had "detained" or held hostage up to five hundred U.N. peacekeepers, all of whom were released several weeks later. Aside from the fighting in the Bihac area, war was waged at a low level, and there was a ceasefire from December 23 to May 1, 1995.

In April and May 1995, Bosnian-Serb forces reclaimed the weapons that they had deposited in U.N. depots around Sarajevo, and

Croatian Serbs joined Bosnian Serbs attacking Bihac. Bosnian-Serb forces resumed heavy shelling of Sarajevo in May, N.A.T.O. responded with two "pinprick" air strikes, and the Bosnian Serbs "detained" more than three hundred U.N. peacekeepers, all of whom were released in June. Bosnian-Serb forces captured Srebrenica on July 11 and Zepa on July 25. Civilian Muslim populations were expelled, and U.N. peacekeepers in the town temporarily "detained" as hostages.

In the same period (the spring and summer of 1995), Croatia moved decisively against secessionist Croatian Serbs. On May 1, Croat forces retook control of the Zagreb-Belgrade highway, thereby severing the land link between Croatian Serbs in the Krajina and their kinsmen in Yugoslavia. On May 2, Croat forces conquered Western Slavonia (eastern Croatia). At the end of July, Croat forces south of the Krajina crossed into eastcentral Bosnia and pushed west toward the Krajina. On August 4, Croat forces launched an assault on the Krajina from the north and achieved complete control by August 7. As a result of the Croat victory in the Krajina, more than 150,000 Croat-Serb refugees fled to Bosnian-Serb territory and Yugoslavia, and the siege of Bihac was relieved. The Croatian armed forces had been greatly strengthened since 1991 by arms purchases and training by former U.S. military personnel. Moreover, although the U.S. government formally condemned the Croat offensive, it threatened no sanctions.

On August 28, Bosnian-Serb forces again indiscriminately shelled Sarajevo and killed thirty-eight civilians. In response, beginning on August 30, N.A.T.O. jets for first time intensively bombed Serb anti-aircraft defenses, communication centers, transportation links, and ammunition depots throughout Bosnia. To prevent Bosnian-Serb hostage taking, the U.N. command had withdrawn peacekeepers from Gorazde by August 25. When, on September 14, Bosnian Serbs agreed to withdraw their heavy weapons and lift the siege of Sarajevo, N.A.T.O. agreed to end the air strikes.

As of September 1, 1995, more than three years of war had left Bosnian Serbs in possession of 70 percent of the territory of Bosnia, 200,000 Bosnians (mainly Muslims) dead, and 2,000,000 Bosnians (also mainly Muslims) refugees. Largely as a result of "ethnic cleansing," the population of the territory occupied by Bosnian-Serb forces was homogeneously Serb, and the population of the territory occupied by Bosnian-Croat and Bosnian-government forces almost homogeneously non-Serb. Although Bosnian-Serb forces in the fall of 1995 vastly outnumbered Bosnian-government forces in tanks (450 to 45) and heavy artillery (800 to 80), the lightly armed Bosnian-government army sizably outnumbered the Bosnian-Serb army (200,000 to 80,000). Moreover, N.A.T.O. maintained complete control of the air, and the British, French, and Dutch had deployed a 12,500-strong rapid-reaction force in Bosnian-government territory.

Beginning on September 9, advances by Bosnian-Croat and Bosnian government forces radically reduced the territory under the control of the Bosnian Serbs; by September 18, Bosnian Serbs controlled about half of Bosnia. On October 5, in preparation for a peace conference in November, the combatants agreed to a ceasefire, which went into effect on October 12.

U.N. and N.A.T.O. Responses

As noted, the U.N. Security Council had on September 25, 1991, imposed a general embargo on the delivery of weapons and military equipment to any part of the former Yugoslavia (S.C. Resolution 713) and on February 21, 1992, established the UNPROFOR peace-keeping unit to operate in the troubled areas of the former Yugoslavia (S.C. Resolution 743).

On May 15, 1992, the Security Council adopted a resolution demanding an immediate end to the fighting in Bosnia, the immediate withdrawal of outside forces (the Yugoslav/Serb army, elements of the Croatian army, and irregulars from Serbia and Croatia), the disbanding and disarmament of local militias, and the end of forcible expulsions and coercion to change the ethnic composition of areas in Bosnia (S.C. Resolution 752). The council, stressing the need for humanitarian assistance, also demanded that all parties cooperate fully with UNPROFOR and respect fully UNPROFOR's freedom of movement and the safety of its personnel.

On May 30, the Security Council voted to impose wide-ranging economic sanctions on Yugoslavia (Serbia-Montenegro), including an air embargo, demanded that the delivery of relief supplies to the Sarajevo area not be impeded, and called for the creation of a security zone around the capital and its airport (S.C. Resolution 757).

On June 8, the Security Council voted to enlarge UNPROFOR, to broaden its mandate to include full responsibility for the operation and security of the Sarajevo airport, and to authorize the secretary general to deploy military personnel to supervise the withdrawal of heavy weapons in Sarajevo to agreed locations in the area (S.C. Resolution 758).

On June 30, the Security Council adopted a resolution authorizing the deployment of additional UNPROFOR personnel to ensure the security and operation of the Sarajevo airport and the delivery of humanitarian assistance, calling for an unconditional ceasefire, and declaring that the council did not exclude "other measures," if necessary, to ensure the delivery of relief supplies to Sarajevo and its environs (S.C. Resolution 761).

After Serb forces withdrew from the Sarajevo airport on July 3, the United Nations began airlifting relief supplies. The airlift was able to function only fitfully because of periodic Serb shelling, and Serb forces exacted a toll of nearly 25 percent of the relief supplies as the price of permitting overland transit of the rest to the city. Moreover, overland truck convoys of relief supplies to Sarajevo and Muslim enclaves in eastern Bosnia were subjected to blockades.

On August 13, the Security Council approved a resolution authorizing "all measures" necessary to facilitate the delivery of relief supplies to Sarajevo and other besieged areas of Bosnia (S.C. Resolution 770). A companion resolution condemned forcible civilian expulsions, demanded full access to Serb detention camps by the International Committee of the Red Cross (I.C.R.C.), and called on all nations and humanitarian agencies to collect evidence of grave breaches of international law (S.C. Resolution 771).

On October 9, in response to Yugoslav air force raids on Bosnian government–held towns, the Security Council voted to ban all military flights over Bosnia but did not authorize enforcement of the ban (S.C. Resolution 781). The resolution also called for the establishment of a commission to try persons accused of war crimes in Bosnia.

On November 16, the Security Council voted to impose a naval blockade on Yugoslavia (Serbia-Montenegro) to enforce the council's embargo on the delivery of weapons and equipment to the area and the council's economic sanctions against Yugoslavia (S.C. Resolution 787; cf. S.C. Resolutions 713 and 757). The navies of member states were authorized to stop merchant vessels bound for the Adriatic ports of Montenegro and to inspect the vessels' cargo. Nations bordering the Danube were authorized to halt and inspect merchant vessels using the river. The resolution also prohibited the shipment of strategic materials through Yugoslavia without prior U.N. inspection. And the resolution called on the secretary general to study the feasibility of creating security zones for civilians in Bosnia.

On February 19, 1993, the Security Council voted to increase the peacekeeping forces in Croatia and Bosnia, and to authorize the peacekeepers to enforce mandates of the council under Chapter VII provisions of the charter (S.C. Resolution 807; cf. S.C. Resolution 770).

On March 31, the Security Council authorized enforcement of the ban on military flights over Bosnia (S.C. Resolution 816; cf. S.C. Resolution 781), and N.A.T.O. planes began enforcing the ban on April 12. There were some thousands of Bosnian-Serb violations of the ban, almost all by helicopters, but few shooting incidents involving N.A.T.O. patrol jets.

On April 16, the Security Council, with China and Russia abstaining, voted new economic sanctions against Yugoslavia (S.C. Resolution 820); the sanctions took effect on April 26, when the Bosnian Serbs failed to meet the resolution-imposed deadline for accepting the Vance-Owen plan. The resolution barred ships from entering Yugoslav territorial waters; banned the transshipment of goods through Yugoslavia; confiscated Yugoslav planes, ships, trucks, and cargo containers in foreign countries; required U.N. permission and monitoring for barges on the Danube passing through Yugoslavia; and froze Yugoslav bank accounts and financial assets in foreign countries.

On May 6, the Security Council declared six besieged Bosnian-government towns (Bihac, Gorazde, Sarajevo, Srebrenica, Tuzla, and Zepa) "safe areas" (S.C. Resolution 824). The resolution demanded that all parties treat the towns as areas "free from armed attack and free from any other hostile act." Bosnian-Serb forces were to cease armed attacks on the towns and withdraw some distance from the towns.

After the Bosnian-Serb parliament's third rejection of the Vance-Owen plan on May 6, 1993, the United States proposed air strikes on Bosnian-Serb artillery positions and lifting the embargo on arms to Bosnian-government forces. Great Britain and France opposed the air strikes because they feared the danger to their nationals in the U.N. peacekeeping forces in Bosnia, and the two Western European nations opposed lifting the embargo because they feared that other nations would then enter and enlarge the war. The European Community foreign ministers rejected the proposals on May 10, and Russia also indicated its opposition. On June 29, the Security Council failed to muster the votes necessary to pass a resolution lifting the embargo on arms to Bosnian-government forces; the United States was the only major power to vote for the resolution.

On May 22, the foreign ministers of France, Great Britain, Russia, Spain, and the United States proposed that U.N. peacekeepers provide an armed shield for the declared "safe areas" and possibly other areas. The United States promised to provide air cover for the peacekeepers but declined to commit ground forces until the warring parties reached a peace settlement. President Izetbegovic of Bosnia rejected the proposal on May 23, and fifty-one Muslim nations denounced it on May 24; in their view, the proposal would have legitimated Bosnian-Serb conquests. Bosnian-Serb leaders opposed the stationing of U.N. peacekeepers in Serb-occupied territory, and Yugoslav Serbs opposed monitoring of the Yugoslav-Bosnian border. On May 26, N.A.T.O. defense ministers declined to endorse the safe-haven plan. On May 28, the secretary general severely criticized the plan, saying that it was impossible to carry it out without the consent of the warring parties. The plan died.

On May 25, the Security Council established a war-crimes tribunal to try those accused of committing war crimes in the area of former Yugoslavia (S.C. Resolution 827). The Commission on Yugoslav War Crimes convened in The Hague (Netherlands) on November 17, and eleven members of the commission were sworn in. The commission subsequently charged twenty-one Serbs with genocide in Bosnia (February 13, 1995) and indicted the Bosnian-Serb president, Radovan Karadzic, and the Bosnian-Serb commander, Ratko Mladic (July 25, 1995).

On June 4, 1993, the Security Council authorized member states (understood to be N.A.T.O.) to employ air strikes, if necessary, to protect U.N. peacekeepers carrying out their mandate in Bosnia, and up to ten thousand more peacekeepers for the designated "safe areas" (S.C. Resolution 836; cf. S.C. Resolution 824). The United States and N.A.T.O. agreed on July 14 to provide air cover for the peacekeepers in Bosnia, subject to U.N. authorization.

On January 11, 1994, N.A.T.O. approved air strikes against Bosnian-Serb forces if such strikes were necessary to support relief airlifts and ground convoys to besieged Bosnian-government enclaves, provided that U.N. commanders requested the strikes, and that the secretary general (subsequently the chief civilian U.N. official in Bosnia) authorized them. On February 5, a mortar shell presumably fired by Bosnian-Serb forces exploded in a Sarajevo marketplace and killed sixty-eight civilians. The widely reported and televised incident aroused public indignation in the United States and Western Europe. On February 9, the North Atlantic Council, representing the sixteen N.A.T.O. members, issued an ultimatum to the Bosnian Serbs demanding that the latter withdraw their heavy weapons (artillery and mortars) twenty kilometers from the center of Sarajevo (excluding the area within a two-kilometer radius of Pale, the Bosnian-Serb capital) or face the consequence of air strikes. By the deadline of February 21, the Bosnian Serbs had either withdrawn most of their weapons the requisite distance or turned them over to U.N. peacekeepers. On March 4, the Security

Council committed the United Nations to the restoration of Sarajevo to normalcy, that is, to repair of the city's utilities and infrastructure, and to protecting the free movement of the city's residents (S.C. Resolution 900).

On April 9, with Bosnian-Serb forces poised to overrun Gorazde, the secretary general, citing Security Council Resolution 836, threatened air strikes unless the Bosnian-Serb forces drew back to the positions they held on March 30. The U.N. commander requested, and the U.N. civilian representative in Bosnia authorized, N.A.T.O. air strikes on April 10 and 11 against Bosnian-Serb positions around Gorazde, and N.A.T.O. planes carried out "pinprick" strikes inflicting little damage on Bosnian-Serb forces. When these air strikes failed to induce the Bosnian Serbs to halt their attack, the North Atlantic Council issued an ultimatum demanding that they withdraw their tanks and heavy weapons twenty kilometers from the center of Gorazde by April 26, and their militias three kilometers by April 23, or face the consequence of areawide air strikes. The Bosnian Serbs substantially did so by the requisite deadlines. On April 23, N.A.T.O. extended the same protection to four other "safe areas" (Bihac, Srebrenica, Tuzla, and Zepa).

In retaliation for Croatian-Serb air attacks on Bihac and its environs in November, the Security Council approved air strikes on the nearby Croatian-Serb airport at Ubdina and surface-to-air missile sites within fifty miles of Bihac (S.C. Resolution 958), and N.A.T.O. jets carried out limited strikes in late November. Bosnian-Serb forces took hundreds of U.N. peacekeepers hostage, and N.A.T.O. suspended flights over Bosnia.

In May 1995, after an ultimatum demanding that Bosnian Serbs return heavy weapons taken from U.N. depots and cease the shelling of Sarajevo, N.A.T.O. jets bombed Pale several times. Bosnian-Serb forces took hundreds of U.N. peacekeepers hostages, and the U.N. command backed down.

In July, N.A.T.O. jets carried out two "pinprick" air strikes against Bosnian-Serb forces attacking Srebrenica. Again, those forces "detained" U.N. peacekeepers, and again the U.N. command backed down.

On July 21, after the Bosnian-Serb conquest of Srebrenica and Zepa, the United States and its Western allies threatened "substantial and decisive" action if Bosnian-Serb forces attacked Gorazde. On August 1, N.A.T.O. extended the ultimatum to cover all of the remaining "safe areas" (Bihac, Gorazde, Sarajevo, and Tuzla). To prevent hostage taking, the U.N. command had withdrawn peacekeepers from Gorazde by August 25.

When, on August 28, Bosnian-Serb forces indiscriminately shelled Sarajevo, the United States called on N.A.T.O. to retaliate. N.A.T.O. jets carried out one thousand sorties against Bosnian-Serb forces throughout Bosnia for three days. On September 3, the United Nations demanded that Bosnian-Serb forces withdraw heavy weapons twenty kilometers from Sarajevo, cease attacks on the besieged government enclaves, allow the Sarajevo airport to reopen, and allow relief convoys overland access to Sarajevo. The Bosnian-Serb forces failed to comply by the deadline date of 11:00 P.M., September 4, and N.A.T.O. jets resumed intensive air strikes on September 5. On September 14, Bosnian-Serb forces agreed to withdraw their heavy weapons and lift the siege of Sarajevo, and N.A.T.O. agreed to end the air strikes.

On November 22, the day after the presidents of Bosnia, Croatia, and Serbia initialed the Dayton Accords, the Security Council voted unanimously to terminate the U.N. mission in Bosnia by January 31, 1996. On December 15, the day after the presidents signed the formal peace agreement in Paris, the Security Council voted unanimously to hand over authority for peacekeeping in Bosnia to N.A.T.O., which would station sixty thousand troops (including twenty thousand Americans) there. On December 20, U.N. forces formally relinquished authority to N.A.T.O. In the course of the U.N. mission, 107 peacekeepers lost their lives.

Peace Negotiations

On December 27, 1992, a conference on the future of Bosnia convened in Geneva, Switzerland, under U.N. auspices. Attending the conference were President Dobrica Cosic of Yugoslavia, President Franjo Tudjman of Croatia, Bosnian president Izetbegovic, Bosnian-Serb leader Karadzic, and Bosnian-Croat leader Mate Bohan.

On January 2, 1993, Cyrus R. Vance, the U.N. representative, and Lord David Owen, the European Community representative, co-chairmen of the conference, proposed a peace plan involving three elements: (1) an agreement to establish an interim government, composed of representatives of the three ethnic groups, to rule the country until a new constitution was adopted; (2) an agreement to end hostilities and disengage military forces; (3) an agreement to establish ten semiautonomous provinces or regions. Under the regional agreement, Bosnian-Serb rebels would give up 39 percent of the land they had conquered but dominate 43 percent of the country's territory. The plan envisioned a large U.N. peacekeeping force to enforce the agreements.

On January 30, the Bosnian leaders were asked to sign the agreements. The Bosnian-Croat leader signed all three; the Bosnian-Serb leader signed the first and third agreements but refused to sign the second, that is, to agree to withdraw artillery and heavy weapons from combat positions and store them under U.N. supervision. The Bosnian-government leader signed only the first agreement and objected strongly to the regional agreement.

The Bosnian government's deteriorating military position induced that government to sign the ceasefire and disengagement agreement on March 3, and the regional agreement, with minor adjustments, on March 25. The same military position, however, emboldened the Bosnian-Serb parliament to reject the Vance-Owen plan in its entirety on April 2, despite Karadzic's recommendation that the plan be conditionally accepted. Russia and Serbia pressured the Bosnian Serbs to accept the plan, but the Bosnian-Serb parliament again rejected it on April 26, and yet again on May 6. In a referendum on May 15–16, Bosnian-Serb voters overwhelmingly (96 percent) disapproved the plan and approved independent sovereignty. The Bosnian Serb parliament ratified the result of the referendum on May 19.

On June 16, negotiations under U.N. auspices resumed in Geneva and continued intermittently during the summer. On July 29, mediators Owen and Thorvald Stoltenberg, who had replaced Vance as the U.N. representative on April 2, proposed that Bosnia become a weak confederation of three ethnic republics: the entire country would be demilitarized, the central government would control foreign affairs and international trade, and the three constituent republics, which could secede from the confederation in two years, would guarantee human rights and the return of private property to expelled owners. On August 20, Owen and Stoltenberg filled out the proposal with a partition map allotting 52 percent of the territory to the Serbs, 30 percent to the Muslims, and 18 percent to the Croats. (The Serbs by August possessed 70 percent of the territory of prewar Bosnia.) The United Nations would presumably be called upon to provide some fifty thousand peacekeepers to carry out the plan.

The Bosnian-Serb parliament accepted the Owen-Stoltenberg plan unconditionally. The Bosnian Croats, while seeking adjustments to the map, accepted the plan and declared a republic in anticipation. The Bosnian-government parliament, however, unanimously rejected the plan on August 28 and overwhelmingly did so again on September 29. In rejecting the plan on September 29, the Bosnian-government parliament demanded that it be modified to provide for the return of "territories seized by force" and to include "international guarantees."

The three warring parties held intermittent peace talks in Geneva and Brussels from November 29, 1993, to February 12, 1994. The Bosnian Serbs offered to relinquish territory that would have enabled the Bosnian government to control some 30 percent of the territory of prewar Bosnia. The Bosnian government rejected this offer for several reasons: the land offered was deemed inferior, there was no provision for the return of property to dispossessed Muslims, there would be no linkage of the enclaves to the core of the Bosnian Republic, and the republic would have no seaport on the Adriatic. The peace talks accordingly failed to produce a settlement.

Following up on their February 23, 1994, ceasefire agreement, the Bosnian Croats and the Bosnian government reached a political agreement on March 1 to form a federal union. That union envisioned three layers of governance: (1) a local or municipal layer; (2) a regional layer of cantons, each of which would be all-Croat, all-Muslim, or of a roughly equal proportion of Croats and Muslims; (3) a federal layer in Sarajevo. The federal government would have control of matters relating to foreign affairs, defense, and commerce. Both parties promised to respect minority rights and the rights of the war's victims to restitution of property and compensation for injuries suffered. There was also to be an economic confederation with Croatia. On March 18, the parties signed a treaty formalizing the agreement.

On May 13, the foreign ministers of the European Union (principally those of France, Great Britain, and Germany) and Russia proposed a territorial division that would give the Bosnian government 51 percent of the land and the Bosnian Serbs 49 percent. The United States endorsed the plan. The Bosnian-government parliament accepted the plan on July 18 but withdrew its unconditional acceptance on July 21. Bosnian-Serb leaders rejected the plan on July 20, and a Bosnian-Serb referendum rejected it overwhelmingly (96 percent) on August 29. The United States, France, Great Britain, Germany, and Russia subsequently indicated that the parties could trade land within the allotted percentages, and that the Bosnian Serbs would be permitted to confederate with Serbia.

The success of the Croat offensive against secessionist Croatian Serbs in the spring and summer of 1995 revived chances for Bosnian-Serb acceptance of the plan, and U.S. diplomats actively promoted the plan. On August 31, the Bosnian Serbs agreed to have their interests in peace talks represented by the government of Yugoslavia. On September 8, the foreign ministers of Yugoslavia, Croatia, and Bosnia, meeting in Geneva, agreed to recognition of a Bosnian nation composed of two "entities": a Bosnian Federation (mainly Croat and Muslim) and a Bosnian-Serb Republic. The Bosnian-Serb Republic would be permitted to form a "special relationship" with Yugoslavia. Both the federation and the Bosnian-Serb Republic would guarantee human rights to ethnic minorities and the restitution of private property. The federation would control 51 percent of the territory, and the Bosnian-Serb Republic 49 percent.

On November 1, the presidents of Bosnia, Croatia, and Serbia met in Dayton, Ohio, to negotiate a peace agreement. On November 21, they initialed a peace accord that followed the lines of the foreign ministers' agreement of September 8, specified a buffer zone of four kilometers between the warring parties, and restricted heavy weapons to certain locations.

SUGGESTED READINGS

Betts, Richard K. "The Delusion of Impartial Intervention." *Foreign Affairs* 73 (November/December 1994): 22–33.

Haass, Richard N. *Intervention: The Use of American Military Force in the Post-Cold-War World.* Washington, D.C.: Brookings, 1994.

Reiff, David. *Slaughterhouse: Bosnia and the Failure of the West.* New York: Simon and Schuster, 1995.

Sekelj, Laslo. *The Process of Disintegration.* Atlantic Studies on Society and Change. Eastern European Monographs. New York: Columbia University Press, 1993.

Weiss, Thomas G. "U.N. Responses in the Former Yugoslavia: Moral and Operational Choices." *Ethics and International Affairs* 8 (1994): 1–22.

Zimmerman, Warren. "The Last Ambassador." *Foreign Affairs* (March/April 1995): 2–20.

QUESTIONS

1. If Croatia had a right to secede from Yugoslavia, did not Bosnia have the right to do so? If Croatia and Bosnia had rights to independence, should not predominantly Serb areas in Croatia and Bosnia have rights to secede from Croatia and Bosnia? Or should the long-standing identity of Croatia and Bosnia as integral territorial units preclude the right of Serbs living there to independence? How should boundaries be determined? What rights should ethnic minorities enjoy, and how should such rights be guaranteed?

2. Germany, other Western European nations, and the United States rapidly recognized the newly declared nations of Slovenia and Croatia. Did those rapid recognitions irreparably undermine any chance for a regional (federal) solution to the problem of old Yugoslavia's ethnic divisions, make war between Croats and Serbs in Croatia inevitable, and incite non-Serb Bosnians to push for independence of Bosnia? If so, were the rapid recognitions nonetheless justified by the principle of self-determination? In any case, how likely was it that nonrecognition, or at least delayed recognition, by Western powers would have made independence-minded Croats and Bosnians more disposed to seek anything less than complete independence?

3. When Bosnian-Serb leaders indicated that they would refuse to accept the results of the referendum on Bosnian independence (April

1992), that is, that they would form their own political unit, what, if anything, should the United Nations and Western nations have done? Should they have threatened to intervene, and done so if the Bosnian Serbs ignored the threat? For what purpose or purposes? To prevent "ethnic cleansing" and guarantee minority rights in Bosnian-Serb and Bosnian-government territory? To prevent the transfer of arms from the Yugoslav army to the Bosnian Serbs? How could any of these aims have been achieved without massive deployment of ground troops? Would Western electorates have supported, or could they have been persuaded to support, such a level of intervention?

4. When there was incontrovertible evidence of "ethnic cleansing" of Muslims by Serbs (and to a lesser extent by Croats) in the war that erupted after the Bosnian independence referendum, what, if anything, could or should the United Nations or Western nations have done?

5. The Security Council voted economic sanctions against Yugoslavia (Serbia-Montenegro) on May 30, 1992, and April 17, 1993 (S.C. Resolutions 757 and 820), and a naval blockade on November 16, 1992 (S.C. Resolution 787). Did those sanctions and blockade have any appreciable effect on the Bosnian-Serb will to wage war or the Bosnian-Serb war conduct?

6. The United Nations has authorized prosecution of war criminals in the former Yugoslavia (S.C. Resolutions 781, 827). Are such threats likely to have any appreciable effect on the behavior of participants in an ethnic war like the Bosnian? In any case, how would the United Nations gain custody of the accused? If, as seems likely, the United Nations cannot gain custody of the principal accused, what is the point of threatening to prosecute them in absentia?

7. Was it wise policy for the United Nations to station peacekeepers in Bosnia in the absence of an agreement by the warring parties to a truce? Did the possibility that the peacekeepers might mitigate the rigors of war on civilians justify the policy, despite its expense and the risks of peacekeepers becoming involved in the war or being taken hostage?

8. In 1991, largely in response to the war in Croatia, the United Nations imposed an embargo on the shipment of weapons and war material into the territory of the former Yugoslavia. Since the outbreak of the war in Bosnia, many (e.g., Baroness Thatcher in 1992) urged lifting application of the embargo with respect to supplying the Bosnian government. Western governments with forces serving as peacekeepers in

Bosnia, and the United States for the most part, opposed lifting the embargo. Opponents argued (1) that external military aid to the Bosnian government would intensify the war and so cause more military and civilian casualties on all sides; (2) that external military aid to the Bosnian government would put U.N. peacekeepers at risk, including the risk of being held hostage; (3) that external military aid to the Bosnian government might induce Russia to aid Bosnian Serbs; (4) that external military aid to the Bosnian government might destabilize other parts of the former Yugoslavia (e.g., Croatia, Macedonia); (5) that if Turkey aided the Bosnian government, Greece might be induced to aid the Bosnian Serbs; (6) that if extremist Muslim nations (e.g., Iran, Libya) aided the Bosnian government, they might stimulate violent anti-Western agitation throughout the Middle East. Critically evaluate these contentions.

9. Assuming that lifting the embargo on military aid to the Bosnian government would have been wise policy, should the United States have done so unilaterally? In other words, did the United States have a moral obligation to adhere to the U.N. embargo? What about the effect of unilateral action by the United States on its Western allies? What if unilateral action would induce France and Great Britain to withdraw their forces from serving as peacekeepers in Bosnia? If the United States lifted the embargo, would the Bosnian government be able to finance the purchase of arms? Would Croatia allow arms for Bosnian Muslims, wherever and however obtained, to pass through its territory? If not, how would the arms be delivered? Would the Bosnian Serbs be likely to remain passive while Bosnian-government forces acquired new weapons and became trained in their use?

10. After Bosnian-Serb forces took hundreds of U.N. peacekeepers hostage at the end of May 1995, France, Great Britain, and the Netherlands undertook to deploy some 12,500 troops as rapid-reaction forces in Bosnia. Would such forces be adequate to defend besieged U.N. peacekeepers in remote areas or outlying posts? To protect "safe areas" from Bosnian-Serb attacks?

11. Assuming no substantial risk of U.N. peacekeepers' being taken hostage (either because the rapid-reaction forces can protect them or because they have been withdrawn from vulnerable areas), were intensive N.A.T.O. air strikes on Bosnian-Serb military targets wise policy? For what purpose or purposes? To deter Bosnian Serbs from shelling or attacking "safe areas"? To protect convoys of food to the civilian pop-

ulations of "safe areas"? To help Bosnian-government forces defend government territory? To help Bosnian-government forces mount a counteroffensive? How much could air power alone achieve? What level of bombing, if any, would be likely to induce Bosnian Serbs to modify their territorial objectives? What if N.A.T.O. planes were shot down, and N.A.T.O. pilots taken prisoner? Would widespread N.A.T.O. air strikes lead to the commitment of ground troops if Bosnian Serbs retaliated against downed pilots or attacked U.N. peacekeepers?

12. Does the Bosnian war indicate the futility or disproportionate costs of military intervention in secessionist wars? Does the war indicate the futility or disproportionate costs of military intervention for humanitarian reasons? Or does it indicate the unwillingness of Western nations and the United Nations until late summer 1995 to use sufficient force to achieve morally desirable purposes? If the latter, what military means for what objectives? What policy would you have recommended in the spring of 1992 before the outbreak of war? What policy would you have recommended in the summer of 1992 after the transfer of Yugoslav arms to the Bosnian Serbs, the Bosnian-Serb offensive, and the "ethnic cleansing"? What policy would you have recommended in the spring of 1995 after the winter truce broke down? What policy would you have recommended in the summer of 1995 after the Bosnian-Serb capture of the eastern Bosnian-government enclaves of Srebrenica and Zepa? Compare the potential benefits and costs of the plans you would have recommended with the benefits and costs of alternate plans.

13. Did the U.S. Constitution require the president to obtain congressional authorization for the participation of the U.S. air force in air strikes against Bosnian-Serb forces? Did the War Powers Resolution require the president to obtain congressional authorization for continuing air strikes beyond a period of sixty days? Did the N.A.T.O. Treaty give the president authority to station ground forces in Bosnia to monitor the peace accord?

THE UNITED NATIONS CHARTER

We, the peoples of the United Nations, determined

to save succeeding generations from the scourge of war, which twice in our lifetime has brought untold sorrow to mankind, and

to reaffirm faith in fundamental human rights, in the dignity and worth of the human person, in the equal rights of men and women and of nations large and small, and

to establish conditions under which justice and respect for the obligations arising from treaties and other sources of international law can be maintained, and

to promote social progress and better standards of life in larger freedom,

and for these ends

to practice tolerance and live together in peace with one another as good neighbors, and

to unite our strength to maintain international peace and security, and

to ensure, by the acceptance of principles and the institution of methods, that armed force shall not be used save in the common interest, and

to employ international machinery for the promotion of the economic and social advancement of all peoples,

have resolved to combine our efforts to accomplish these aims.

Accordingly, our respective governments, through representatives assembled in the city of San Francisco, who have exhibited their full

U.S. Department of State, Publication 2368. Asterisks indicate elided articles.

powers found to be in good and due form, have agreed to the present Charter of the United Nations and do hereby establish an international organization to be known as the United Nations.

Chapter I. Purposes and Principles

Article 1

The purposes of the United Nations are:

1. to maintain international peace and security, and to that end to take effective collective measures for the prevention and removal of threats to the peace and for the suppression of acts of aggression or other breaches of the peace, and to bring about by peaceful means and in conformity with the principles of justice and international law adjustment or settlement of international disputes or situations which might lead to a breach of the peace,

2. to develop friendly relations among nations based on respect for the principle of equal rights and self-determination of peoples, and to take other appropriate measures to strengthen universal peace,

3. to achieve international cooperation in solving international problems of an economic, social, cultural, or humanitarian character, and in promoting and encouraging respect for human rights and for fundamental freedom for all without distinction as to race, sex, language, or religion, and

4. to be a center for harmonizing the actions of nations in the attainment of these common ends.

Article 2

The Organization and its members, in pursuit of the purposes stated in Article 1, shall act in accordance with the following principles.

1. The Organization is based on the principle of the sovereign equality of all its members.

2. All members, in order to ensure to all of them the rights and benefits resulting from membership, shall fulfill in good faith the obligations assumed by them in accordance with the present Charter.

3. All members shall settle their international disputes by peaceful means in such a manner that international peace and security, and justice, are not endangered.

4. All members shall refrain in their international relations from the threat or use of force against the territorial integrity or political independence of any state, or in any other manner inconsistent with the purpose of the United Nations.

5. All members shall give the United Nations every assistance in any action it takes in accordance with the present Charter, and shall refrain

from giving assistance to any state against which the United Nations is taking preventive or enforcement action.

6. The Organization shall ensure that states which are not members of the United Nations act in accordance with these principles so far as may be necessary for the maintenance of international peace and security.

7. Nothing contained in the present Charter shall authorize the United Nations to intervene in matters which are essentially within the domestic jurisdiction of any state or shall require the members to submit such matters to settlement under the present Charter, but this principle shall not prejudice the application of enforcement measures under Chapter VII.

Chapter II. Membership

*   *   *

Article 5

A member of the United Nations against which preventive or enforcement action has been taken by the Security Council may be suspended from the exercise of the rights and privileges of membership by the General Assembly upon the recommendation of the Security Council. The exercise of these rights and privileges may be restored by the Security Council.

Article 6

A member of the United Nations which has persistently violated the principles contained in the present Charter may be expelled from the Organization by the General Assembly upon the recommendation of the Security Council.

Chapter III. Organs

Article 7

1. There are established as the principal organs of the United Nations: a General Assembly, a Security Council, an Economic and Social Council, a Trusteeship Council, an International Court of Justice, and a Secretariat.

2. Such subsidiary organs as may be found necessary may be established in accordance with the present Charter.

*   *   *

Chapter IV. The General Assembly

Article 9

1. The General Assembly shall consist of all the members of the United Nations.

2. Each member shall have not more than five representatives in the General Assembly.

Article 10

The General Assembly may discuss any questions or any matters within the scope of the present Chapter or relating to the powers and functions of any organs provided for in the present Charter, and, except as provided in Article 12, may make recommendations to the members of the United Nations or to the Security Council or to both on any such questions or matters.

Article 11

1. The General Assembly may consider the general principles of co-operation in the maintenance of international peace and security, including the principles governing disarmament and the regulation of armaments, and may make recommendations with regard to such principles to the members or to the Security Council or to both.

2. The General Assembly may discuss any questions relating to the maintenance of international peace and security brought before it by any member of the United Nations or by the Security Council or by a state which is not a member of the United Nations, in accordance with Article 35, paragraph 2, and, except as provided in Article 12, may make recommendations with regard to any such questions to the state or states concerned or to the Security Council or to both. Any such question on which action is necessary shall be referred to the Security Council by the General Assembly either before or after discussion.

3. The General Assembly may call the attention of the Security Council to situations which are likely to endanger international peace and security.

4. The powers of the General Assembly set forth in this Article shall not limit the general scope of Article 10.

Article 12

1. While the Security Council is exercising in respect of any dispute or situation the functions assigned to it in the present Charter, the General Assembly shall not make any recommendation with regard to that dispute or situation unless the Security Council so requests.

2. The Secretary General, with the consent of the Security Council,

shall notify the General Assembly at each session of any matters relative to the maintenance of international peace and security which are being dealt with by the Security Council, and shall similarly notify the General Assembly, or the members of the United Nations if the General Assembly is not in session, immediately the Security Council ceases to deal with such matters.

* * *

Article 14

Subject to the provisions of Article 12, the General Assembly may recommend measures for the peaceful adjustment of any situation, regardless of origin, which it deems likely to impair the general welfare or friendly relations among nations, including situations resulting from a violation of the provisions of the present Charter setting forth the purposes and principles of the United Nations.

Article 15

1. The General Assembly shall receive and consider annual and special reports from the Security Council; these reports shall include an account of the measures that the Security Council has decided upon or taken to maintain international peace and security.

2. The General Assembly shall receive and consider reports from the other organs of the United Nations.

Article 16

The General Assembly shall perform such functions with respect to the international trusteeship system as are assigned to it under Chapters XII and XIII, including the approval of the trusteeship agreements for areas not designated as strategic.

Article 17

1. The General Assembly shall consider and approve the budget of the Organization.

2. The expenses of the Organization shall be borne by the members as apportioned by the General Assembly.

3. The General Assembly shall consider and approve any financial and budgetary arrangements with specialized agencies referred to in Article 57 and shall examine the administrative budgets of such specialized agencies with a view to making recommendations to the agencies concerned.

Article 18

1. Each member of the General Assembly shall have one vote.

2. Decisions of the General Assembly on important questions shall

be made by a two-thirds majority of the members present and voting. These questions shall include: recommendations with respect to the maintenance of international peace and security, the election of non-permanent members of the Security Council, the election of the members of the Economic and Social Council, the election of members of the Trusteeship Council in accordance with paragraph 1(c) of Article 86, the admission of new members to the United Nations, the suspension of the rights and privileges of membership, the expulsion of members, questions relating to the operation of the trusteeship system, and budgetary questions.

3. Decisions on other questions, including the determination of additional categories of questions to be decided by a two-thirds majority, shall be made by a majority of the members present and voting.

Article 19

A member of the United Nations which is in arrears in the payment of financial contributions to the Organization shall have no vote in the General Assembly if the amount of its arrears equals or exceeds the amount of the contributions due from it for the preceding two full years. The General Assembly may nevertheless permit such a member to vote if it is satisfied that the failure to pay is due to conditions beyond the control of the member.

*　*　*

Chapter V. The Security Council

Article 23

1. [as amended, 1965] The Security Council shall consist of fifteen members of the United Nations. The Republic of China [now the People's Republic of China], France, the Union of Soviet Socialist Republics [now Russia], the United Kingdom of Great Britain and Northern Ireland, and the United States of America shall be permanent members of the Security Council. The General Assembly shall elect ten other members of the United Nations to be nonpermanent members of the Security Council, due regard being specially paid in the first instance to the contribution of members of the United Nations to the maintenance of international peace and security and to the other purposes of the Organization, and also to equitable geographical distribution.

2. [as amended, 1965] The nonpermanent members of the Security Council shall be elected for a term of two years. In the first election of the nonpermanent members after the increase of the membership of the Security Council from eleven to fifteen, two of the four additional mem-

bers shall be chosen for a term of one year. A retiring member shall not be eligible for immediate re-election.

3. Each member of the Security Council shall have one representative.

Article 24

1. In order to ensure prompt and effective action by the United Nations, its members confer on the Security Council primary responsibility for the maintenance of international peace and security and agree that, in carrying out its duties under this responsibility, the Security Council acts on their behalf.

2. In discharging these duties, the Security Council shall act in accordance with the purposes and principles of the United Nations. The specific powers granted to the Security Council for the discharge of these duties are laid down in Chapters VI, VII, VIII, and XII.

3. The Security Council shall submit annual and, when necessary, special reports to the General Assembly for its consideration.

Article 25

The members of the United Nations agree to accept and carry out the decisions of the Security Council in accordance with the present Charter.

Article 26

In order to promote the establishment and maintenance of international peace and security with the least diversion for armaments of the world's human and economic resources, the Security Council shall be responsible for formulating, with the assistance of the Military Staff Committee referred to in Article 47, plans to be submitted to the members of the United Nations for the establishment of a system for the regulation of armaments.

Article 27

1. Each member of the Security Council shall have one vote.

2. [as amended, 1965] Decisions of the Security Council on procedural matters shall be made by an affirmative vote of nine members.

3. [as amended, 1965] Decisions of the Security Council on all other matters shall be made by an affirmative vote of nine members, including the concurring votes of the permanent members, provided that, in decisions under Chapter VI and under paragraph 3 of Article 52, a party to a dispute shall abstain from voting.

* * *

Chapter VI. Pacific Settlement of Disputes

Article 33

1. The parties to any dispute, the continuance of which is likely to endanger the maintenance of international peace and security, shall first of all seek a solution by negotiation, enquiry, mediation, conciliation, arbitration, judicial settlement, resort to regional agencies or arrangements, or other peaceful means of their own choice.

2. The Security Council shall, when it deems necessary, call upon the parties to settle their disputes by such means.

Article 34

The Security Council may investigate any dispute, or any situation which might lead to international friction or give rise to a dispute, in order to determine whether the continuance of the dispute or situation is likely to endanger the maintenance of international peace and security.

Article 35

1. Any member of the United Nations may bring any dispute, or any situation of the nature referred to in Article 34, to the attention of the Security Council or of the General Assembly.

2. A state which is not a member of the United Nations may bring to the attention of the Security Council or of the General Assembly any dispute to which it is a party if it accepts in advance, for the purposes of the dispute, the obligations of the pacific settlement provided in the present Charter.

3. The proceedings of the General Assembly in respect of matters brought to its attention under this Article will be subject to the provisions of Articles 11 and 12.

Article 36

1. The Security Council may at any stage of a dispute of the nature referred to in Article 33 or of a situation of like nature recommend appropriate procedures or methods of adjustment.

2. The Security Council should take into consideration any procedures for the settlement of the dispute which have already been adopted by the parties.

3. In making recommendations under this Article, the Security Council should also take into consideration that legal disputes should as a rule be referred by the parties to the International Court of Justice in accordance with the provisions of the Statute of the Court.

Article 37

1. Should the parties to a dispute of the nature referred to in Article 33 fail to settle it by the means indicated in that Article, they shall refer it to the Security Council.

2. If the Security Council deems that the continuance of the dispute is in fact likely to endanger the maintenance of international peace and security, it shall decide whether to take action under Article 36 or to recommend such terms of settlement as it may consider appropriate.

Article 38

Without prejudice to the provisions of Articles 33 to 37, the Security Council may, if all the parties so request, make recommendations to the parties with a view to a pacific settlement of the dispute.

Chapter VII. Action with Respect to Threats to the Peace, Breaches of the Peace, and Acts of Aggression

Article 39

The Security Council shall determine the existence of any threat to the peace, breach of the peace, or act of aggression and shall make recommendations, or decide what measures shall be taken in accordance with Articles 41 and 42, to maintain or restore international peace and security.

Article 40

In order to prevent an aggravation of the situation, the Security Council may, before making the recommendations or deciding upon the measures provided for in Article 39, call upon the parties concerned to comply with such provisional measures as it deems necessary or desirable. Such provisional measures shall be without prejudice to the rights, claims, or position of the parties concerned. The Security Council shall duly take account of failure to comply with such provisional measures.

Article 41

The Security Council may decide what measures not involving the use of armed force are to be employed to give effect to its decisions, and it may call upon the members of the United Nations to apply such measures. These may include complete or partial interruption of economic relations and of rail, sea, air, postal, telegraphic, radio, or other means of communication, and the severance of diplomatic relations.

Article 42

Should the Security Council consider that measures provided for in Article 41 would be inadequate or have proved to be inadequate, it may take such action by air, sea, or land forces as may be necessary to maintain or restore international peace and security. Such action may include demonstrations, blockade, and other operations by air, sea, or land forces of members of the United Nations.

Article 43

1. All members of the United Nations, in order to contribute to the maintenance of international peace and security, undertake to make available to the Security Council, on its call and in accordance with a special agreement or agreements, armed forces, assistance, and facilities, including rights of passage, necessary for the purpose of maintaining international peace and security.

2. Such agreement or agreements shall govern the numbers and types of forces, their degree of readiness and general location, and the nature of the facilities and assistance to be provided.

3. The agreement or agreements shall be negotiated as soon as possible on the initiative of the Security Council. They shall be concluded between the Security Council and members, or between the Security Council and groups of members, and shall be subject to ratification by the signatory states in accordance with their respective constitutional processes.

Article 44

When the Security Council has decided to use force, it shall, before calling upon a member not represented on it to provide armed forces in fulfillment of the obligations assumed under Article 43, invite that member, if the member so desires, to participate in the decisions of the Security Council concerning the employment of contingents of that member's armed forces.

Article 45

In order to enable the United Nations to take urgent military measures, members shall hold immediately available national air force contingents for combined international enforcement action. The strength and degree of readiness of these contingents and plans for their combined action shall be determined, within the limits laid down in the special agreement or agreements referred to in Article 43, by the Security Council with the assistance of the Military Staff Committee.

Article 46

Plans for the application of armed force shall be made by the Security Council with the assistance of the Military Staff Committee.

Article 47

1. There shall be established a Military Staff Committee to advise and assist the Security Council on all questions relating to the Security Council's military requirements for the maintenance of international peace and security, the employment and command of forces placed at its disposal, the regulation of armaments, and possible disarmament.

2. The Military Staff Committee shall consist of the Chiefs of Staff of the permanent members of the Security Council or their representatives. Any member of the United Nations not permanently represented on the Committee shall be invited by the Committee to be associated with it when the efficient discharge of the Committee's responsibilities requires the participation of that member in its work.

3. The Military Staff Committee shall be responsible under the Security Council for the strategic direction of any armed forces placed at the disposal of the Security Council. Questions relating to the command of such forces shall be worked out subsequently.

4. The Military Staff Committee, with the authorization of the Security Council and after consultation with appropriate regional agencies, may establish regional subcommittees.

Article 48

1. The action required to carry out the decisions of the Security Council for the maintenance of international peace and security shall be taken by all members of the United Nations or by some of them, as the Security Council may determine.

2. Such decisions shall be carried out by the members of the United Nations directly or through their action in the appropriate international agencies of which they are members.

Article 49

The members of the United Nations shall join in affording mutual assistance in carrying out the measures decided upon by the Security Council.

Article 50

If preventive or enforcement measures against any state are taken by the Security Council, any other state, whether a member of the United Nations or not, which finds itself confronted with special economic problems arising from the carrying out of those measures shall have the right to consult the Security Council with regard to a solution of those problems.

Article 51

Nothing in the present Charter shall impair the inherent right of individual or collective self-defense if an armed attack occurs against a member of the United Nations, until the Security Council has taken the measures necessary to maintain international peace and security. Measures taken by members in the exercise of this right of self-defense shall be immediately reported to the Security Council and shall not in any way affect the authority and responsibility of the Security Council under the present Charter to take at any time such action as it deems necessary in order to maintain or restore international peace and security.

Chapter VIII. Regional Arrangements

Article 52

1. Nothing in the present Charter precludes the existence of regional arrangements or agencies for dealing with such matters relating to the maintenance of international peace and security as are appropriate for regional action, provided that such arrangements or agencies and their activities are consistent with the purposes and principles of the United Nations.

2. The members of the United Nations entering into such arrangements or constituting such agencies shall make every effort to achieve pacific settlement of local disputes through such regional arrangements or by such regional agencies before referring them to the Security Council.

3. The Security Council shall encourage the development of pacific settlement of local disputes through such regional arrangements or by such regional agencies either on the initiative of the states concerned or by reference from the Security Council.

4. This Article in no way impairs the application of Articles 34 and 35.

Article 53

1. The Security Council shall, where appropriate, utilize such regional arrangements or agencies for enforcement action under its authority. But no enforcement action shall be taken under regional arrangements or by regional agencies without the authorization of the Security Council, with the exception of measures against any enemy state, as defined in paragraph 2 of this Article, provided for pursuant to

Article 107 or in regional arrangements directed against renewal of aggressive policy on the part of any state, until such time as the Organization may, on the request of the governments concerned, be charged with the responsibility for preventing further aggression by such a state.

2. The term "enemy state" as used in paragraph 1 of this Article applies to any state which during the Second World War has been an enemy of any signatory of the present Charter.

Article 54

The Security Council shall at all times be kept fully informed of activities undertaken or in contemplation under regional arrangements or by regional agencies for the maintenance of international peace and security.

* * *

Chapter XI. Declaration Regarding Non-Self-Governing Territories

Article 73

Members of the United Nations which have or assume responsibilities for the administration of territories whose peoples have not yet attained a full measure of self-government recognize the principle that the interests of the inhabitants of these territories are paramount and accept as a sacred trust the obligation to promote to the utmost, within the system of international peace and security established by the present Charter, the well-being of the inhabitants of these territories, and to this end:

a. to ensure, with due respect for the culture of the peoples concerned, their political, economic, social, and educational advancement, their just treatment, and their protection against abuses,

b. to develop self-government to take due account of the political aspirations of the peoples and to assist them in the progressive development of their free political institutions, according to the particular circumstances of each territory and its peoples and their varying stages of development,

c. to further international peace and security,

d. to promote constructive measures of development, to encourage research, and to cooperate with one another and, when and where appropriate, with specialized international bodies with a view to the practical achievement of the social, economic, and scientific purposes set forth in this Article, and

e. to transmit regularly to the Secretary General for information pur-

poses, subject to such limitation as security and constitutional considerations may require, statistical and other information of a technical
nature relating to economic, social, and educational conditions in the
territories for which they are respectively responsible, other than those
territories to which Chapters XII and XIII apply.

Article 74

Members of the United Nations also agree that their policy in respect
of the territories to which this Chapter applies, no less than in respect
of their metropolitan areas, must be based on the general principle of
good-neighborliness, due account being taken of the interests and well-
being of the rest of the world in social, economic, and commercial
matters.

Chapter XII. International Trusteeship System

Article 75

The United Nations shall establish under its authority an international trusteeship system for the administration and supervision of such
territories as may be placed thereunder by subsequent individual agreements. These territories are hereinafter referred to as trust territories.

Article 76

The basic objectives of the trusteeship system, in accordance with the
purposes of the United Nations laid down in Article 1 of the present
Charter, shall be:

a. to further international peace and security,

b. to promote the political, economic, social, and educational advancement of the inhabitants of the trust territories, and their progressive development towards self-government or independence as may be
appropriate to the particular circumstances of each territory and its peoples and the freely expressed wishes of the peoples concerned, and as
may be provided by the terms of each trusteeship agreement,

c. to encourage respect for human rights and for fundamental freedoms for all without distinction as to race, sex, language, or religion,
and to encourage recognition of the interdependence of the peoples of
the world, and

d. to ensure equal treatment in social, economic, and commercial
matters for all members of the United Nations and their nationals, and
also equal treatment for the latter in the administration of justice, without prejudice to the attainment of the foregoing objectives and subject
to the provisions of Article 80.

Article 77

1. The trusteeship system shall apply to such territories in the following categories as may be placed thereunder by means of trusteeship agreements:

a. territories now held under mandate,

b. territories which may be detached from enemy states as a result of the Second World War, and

c. territories voluntarily placed under the system by states responsible for their administration.

2. It will be a matter for subsequent agreement as to which territories in the foregoing categories will be brought under the trusteeship system and upon what terms.

Article 78

The trusteeship system shall not apply to territories which have become members of the United Nations, relationship among which shall be based on respect for the principle of sovereign equality.

Article 79

The terms of trusteeship for each territory to be placed under the trusteeship system, including any alteration or amendment, shall be agreed upon by the states directly concerned, including the mandatory power in the case of territories held under mandate by a member of the United Nations, and shall be approved as provided for in Articles 83 and 85.

Article 80

1. Except as may be agreed upon in individual trusteeship agreements made under Articles 77, 79, and 81 placing each territory under the trusteeship system, and until such agreements have been concluded, nothing in this Chapter shall be construed in or of itself to alter in any manner the rights whatsoever of any states or any peoples or the terms of existing international instruments to which members of the United Nations may respectively be parties.

2. Paragraph 1 of this Article shall not be interpreted as giving grounds for delay or postponement of the negotiation and conclusion of agreements for placing mandated and other territories under the trusteeship system as provided for in Article 77.

Article 81

The trusteeship agreement shall in each case include the terms under which the trust territory will be administered, and designate the authority which will exercise the administration of the trust territory. Such authority, hereinafter called the administering authority, may be one or more states or the Organization itself.

Article 82

There may be designated in any trusteeship agreement a strategic area or areas, which may include part or all of the trust territory to which the agreement applies, without prejudice to any special agreement or agreements made under Article 43.

Article 83

1. All functions of the United Nations relating to strategic areas, including the approval of the terms of the trusteeship agreements and of their alteration or amendment, shall be exercised by the Security Council.

2. The basic objectives set forth in Article 76 shall be applicable to the people of each strategic area.

3. The Security Council shall, subject to the provisions of the trusteeship agreements and without prejudice to security considerations, avail itself of the assistance of the Trusteeship Council to perform those functions of the United Nations under the trusteeship system relating to political, economic, social, and educational matters in the strategic areas.

Article 84

It shall be the duty of the administering authority to ensure that the trust territory shall play its part in the maintenance of international peace and security. To this end, the administering authority may make use of volunteer forces, facilities, and assistance from the trust territory in carrying out the obligations towards the Security Council undertaken in this regard by the administering authority, as well as for local defense and the maintenance of law and order within the trust territory.

Article 85

1. The functions of the United Nations with regard to trusteeship agreements for all areas not designated as strategic, including the approval of the terms of the trusteeship agreements and of their alteration or amendment, shall be exercised by the General Assembly.

2. The Trusteeship Council, operating under the authority of the General Assembly, shall assist the General Assembly in carrying out these functions.

*   *   *

Chapter XIV. The International Court of Justice

Article 92

The International Court of Justice shall be the principal judicial organ of the United Nations. It shall function in accordance with the annexed Statute, which is based upon the Statute of the Permanent Court of International Justice and forms an integral part of the present Charter.

Article 93

1. All members of the United Nations are ipso facto parties to the Statute of the International Court of Justice.

2. A state which is not a member of the United Nations may become a party to the Statute of the International Court of Justice on conditions to be determined in each case by the General Assembly upon the recommendation of the Security Council.

Article 94

1. Each member of the United Nations undertakes to comply with the decision of the International Court of Justice in any case to which it is a party.

2. If any party to a case fails to perform the obligations incumbent upon it under a judgment rendered by the Court, the other party may have recourse to the Security Council, which may, if it deems necessary, make recommendations or decide upon measures to be taken to give effect to the judgment.

Article 95

Nothing in the present Chapter shall prevent members of the United Nations from entrusting the solution of their differences to other tribunals by virtue of agreements already in existence or which may be concluded in the future.

Article 96

1. The General Assembly or the Security Council may request the International Court of Justice to give an advisory opinion on any legal question.

2. Other organs of the United Nations and specialized agencies, which may at any time be so authorized by the General Assembly, may also request advisory opinions of the Court on legal questions arising within the scope of their activities.

Chapter XV. The Secretariat

Article 97

The Secretariat shall comprise a Secretary General and such staff as the Organization may require. The Secretary General shall be appointed by the General Assembly upon the recommendation of the Security Council. He shall be the chief administrative officer of the Organization.

Article 98

The Secretary General shall act in that capacity in all meetings of the General Assembly, of the Security Council, of the Economic and Social Council, and of the Trusteeship Council, and shall perform such other functions as are entrusted to him by these organs. The Secretary General shall make an annual report to the General Assembly on the work of the Organization.

Article 99

The Secretary General may bring to the attention of the Security Council any matter which in his opinion may threaten the maintenance of international peace and security.

Article 100

1. In the performance of their duties, the Secretary General and the staff shall not seek or receive instructions from any government or from any other authority external to the Organization. They shall refrain from any action which might reflect on their position as international officials responsible only to the Organization.

2. Each member of the United Nations undertakes to respect the exclusively international character of the responsibilities of the Secretary General and the staff and not to seek to influence them in the discharge of their responsibilities.

Article 101

1. The staff shall be appointed by the Secretary General under regulations established by the General Assembly.

2. Appropriate staffs shall be permanently assigned to the Economic and Social Council, the Trusteeship Council, and, as required, to other organs of the United Nations. These staffs shall form a part of the Secretariat.

3. The paramount consideration in the employment of the staff and in the determination of the conditions of service shall be the necessity of securing the highest standards of efficiency, competence, and integ-

rity. Due regard shall be paid to the importance of recruiting the staff on as wide a geographical basis as possible.

* * *

Chapter XVII. Transitional Security Arrangements

Article 106

Pending the coming into force of such special agreements referred to in Article 43 as in the opinion of the Security Council enable it to begin the exercise of its responsibilities under Article 42, the parties to the Four-Nation Declaration, signed at Moscow, October 30, 1943, and France, shall, in accordance with the provisions of paragraph 5 of that Declaration, consult with one another and as occasion requires with other members of the United Nations, with a view to such joint action on behalf of the Organization as may be necessary for the purpose of maintaining international peace and security.

* * *

Chapter XVIII. Amendments

Article 108

Amendments to the present Charter shall come into force for all members of the United Nations when they have been adopted by a vote of two thirds of the members of the General Assembly and ratified in accordance with their respective constitutional processes by two thirds of the members of the United Nations, including all the permanent members of the Security Council.

Article 109

1. [as amended, 1968] A general conference of the members of the United Nations for the purpose of reviewing the present Charter may be held at a date and place to be fixed by a two-thirds vote of the members of the General Assembly and by a vote of any nine members of the Security Council. Each member of the United Nations shall have one vote in the conference.

2. Any alteration of the present Charter recommended by a two-thirds vote of the conference shall take effect when ratified in accordance with their respective constitutional processes by two thirds of the members of the United Nations, including all the permanent members of the Security Council.

* * *

WAR POWERS RESOLUTION
November 7, 1973

Sec. 2 [#1541]. Purpose and Policy

a. It is the purpose of this chapter to fulfill the intent of the framers of the Constitution of the United States and insure that the collective judgment of both the Congress and the President will apply to the introduction of United States Armed Forces into hostilities, or into situations where imminent involvement in hostilities is clearly indicated by the circumstances, and to the continued use of such forces in hostilities or in such situations.

b. Under Article I, sec. 8., of the Constitution, it is specifically provided that the Congress shall have the power to make all laws necessary and proper for carrying into execution not only its own powers but also all other powers vested by the Constitution in the Government of the United States or in any department or officer thereof.

c. The constitutional powers of the President as commander in chief to introduce United States Armed Forces into hostilities, or into situations where imminent involvement in hostilities is clearly indicated by the circumstances, are exercised only pursuant to (1) a declaration of war, (2) specific statutory authorization, or (3) a national emergency created by attack upon the United States, its territories or possessions, or its armed forces.

Sec. 3 [#1542]. Consultation with Congress

The President in every possible instance shall consult with Congress before introducing United States Armed Forces into hostilities or into situations where imminent involvement in hostilities is clearly indicated by the circumstances, and after every such introduction shall consult

87 Stat. 555, 50 U.S.C. nos. 1541–48 (1982 ed.)

regularly with the Congress until the United States Armed Forces are no longer engaged in hostilities or have been removed from such situations.

Sec. 4 [#1543]. Reporting to Congress

a. In the absence of a declaration of war, in any case in which the United States Armed Forces are introduced (1) into hostilities or into situations where imminent involvement in hostilities is clearly indicated by the circumstances, (2) into the territory, airspace, or waters of a foreign nation while equipped for combat, except for deployments which relate solely to supply, replacement, repair, or training of such forces, or (3) in numbers which substantially enlarge United States Armed Forces equipped for combat already located in a foreign nation, the President shall submit within forty-eight hours to the Speaker of the House of Representatives and to the President pro tempore of the Senate a report in writing setting forth (A) the circumstances necessitating the introduction of United States Armed Forces, (B) the constitutional and legislative authority under which such introduction took place, and (C) the estimated scope and duration of the hostilities or involvement.

b. The President shall provide such other information as the Congress may request in the fulfillment of its constitutional responsibilities with respect to committing the nation to war and to the use of United States Armed Forces abroad.

c. Whenever the United States Armed Forces are introduced into hostilities or into any situation described in subsection (a) of this section, the President shall, so long as such armed forces continue to be engaged in such hostilities or situation, report to Congress periodically on the status of such hostilities or situation, as well as on the scope and duration of such hostilities or situation, but in no event shall he report to the Congress less often than once every six months.

Sec. 5 [#1544]. Congressional Action

a. Each report submitted pursuant to section 4(a)(1) shall be transmitted to the Speaker of the House of Representatives and to the President pro tempore of the Senate on the same calendar day. Each report so transmitted shall be referred to the Committee on Foreign Affairs of the House of Representatives and to the Committee on Foreign Relations of the Senate for appropriate action. If, when the report is transmitted, the Congress has adjourned sine die or has adjourned for any period in excess of three calendar days, the Speaker of the House of Representatives and the President pro tempore of the Senate, if they deem it advisable (or if petitioned by at least thirty percent of the membership of their respective House) shall jointly request the President to convene

Congress in order that it may consider the report and take appropriate action pursuant to this section.

b. Within sixty calendar days after a report is submitted or is required to be submitted pursuant to section 4(a)(1), whichever is earlier, the President shall terminate any use of United States Armed Forces with respect to which such report was submitted (or required to be submitted) unless the Congress (1) has declared war or has enacted a specific authorization for such use of United States Armed Forces, (2) has extended by law such sixty-day period, or (3) is physically unable to meet as a result of an armed attack upon the United States. Such sixty-day period shall be extended for not more than an additional thirty days if the President determines and certifies to the Congress in writing that unavoidable military necessity respecting the safety of United States Armed Forces requires the continued use of such armed forces in the course of bringing about a prompt removal of such forces.

c. Notwithstanding subsection (b) of this section, at any time that United States Armed Forces are engaged in hostilities outside the territory of the United States, its possessions, and territories without a declaration of war or specific statutory authorization, such forces shall be removed by the President if the Congress so directs by concurrent resolution.

Sec. 6 [#1545]. Congressional Procedures for a Joint Resolution or Bill

a. Any joint resolution or bill introduced pursuant to section 5(b) at least thirty calendar days before the expiration of the sixty-day period specified in such section shall be referred to the Committee on Foreign Affairs of the House of Representatives or the Committee on Foreign Relations of the Senate, as the case may be, and such committee shall report one such joint resolution or bill, together with its recommendations, not later than twenty-four calendar days before the expiration of the sixty-day period specified in such section, unless such House shall otherwise determine by the yeas and nays.

b. Any joint resolution or bill so reported shall become the pending business of the House in question (in the case of the Senate, the time for debate shall be equally divided between the proponents and opponents) and shall be voted on within three calendar days thereafter unless the House shall otherwise determine by yeas and nays.

c. Such a joint resolution or bill passed by one House shall be referred to the committee of the other House named in subsection (a) of this section and shall be reported out not later than fourteen calendar days before the expiration of the sixty-day period specified in section 5(b). The joint resolution or bill so reported shall become the pending business of the House in question and shall be voted on within three calendar days after it has been reported unless such House shall otherwise determine by yeas and nays.

d. In the case of any disagreement between the two Houses of Congress with respect to a joint resolution or bill passed by both Houses, conferees shall be promptly appointed, and the committee of conference shall make and file a report with respect to such resolution or bill not later than four calendar days before the expiration of the sixty-day period specified in section 5(b). In the event the conferees are unable to agree within forty-eight hours, they shall report back to their respective Houses in disagreement. Notwithstanding any rule in either House concerning the printing of conference reports in the Record or concerning any delay in the consideration of such reports, such report shall be acted upon by both Houses not later than the expiration of the sixty-day period.

Sec. 7 [#1546]. Congressional Procedures for a Concurrent Resolution

a. Any concurrent resolution introduced pursuant to section 5(c) shall be referred to the Committee on Foreign Affairs of the House of Representatives or the Committee on Foreign Relations of the Senate, as the case may be, and one such concurrent resolution shall be reported out by such committee, together with its recommendations, within three calendar days, unless such House shall otherwise determine by the yeas and nays.

b. Any concurrent resolution so reported shall become the pending business of the House in question (in the case of the Senate, the time for debate shall be equally divided between the proponents and the opponents) and shall be voted on within three calendar days thereafter unless such House shall otherwise determine by yeas and nays.

c. Such a concurrent resolution passed by one House shall be referred to the committee of the other House named in subsection (a) of this section and shall be reported out by such committee, together with its recommendations, within fifteen calendar days and shall thereupon become the pending business of such House and shall be voted upon within three calendar days, unless such House shall otherwise determine by yeas and nays.

d. In the case of any disagreement between the two Houses of Congress with respect to a concurrent resolution passed by both Houses, conferees shall be promptly appointed, and the committee of conference shall make and file a report with respect to such concurrent resolution within six calendar days after the legislation is referred to the committee of conference. Notwithstanding any rule in either House concerning the printing of conference reports in the Record or concerning any delay in the consideration of such reports, such report shall be acted upon by both Houses not later than six calendar days after the conference report is filed. In the event the conferees are unable to agree within forty-eight hours, they shall report back to their respective Houses in disagreement.

Sec. 8 [#1547]. Interpretation of a Joint Resolution

a. Authority to introduce United States Armed Forces into hostilities or into situations wherein involvement in hostilities is clearly indicated by the circumstances shall not be inferred (1) from any provision of law (whether or not in effect before the date of enactment of this resolution), including any provision contained in any appropriation act, unless such provision specifically authorizes the introduction of United States Armed Forces into hostilities or into such situations and states that it is intended to constitute specific statutory authorization within the meaning of this resolution, or (2) from any treaty heretofore or hereafter ratified, unless such treaty is implemented by legislation specifically authorizing the introduction of United States Armed Forces into hostilities or into such situations and stating that it is intended to constitute specific statutory authorization within the meaning of this resolution.

b. Nothing in this resolution shall be construed to require any further specific statutory authorization to permit members of United States Armed Forces to participate jointly with members of the armed forces of one or more foreign countries in the headquarters operations of high-level military commands which were established prior to the date of enactment of this resolution and pursuant to the United Nations Charter or any treaty ratified by the United States prior to such date.

c. For purposes of this resolution, the term "introduction of United States Armed Forces" includes the assignment of members of such armed forces to command, coordinate, participate in the movement of, or accompany the regular or irregular military forces of any foreign country or government when such military forces are engaged, or there exists an imminent threat that such forces will become engaged, in hostilities.

d. Nothing in this resolution (1) is intended to alter the constitutional authority of the Congress or of the President, or the provisions of existing treaties, or (2) shall be construed as granting any authority to the President with respect to the introduction of United States Armed Forces into hostilities or into situations wherein involvement in hostilities is clearly indicated by the circumstances, which authority he would not have had in the absence of this resolution.

Sec. 9 [#1548]. Separability of Provisions

If any provision of this resolution or the application thereof to any person or circumstance is held invalid, the remainder of the resolution and the application of such provision to any other person or circumstance shall not be affected thereby.

SELECTED BIBLIOGRAPHY

Early Christian Attitudes on War

Texts

Swift, Louis J. *The Early Fathers on War and Military Service*. Wilmington, Del.: Glazier, 1983.

Pacifist Interpretation

Hornus, Jean M. *It Is Not Lawful for Me to Fight: Early Christian Attitudes Toward War, Violence, and the State*. Translated by Alan Kreider and Oliver Coburn. Scottsdale, Pa.: Herald Press, 1980.

Nonpacifist Interpretation

Ryan, Edward A. "The Rejection of Military Service by the Early Christians." *Theological Studies* 13 (March 1952): 1–32.

Contemporary Pacifist Exposition

Zahn, Gordon C. *War, Conscience, and Dissent*. New York: Hawthorn, 1967.

Just-War Theory

Classical Texts and Commentaries

Aquinas, St. Thomas. *Summa theologiae*. II–II, Q. 40, A. 1; Q. 64, AA. 6, 7.

de la Brière, Yves. *Le droit de juste guerre*. Paris: Pedone, 1933.

de Vitoria, Francisco. *Reflectiones: De Indis et de jure belli*. Edited by Ernest Nys. Washington, D.C.: Carnegie Endowment for International Peace, 1917.

Suárez, Francisco. *De triplici virtute theologica: De caritate, disputatio 13 [de bello]*. In *Selections from Three Works*. Edited by James Brown Scott. 2 vols. [Latin text and English translation.] Oxford: Clarendon Press, 1944.

Vanderpol, Alfred. *La doctrine scolastique du droit de guerre*. Paris: Pedone, 1919.

Walters, Leroy. "Five Classic Just-War Theories: A Study in the Thought of Thomas Aquinas, Vitoria, Suárez, Gentili, and Grotius." Ph.D. Dissertation, Yale University Press, 1971.

Contemporary Expositions

Bailey, Sydney D. *Prohibitions and Restraints in War.* London: Oxford University Press, 1972.

Childress, James F. "Just-War Criteria." In *War or Peace: The Search for New Answers,* pp. 40–58. Edited by Thomas A. Shannon. Maryknoll, N.Y.: Orbis, 1980.

———. "Just-War Theories." *Theological Studies* 39 (December 1978): 427–45.

Hehir, J. Bryan. "The Just-War Ethic and Catholic Theology." In *War or Peace: The Search for New Answers,* pp. 15–39. Edited by Thomas A. Shannon. Maryknoll, N.Y.: Orbis, 1980.

Johnson, James T. *Can Modern War Be Just?* New Haven, Conn.: Yale University Press, 1984.

———. *Ideology, Reason, and Limitation of War.* Princeton, N.J.: Princeton University Press, 1975.

———. *Just-War Tradition and the Restraint of War.* Princeton, N.J.: Princeton University Press, 1981.

———. *The Quest for Peace.* Princeton, N.J.: Princeton University Press, 1987.

———, and George Weigel, eds. *Just War and Gulf War.* Washington, D.C.: Ethics and Public Policy, 1991.

McCormick, Richard A. "War, Morality of." In *New Catholic Encyclopedia.* Vol. 14. pp. 802–9. New York: McGraw-Hill, 1967.

McKenna, Joseph C. "Ethics and War: A Catholic View." *American Political Science Review* 54 (September 1960): 647–58.

Murray, John C. "A Use of Doctrine in the Uses of Force." In *We Hold These Truths,* pp. 249–73. New York: Sheed and Ward, 1960.

O'Brien, William V. *The Conduct of Just and Limited War.* New York: Praeger, 1981. (This book is the most systematic interpretation and application of just-war theory to modern war. It also integrates current understandings of international law with treatment of moral questions. The bibliography, as of 1981, is comprehensive.)

Osgood, Robert E., and Robert W. Tucker. *Force, Order, and Justice.* Baltimore: Johns Hopkins University Press, 1967.

Ramsey, Paul. *The Just War: Force and Political Responsibility.* New York: Charles Scribner's Sons, 1968.

———. *War and the Christian Conscience: How Shall Modern War Be Conducted Justly?* Durham, N.C.: Duke University Press, 1961.

Tucker, Robert W. *The Just War.* Baltimore: Johns Hopkins University Press, 1960.

Walzer, Michael. *Just and Unjust Wars*. New York: Basic Books, 1977.
Wasserstrom, Richard A., ed. *War and Morality.* Belmont, Calif.: Wadsworth, 1970.

Humanitarian Intervention

Hehir, J. Bryan. "Intervention: From Theories to Cases." *Ethics and International Affairs* 9 (1995): 1–13.
Laberge, Pierre. "Humanitarian Intervention: Three Ethical Positions." *Ethics and International Affairs* 9 (1995): 15–35.

Intervention in Revolutionary Wars

O'Brien, William V. *U.S. Military Intervention: Law and Morality.* Washington Papers, No. 68. Beverly Hills, Calif.: Sage, 1979.
Regan, Richard J. *The Moral Dimensions of Politics*, pp. 180–95. New York: Oxford University Press, 1986.

Nuclear Weapons

Martino, Joseph P. *A Fighting Chance: The Moral Use of Nuclear Weapons.* San Francisco: Ignatius Press, 1988.
O'Brien, William V. "Just-War Conduct in a Nuclear Context." *Theological Studies* 44 (June 1983): 191–220.
Regan, Richard J. *The Moral Dimensions of Politics.* pp. 160–79. New York: Oxford University Press, 1986.
Reiss, Mitchell. *Why Nations Constrain Their Nuclear Capabilities.* Baltimore: Johns Hopkins University Press, 1995.
Sagan, Scott D., and Kenneth N. Waltz. *The Spread of Nuclear Weapons: A Debate.* New York: Norton, 1995.
Schall, James V., ed. *Out of Justice, Peace: Joint Pastoral Letter of the West German Bishops; Winning the Peace: Joint Pastoral Letter of the French Bishops.* San Francisco: Ignatius Press, 1984.
U.S. Catholic Bishops. *The Challenge of Peace: God's Promise and Our Response.* Washington, D.C.: U.S. Catholic Conference, 1983.

Moral "Realist" Views on War

Niebuhr, Reinhold. *Christianity and Power Politics.* New York: Charles Scribner's Sons, 1940.
Thompson, Kenneth W. *Political Realism and the Crisis of World Politics.* Princeton, N.J.: Princeton University Press, 1960.

U.S. Law

Fisher, Louis. *Presidential War Power.* Lawrence, Kans.: University of Kansas Press, 1995.

International Law

General

Brownlie, Ian. *System of the Law of Nations.* Oxford: Oxford University Press, 1983.
Kelsen, Hans. *Principles of International Law.* Edited by Robert W. Tucker. 2d rev. ed. New York: Holt, Rinehart, and Winston, 1966.
Lauterpacht, Hersch. *International Law.* Vols. 3 and 4. *The Law of Peace.* Cambridge: Cambridge University Press, 1977, 1978.
Maris, Gary L. *International Law.* Lanham, Md.: University Press of America, 1984.
Van Glahen, Gerhard. *Law Among Nations.* 5th ed. New York: Macmillan, 1986.

Right to Wage War

Brownlie, Ian. *International Law and the Use of Force by States.* Oxford: Clarendon Press, 1963.
Feliciano, Florentino P., and Myres S. McDougal. *Law and Minimum World Public Order,* pp. 121–383. New Haven, Conn.: Yale University Press, 1961.
Henkin, Louis. *How Nations Behave,* pp. 135–64, 250–312. 2d ed. New York: Columbia University Press, 1979.

The United Nations, U.N. Charter Articles 42 and 51, and the Gulf War

Franck, Thomas M., and Faiza Patel. "U.N. Police Action in Lieu of War: 'The Old Order Changeth.'" *American Journal of International Law* 85 (January 1991): 63–74.
Glennon, Michael J. "The Constitution and Chapter VII of the U.N. Charter." *American Journal of International Law* 85 (January 1991): 74–88.
Moore, John N. *Crisis in the Gulf: Enforcing the Rule of Law.* Dobbs Ferry, N.Y.: Oceana, 1992.
Rostow, Eugene V. "Until What? Enforcement Action or Collective Security?" *American Journal of International Law* 85 (July 1991): 506–16.
Schachter, Oscar. "United Nations Law in the Gulf Conflict." *American Journal of International Law* 85 (July 1991): 452–73.

Reprisals

O'Brien, William V. *The Conduct of Just and Limited War,* pp. 24–27. New York: Praeger, 1981.

————. *The Law of Limited International Conflict,* pp. 23–32, 35–38. Washington, D.C.: Georgetown University Press, 1965.

Humanitarian Intervention

Bowett, Derek W. "The Interrelation of Theories of Intervention and Self-Defense." In *Law and Civil War in the Modern World,* pp. 38–50, especially pp. 44–46. Edited by John Norton Moore. Baltimore: Johns Hopkins University Press, 1974.

Brownlie, Ian. "Humanitarian Intervention." In *Law and Civil War in the Modern World,* pp. 218–27. Edited by John Norton Moore. Baltimore: Johns Hopkins University Press, 1974.

Lillich, Richard B. "Humanitarian Intervention: A Reply to Ian Brownlie and a Plea for Constructive Alternatives." In *Law and Civil War in the Modern World,* pp. 229–51. Edited by John Norton Moore. Baltimore: Johns Hopkins University Press, 1974.

O'Brien, William V. *U.S. Military Intervention: Law and Morality,* pp. 22–23, 30–36. Washington Papers, No. 68. Beverly Hills, Calif.: Sage, 1979.

INDEX

Achille Loro incident, 55
Aidid, Mohammed Farah, 71, 181–87
Albright, Madeleine K., 175
Alsace-Lorraine, 130
Anabaptists, 5
Anatolia, 131
Aquinas, St. Thomas, 17–18
Arabs, 62–63, 83, 94, 113
Arafat, Yasir, 170
Argentina, 61, 151–56
Aristotle, 14–19
Armenia, 83
assassination of political leaders, 88–89
atomic bombing of Japan, 91–92
Augustine, St., 14, 17
Austria-Hungary, 123–27, 129–31, 192
Azerbaijan, 82–83

Bao Dai, Emperor, 138–40
Barbary Coast pirates, 24
Barre, Mohammed Said, 180–82
Belarus, 114n., 117–18
Belgium, 126, 130
Benedict XV, Pope, 130
Bohan, Mate, 204
Bosnia, 73–74, 77, 82, 192–93. *See also* Bosnian Federation; Bosnian-Serb Republic; Bosnian War
Bosnian Federation, 206–7
Bosnian-Serb Republic, 207
Bosnian War: 34, 81–82; diplomatic efforts to end, 204–8; military history, 193–98; U.N. and N.A.T.O. activity, 198–204

Boutros-Ghali, Boutros, 182, 195n., 201–2
Brest-Litovsk, Treaty of, 130
Brethren, 5
British Commonwealth, 154
Buchanan, James, 24
Bulgaria, 124, 127, 130–31
Bush, George H. W., 33, 39, 173–74, 183

Cambodia, 36–37
Central Intelligence Agency, 115, 160–61
Chamorro, Violeta Barrios de, 161–62
China: 26, 45–46, 115–16, 137–40, 200; and nuclear weapons, 108–11, 112n., 115–16
Christiani, Alfredo, 167, 169
Churchill, Winston, 101
Cicero, M. Tullius, 14, 16
Civil War, American, 24
civil wars, 68–73
Clement of Alexandria, 5
Clinton, William J., 174, 187
colonialism and the United Nations, 35–36
Colombia, 60
Constantine, Emperor, 5
Contras, 160–62
Cosic, Dobrica, 204
Croatia, 193, 195, 197–98, 200, 204, 207
Crusades, 9
Cuba, 58, 159–60
Czechoslovakia, 131

Dardanelles, 131–32
D'Aubuisson, Roberto, 166–67
Dayton Accords, 204, 207–8
Denmark, 127
Diem, Ngo Dinh, 140–42
Dien Bien Phu, 139
Dominican Republic, 58
double effect, principle of, 95–96
Duarte, José, 165–67

Eastern Europe, 79, 83, 110
economic sanctions, 25, 56–57, 65–66, 199–201
Egypt, 62, 113
Ekeus, Rolf, 175
El Salvador, 36–37, 165–69
Estonia, 130
Ethiopia, 180
European Community, 65, 113, 194, 205

Falklands War, 61, 151–56
Finland, 130
Fourteenth Amendment, 21
France: 26, 45, 108n., 114; and the Bosnian War, 198, 201, 207; and Vietnam, 136–40; and World War I, 125–27, 130
Franz Joseph, Emperor, 123

Gandhi, Mahatma, 6
Geneva Accord (Final Declaration of the 1954 Convention on Vietnam), 140
Geneva Conference, 139–40
Georgia, 82
Germany: 60, 67n., 92n., 95–98, 207; and World War I, 123–30
God's will and war, 8–10
Gorbachev, Mikhail, 173
Great Britain: 26, 45, 61, 73–74, 101, 108n., 114, 138, 171, 179; and the Bosnian War, 198, 207; and the Falklands, 151–56; and World War I, 124–25, 127–29
Greece, 1, 55, 131
Gulf of Sidra incident, 50–51
Gulf War, 28–29, 37, 112, 172–75

Haig, Alexander, 153
Haiti, 58
Harris, Sir Arthur, 92n.

Hindus, 83
Hitler, Adolph, 49, 60, 132
Hobbes, Thomas, 1, 6
Ho Chi Minh, 137–38
Hungary, 124, 131

India, 83, 111, 114–16
Indian-Pakistani conflict, 36
Indian wars, American, 24
Indochina, 137–39, 144
Indonesia, 35
International Atomic Energy Agency, 115
international conventions, 38, 50, 88–89, 98–99
international law, 39, 50, 59, 88–89
Iran, 36–37, 52–53, 112, 114
Iraq, 28–29, 33, 36–37, 45, 49, 66n., 112, 172–75
Iraqi-Iranian War, 36
Ireland, 60, 73–74, 154
Irish Republican Army, 89, 94
Israel, ancient, 9
Israel, modern: 36, 55–56, 60–63, 112n., 113; and nuclear weapons, 111–13, 116
Italy, 127, 131, 154, 179
Izetbegovic, Alija, 194, 201, 204, 207

Japan, 109, 111, 115–16, 127, 137–38
Jesus, 4–7
Johnson, Lyndon B., 39, 143
Jordan, 62
Justin Martyr, 5
just-war theory, 14–19

Karadzic, Radovan, 202, 204–5
Karl, Emperor, 129–30
Kashmir, 83, 114
Kazakhstan, 107n., 114n., 117–18
Kellogg-Briand Pact, 59
King, Martin Luther, 5–6
Korean War, 28–29, 32–33
Kosovo, 82
Krajina, 197
Kurdistan, 131
Kurds, 54, 174
Kuwait, 28–29, 33, 36, 49, 60, 172–74

Laos, 146

Latvia, 130
Lausanne, Treaty of, 132
League of Nations, 130
Lebanon, 9, 55–56, 62
Libya, 50–51, 55
Lincoln, Abraham, 21
Lithuania, 130–31
Lusitania, sinking of, 128

Macedonia, 82, 192
Mahdi, Mohammed Ali, 181–87
Marxism and war, 7–8
Mennonites, 5
Mexican-American War, 24, 50
Mexico, 60
Middle East, 112, 114–15
Milan, Edict of, 5
Mladic, Ratko, 202
Monte Cassino, bombing of, 96–97
Montenegro, 127, 130, 192
Muslims, 83, 112–13, 114n., 115

Nasser, Gamel Abdel, 62
National Council of Churches, 19
National Liberation Front, 141, 143–44
Netherlands, 35, 127, 198
Neuilly, Treaty of, 131
Nicaragua, 58, 159–62
Nicholas II, Emperor, 124–26
Niebuhr, Reinhold, 18–19
Nimibia, 35
Nixon, Richard M., 39
North Atlantic Council, 202
North Atlantic Treaty, 41
North Atlantic Treaty Organization: 105–6; and the Bosnian War, 196–98, 200–204
North Korea, 13, 28–29, 32, 45, 114–15
North Vietnam, 140–47
Nuclear Nonproliferation Treaty, 115–16
nuclear weapons and just war conduct: 100–101; China context, 108–11; Cold War context, 101–6; development of nuclear capability and proliferation, 111–17; new superpower context, 106–8; proliferation and terrorism, 117–19

O'Brien, William V., 93–94

Organization of American States, 65, 154
Origen, 5
Ortega, Daniel, 160–61
Owen, Lord David, 205–6
Owen-Stoltenberg plan, 205–6
Owen-Vance plan. *See* Vance-Owen plan

pacifism, 4–7
Pakistan, 83, 111–12, 114–16
Palestine, 9, 62–63, 113
Palestinian Liberation Organization, 55–56, 62, 113
Panama, 60
Penn, William, 5
Pérez de Cuéllar, Javier, 154
Peter, St., 5
Platt Amendment, 58
Poland, 49, 130–32
Ponce, René Emilio, 169
Portugal, 35

Quakers, 5

reason and war, 10–14, 20–23, 63–64, 80–81, 84–85
Reformation, 5, 9
reparations, 67
residential bombing of German cities, 92
Rhineland, 131
Rome, 1
Romania, 127, 130–31
Romero, Oscar, 165, 167
Russia: 26, 45, 82, 106–7; and the Bosnian War, 200–201, 207; and nuclear weapons, 100, 106–13, 114n., 117; and World War I, 124–27, 130, 132

Saar, 130
Saddam Hussein, 60
Saint Germain-en-Laye, Treaty of, 131
Sandinistas, 159–62, 168
secessionist wars, 68, 73–83
secretary general of the United Nations, 46, 65
senators, U.S.: and Korean War, 32–33; and U.N. Charter, 30–32
Serbia: 77, 192, 194–95, 204, 207;

Serbia *(continued)*
and World War I, 123–25, 127, 130
Sèvres, Treaty of, 131–32
Shakers, 5
Slavonia, 197
Slovenia, 192–93
Somalia, 33–34, 37–38, 179–88
Somoza, Anastasio, 159
South Africa, 35–36
South Korea, 28–29, 114
South Vietnam, 140–47
Southern Rhodesia, 35
Soviet Union: 37, 82, 108, 130, 168; and ethnic problems after collapse, 73, 79, 82; and Nicaragua, 159–60; and nuclear problems for successor states, 112n., 113–14, 117–18; and nuclear threat during the Cold War, 95, 100–106; and prospects for cooperation with Russia after collapse, 45–46; and split with Tito, 192; and support of North Vietnam, 145; and support of Somalia and Ethiopia, 180
Spain, 201
Spanish-American War, 24
Stimson, Henry L., 91
Stoltenberg, Thorvald, 205–6
Suárez, Francisco, 18
Sudan, 83
Syria, 37, 62, 112

Taiwan, 111
Terrorism, 53–56, 94–95, 118–19
Terry, Fernando Belaunde, 153
Thatcher, Baroness Margaret, 77
Thieu, Nguyen Van, 142, 146
Thirty Years War, 9
Thrace, 133
Tito, Josip, 192
Trianon, Treaty of, 131
Triple Alliance, 123
Truman, Harry S., 32
Tudjman, Franjo, 204, 207
Turkey: 37, 83, 192; and World War I, 127, 130–31

Ukraine, 82, 107n., 114n., 117–18, 130
United Nations: 29–30, 59–62, 112; and Bosnia, 34, 81–82, 193, 196–206; and Cambodia, 37, 72; and control of nuclear proliferation, 113, 115–17, 119; and El Salvador, 36–37, 167–69; and the Falklands, 152–54, 156; and the Gulf War, 28–29, 33, 37, 172–75; and human rights, 50–57, 118–19; Secretariat of, 46–47; Security Council of, 20, 25–37, 39, 53–54, 71–72; and Somalia, 33, 38, 71, 181–88; and South Korea, 28–29, 32; and U.S. Constitution, 34–37, 105; and Yugoslavia, 193, 196–205
United States: 75n.; and the Bosnian War, 194, 201–2, 207; and El Salvador, 165–67, 169; and the Falklands War, 153–54, 156; and the Grenada invasion, 71; and Iran, 52–53; and Iraq, 173–75; and Libya, 51, 55; and Nicaragua, 58, 159–62; and North Korea, 13, 115; and nuclear weapons, 100–111, 113–15, 117, 119; and Panama invasion, 71; and Somalia, 71, 180, 182–88; and South Korea, 32; and Vietnam, 39, 70, 78–79, 98, 141–47; and World War I, 128–30
Uzbekistan, 114n., 117

Vance, Cyrus R., 205
Vance-Owen plan, 201, 205
Versailles, Treaty of, 45n., 66n., 130–32
Viet Cong, 70, 141–46
Viet Minh, 137–40
Vietnam: 39, 70, 78–79, 98; colonial period, 136–38; division of, 139–41; war for independence, 138–40; war in South, 141–47
Vitoria, Francisco de, 18

Walzer, Michael, 90
war: and God's will, 8–10; and just cause. *See* war, just causes for; and just war conduct. *See* war, just conduct of; and just-war-theory, 14–19; and legal authority. *See* war, legal authority for; and Marxism, 7–8; need to justify, 3–4; and pacifism, 4–7; and reason, 10–14, 63–64, 81, 84–85; and right intention, 17, 84–86

War of 1812, 24
war, just causes for: 17–18, 48; and cessation of cause, 66–67; in civil wars, 68–73; defense of territory and space, 48–52; as last resort, 64–66; and proportionality, 63–64; rectification of economic injury, 56–58; rescue of nationals, 52–53; response to terrorism, 53–56; in secessionist wars, 68, 73–83; vindication of territorial claims, 59–63
war, just conduct of: 18; effect of unjust conduct on justice of cause, 98; and international conventions, 98–99; and nuclear weapons. *See* nuclear weapons and just war conduct; and principle of discrimination, 87–95; and principle of proportionality, 95–98

war, legal authority for: 17, 20–23; and U.N. Charter, 24–39, 41–42, 45, 51; and U.S. Constitution, 23–24, 28–34; and War Powers Resolution, 39–43
War Powers Resolution, 39–41
Warsaw Pact, 105–6
Western Europe, 100–101, 105–6
Wilhelm II, Emperor, 123–26, 130–31
Wilson, Woodrow, 128–29
World War I: 24, 59, 88–89, 192; casualties and costs, 132; diplomatic efforts to end, 129–30; naval blockades during, 127–28; origins, 123–27; termination, 130–32
World War II, 24, 79, 92, 96–97

Yugoslavia: former, 82, 192–94, 198, 202; present, 81, 197, 200, 207

Just War was composed in Meridien by Brevis Press, Bethany, Connecticut; printed on 60-pound Booktext Natural and bound by BookCrafters, Chelsea, Michigan; and designed and produced by Kachergis Book Design, Pittsboro,